Invoking Humanity

POLITICAL THEORY AND CONTEMPORARY POLITICS

Series Editors: Richard Bellamy, University of Reading, Jeremy Jennings, University of Birmingham, and Paul Kelly, London School of Economics and Political Science

This series aims to examine the interplay of political theory and practical politics at the beginning of the twenty-first century. It explores the way in which the concepts and ideologies that we have inherited from the past have been transformed or need to be rethought in the light of contemporary political debates. The series comprises concise single-authored books, each representing an original contribution to the literature on a key theme or concept.

Also published in this series:

Love and Politics: Women Politicians and the Ethics of Care
Fiona Mackay

Political Morality: A Theory of Liberal Democracy
Richard Vernon

Liberalism and Value Pluralism
George Crowder

Forthcoming titles:

Defending Liberal Neutrality
Jonathan Seglow

Democracy and Global Warming
Barry Holden

Seductive Virtue: The Socratic Art of Civic Education
Russell Bentley

The Politics of Civil Society
James Martin

Political Theory and the Media
Alan Finlayson

Invoking Humanity

War, Law and Global Order

Danilo Zolo

Translated by Federico and Gordon Poole

continuum
LONDON • NEW YORK

Continuum
The Tower Building, 11 York Road, London, SE1 7NX
370 Lexington Avenue, New York, NY 10017-6503

First published in English 2002

Originally published in Italian as *Chi dice umanità. Guerra, diritto e ordine globale* by Einaudi Editore, Torino, 2000

British Library Cataloguing-in-Publication Data
A catalogue record for this book is available from the British Library.

ISBN 0-8264-5655-3 (hardback)
0-8264-5656-1 (paperback)

Library of Congress Cataloging-in-Publication Data
Zolo, Danilo.
[Chi dice umanità. English]
Invoking humanity: war, law and global order/Danilo Zolo; translated by Federico and Gordon Poole.
p. cm. — (Political theory and contemporary politics)
Includes bibliographical references and index.
ISBN 0-8264-5655-3 — ISBN 0-8264-5656-1 (pbk).
1. Kosovo (Serbia—History—Civil War, 1998– 2. Europe—Politics and government—1989– I. Title. II. Series.

DR2087 .Z6513 2002
949.7103—dc21   2001047479

Typeset by YHT, London
Printed and bound in Great Britain by MPG Books, Bodmin, Cornwall

Contents

Preface to the English Edition

I am writing these lines in March 2002, while the whole world is noting, with growing alarm, a series of weighty events that are pertinent to the political and theoretical perspective of the present book. These events – I say this without any hesitation but also without any sense of satisfaction – bear out the analyses and predictions I expressed in this book two years ago.

I am referring to the terrorist attack of September 11, the war unleashed by the United States against Afghanistan, and the alarming prospect of its extension to Iraq. I am also thinking about the arrest and extradition of former Yugoslav president Slobodan Milošević and his subsequent trial.

There are those who say that the events of September 11 fundamentally changed the world. It is easy to object that in an important sense what happened on that day was an inevitable consequence of international phenomena that had been evolving for the past decade. It was a clearly foreseeable consequence: it is no accident that in the final pages of this book there was an explicit reference both to the growing danger posed by 'global terrorism', and to the importance of Al Qaeda and its leader, Osama bin Laden. In addition, the United States had already been the victim of a long series of terrorist attacks, in the Middle East, in Africa and on its own territory. The US administration had deluded itself into thinking it could make itself immune to this threat by relaunching Reagan's 'Star Wars' project, seen as a defence against so-called 'rogue states'.

In the course of the last decade of the twentieth century, after the end of the Cold War and the collapse of the Soviet empire, the United States established itself as the sole absolute global super-power. Never, perhaps, in human history has a single nation seemed to possess such overwhelming political power and such invincible military might. Under its leadership, Western states became involved in a form of power politics that was perceived by non-Western nations – especially in the Islamic world and east Asia – as an increasing challenge to their territorial integrity, their political independence and their very identities as societies.

The series of armed interventions launched by the United States since the Gulf War, in the name of 'world order' and 'global security' has revealed the increasing gap between the military strength of the American superpower (and thus its advantage in trade, science, technology and computing) and that of the rest of the world. In the Balkans in particular, under the pretext that it was defending human rights, the United States pursued a policy of global hegemony. In pursuit of this strategic aim, it did not hesitate to blatantly violate the United Nations Charter and international law. It also marginalized the UN Security Council, humiliating permanent non-Western members such as Russia and China. Nato's 'humanitarian war' against the Yugoslav Federation could not but provoke a wave of alarm and at the same time exacerbate the deep bitterness and desire for revenge already widespread in the non-Western world.

From this perspective, therefore, the attack on the Twin Towers comes as no surprise. But the novelty of the event lies in its extraordinarily spectacular quality, probably due to very skilful handling of the media, which terrorism borrowed pragmatically from Western television, CNN in particular. To see the leading world power vulnerable in this way filled the Western world with a deep sense of insecurity, fed by the bellicose rhetoric of the US administration. Furthermore, the 'new war' pursued by the Bush administration against Afghanistan did not have the effect of balancing the violence of the terrorist attack with a specific act of retaliation and retribution (even though the number of innocent civilians sacrificed in Afghanistan now far exceeds that of the victims of September 11).

Instead, a prospect of permanent war has opened up, without territorial borders or time-limits, largely secret and beyond the control of international law on war. Now as never before,

Western politico-military élites have shown they are determined to ensure the security and welfare of the industrialized countries by resorting to increased military pressure on the entire world. These countries are reproducing on a global scale what the colonial (old-style Zionist) policies of the state of Israel are currently imposing on the Palestinian people in the microcosm of the Middle East.

It is now clear that the war in Afghanistan is only the beginning of total war on the 'axis of evil'. Iraq will also be attacked sooner or later, in a scenario with huge potential for conflict, all the more so since Israel will almost certainly be drawn in, with its intelligence apparatus and possibly even its nuclear weapons. The recent letter signed by sixty leading American intellectuals, headed by the philosopher and militant Zionist Michael Walzer, in which they applaud the 'new war' as a 'just war' <http://www.propositionsonline.com/html/fighting_for.html> is one of the most disquieting signs that the extension of the war into the Persian Gulf is already in the political, diplomatic and ideological planning stages.

In fact, the strategic objectives of the United States go far beyond suppression of 'global terrorism', as the recent *Quadrennial Defense Review Report* of the Department of Defense shows in the clearest possible way <http://www.defenselink.mil/pubs/gdr2001.pdf>. Its objective is to consolidate its own worldwide hegemony, assuring itself of a permanent military presence in the heart of central Asia. This means controlling, in addition to Afghanistan and Pakistan (where a permanent military base is already under construction at Jacobabad), countries in the Caucasus, and the Caspian and Transcaspian areas, such as Georgia, Azerbaijan, Turkmenistan, Uzbekistan and Tajikistan. The plan is not only to control the enormous underground energy resources of these fomer Soviet republics but, most importantly, to bring about the double political and military isolation of Russia in the West and China in the East. Thus the idea of reviving a particularly aggressive neo-colonial policy, justified by the necessity of defeating terrorism, now becomes of pressing interest. After the hiatus of the cold war and the formal liberation of the colonized countries of Africa and Asia, the West's ancient mission to control, occupy and 'civilize' the non-Western world is returning with full force and can only provoke, as a bloody counterpoint, a 'global terrorism' that is ever more ruthless and effective.

Meanwhile, we are witnessing the actual collapse of the international legal system, both a cause and a consequence of the paralysis of the United Nations, which has been completely marginalized by the desire for unchallenged predominance on the part of the United States and its closest allies. In this situation it is not going too far to speak of a failure of the 'institutional' or 'juridical' pacifism which, from Kant to Hans Kelsen, Norberto Bobbio and Jürgen Habermas, has pointed to law and international institutions as the main – if not the only – tools for achieving peace and protecting fundamental rights. Now more than ever, Kelsen's formula, 'peace through law', looks like an Enlightenment illusion, with its prescriptive optimism and naive cosmopolitan universalism. From the end of the two-superpower system to the present day, the Western powers have not only used force in systematic violation of international law, but have explicitly contested its functions in the name of their unconditional *jus ad bellum*, the right to make war. It is clear that a normative system can have the effect of ritualizing the international use of force – subjecting it to predetermined procedures and general rules – only on condition that no party involved can, thanks to its overwhelming power, consider itself *legibus solutus* – not bound by law.

The great institutional invention of the twentieth century, international criminal jurisdiction, is not exempt from this disastrous state of affairs. The experience of the International Criminal Tribunal for the former Yugoslavia (the Hague Tribunal) has shown that an international criminal court cannot but be, in the absence of an international system that is to a minimal degree based on the model of the 'rule of law', a partisan instrument, in this case an instrument of NATO, which has shown itself not only ineffective but actually counterproductive, as the case against Slobodan Milošević is amply demonstrating.

Slobodan Milošević, demonized by the West as the prime – if not the only – person responsible for the Balkan tragedy, was first arrested in his homeland and then turned over by the Serb government to the International Hague Tribunal thanks to economic blackmail on the part of the victors and the military collaboration of NATO. Apart from the grave political responsibilities of Milošević, it is easy to foresee that the trial will consist in his being victimized, degraded and made into a scapegoat, a far cry from the principles of rule of law and devoid of any preventive or pacifying effect. The whole business of the incrimination, arrest and extradition of the Serbian leader is an eloquent confirmation of evaluations and predictions to be found in the fourth chapter of the present book. It bears out how the Hague Tribunal is subject to the whims of the NATO countries, which continue to finance it and furnish organizational, judicial and military assistance in exchange for an *a priori* immunity from being accused, let alone brought to justice (a complicity that has been criticized not only by Harold Pinter but even by the former presiding judge of the Tribunal, Antonio Cassese). Just after Milošević was extradited, the General Prosecutor Carla Del Ponte went so far as to declare that she was proud of having received immediate congratulations from former State Secretary Madeleine Albright, whom once again she fondly called the 'godmother of the Tribunal'.

It is clear that the winners are imposing on the losers, by means of overbearing political and economic conditioning, a twofold imperial strategy of territorial fragmentation and political sub-ordination of an entire region. In fact, one of the likely consequences of Milošević's (illegal) extradition is the marginalizing of Vojslav Kostunica, a leader of great prestige and moral integrity, against whom serious accusations have been made by prosecutor Carla Del Ponte. Equally probable is the division and political dependency of the Yugoslavian peoples, increasingly drawn into the neo-Atlantic orbit. The long military conflicts that after the war disrupted southern Serbia and devastated Macedonia fulfil my prediction of enduring instability in the Balkan region. The NATO military occupation and politico-economic invasion of broad zones of the former Yugoslavia, which the war has reduced to pre-industrial conditions, have not put a stop to the violence and systematic violation of basic rights directed against the defeated minorities.

Acknowledgements

I am very happy that this book of mine should appear in an English edition, especially with a publisher such as Continuum with a wide international outreach. I wish to thank the persons who have made this English edition of my book possible, recommending that it be published or collaborating directly. With special gratitude I remember Richard Bellamy, Cristina Bicchieri, Diana Johnston, Federico Poole, Gordon Poole and Caroline Wintersgill.

I am glad for at least three reasons. The first is that I wrote this book with an ideal interlocutor in mind, a non-Western reader. For one who writes in Italian, the only way to cross over the boundaries of one's cultural province is to take up that cosmopolitan (and hegemonic) instrument which is the English language. Through this language I can hope to make contact with possible non-Western readers who may be interested in the contents of these pages. I also hope that they may be willing to engage with my theoretical and political proposals, perhaps over the internet.[1] I refer especially to the central assumption of my book: the need for the world's complexity to be preserved; that is, the differences and the particularities of cultures, moral values, lifestyles and natural environments, which the hegemony of the Western powers today is destroying, even by force of arms, in the name of a colonial universalism.

Another reason I am glad this English edition is being published is that I wrote my book with an implicit dedication – a sort of inside epigraph – to the citizens of the countries of former Yugoslavia, to whom I am sentimentally bound for reasons of origin. Unfortunately, the plan to have this book translated into Serbo-Croat has proved infeasible for now on account of economic and organizational problems due to the ravages of war and the continued political instability in the area. The war for Kosovo put me in touch with a lot of Yugoslav citizens, many of them via a long television interview with me in Belgrade a few weeks after the end of the conflict; this was the same television station that my country, Italy, had helped to bomb in April 1999, thus lengthening the list of civil victims of the 'humanitarian war'. My sharp opposition to the regime of Slobodan Milošević did not keep me, during the course of the interview, from asking the Serbian people for forgiveness for the aggression they had undergone once again from my country (and the NATO countries in general). Likewise, my deep dissent from the strategy and objectives of the UÇK did not hinder me from expressing my solidarity with the Kosovar-Albanian people, who were innocent victims first of the atrocities of the civil war and then of the NATO bombings. Now I hope, thanks to the English edition of my book, that a new, more inclusive and pondered message may reach some of my interlocutors in the Balkans.

Third, I am interested in communicating with those in Great Britain and, above all, the United States who share my sense of civil responsibility for the effects that the NATO 'humanitarian war' has had in the Balkans, the Eurasian continent and worldwide. In my opinion, it is unrealistic to think that the hegemonic strategy the present administration of the United States is currently pursuing (seconded by the governments of Great Britain, Spain and Italy) can be defeated without the help of an internal opposition and widespread civil dissent. In this respect, it may be important that between the two shores of the Atlantic a cultural dialogue springs up that is not aligned with the 'Atlantic' philosophy that informed the NATO war against the Federal Republic of Yugoslavia and which is now the inspiration for European support of the war being waged by the Bush administration against the 'axis of evil'.

Florence, March 2002

Note

1. My e-mail address is <zolo@tsd.unifi.it.>. May I be allowed to suggest as well that one log onto the website JURA GENTIUM, Center for Philosophy of International Law and Global Politics, <http://dex1.tsd. unifi.it/juragentium>, available in English, Spanish, Arabic, Chinese and Italian, which I have co-ordinated for the last two years at the Dipartimento di Teoria e Storia del Diritto (Department of Theory and History of Law) of the University of Florence.

Here one is reminded of a somewhat modified expression of Proudhon's: whoever invokes humanity is trying to cheat.

Carl Schmitt, *The Concept of the Political*

Introduction

In this book I offer an interpretation of the 'humanitarian war' waged by nineteen NATO countries against the Federal Republic of Yugoslavia in the spring of 1999. My main purpose is to investigate the strategic reasons for the war and envisage what consequences it may have on the system of international relations in the years to come. Of course, I do not claim to have provided an exhaustive account of the causes and effects of such a complex and elusive event, nor to have made accurate predictions about later developments. War is always the victory of 'invisible power'. Moreover, few conflicts over the past fifty years have been as puzzling and controversial as the war for Kosovo. One has only to think of the enigma of the 'true' motivations of the Western powers' decision to launch the war, or, going more into detail, of the diplomatic labyrinth of Rambouillet, the mysterious bombing of the Chinese embassy in Belgrade, or the puzzling judicial manoeuvres that led to the Hague Tribunal's incrimination of Slobodan Milošević.

To fully appreciate the complexity of the situation, one should place it in the context of the uncertainty and instability of the international scene ever since the end of the Cold War and the collapse of the Soviet empire. The age of the 'balance of terror' was not followed by an age of stable, universal peace, the 'new world order' hoped for by many on both sides of the Atlantic. Nor did the post-Cold War period witness a worldwide deployment of economic and financial policies to promote a more equitable distribution of

1

resources among the rich and poor areas of the planet. It could hardly be claimed that this objective has been pursued by economic organizations such as the World Bank, the International Monetary Fund or the World Trade Organization, whose policies have been the butt of continuous protest ever since Seattle. On the contrary, the irresistible advance of globalization and the worldwide informatics revolution has been accompanied by growing tensions: local wars for ethnic or religious identity, dizzying financial crises, migratory streams, famines and epidemics in the weaker countries, environmental disasters, drug and arms trafficking, unemployment, and urban violence – a list that could be extended.

The following pages are first and foremost the result of ideas I have been working on, often publicly, while thinking my way through many debates, seminars and newspaper articles. Since the end of the conflict, in a less highly strung, polemical climate, I have concentrated on some general themes that I feel have important theoretical, even more than political, implications.

First of all, I have tried to reconstruct, although in an inevitably concise and selective form, the historical premises and geopolitical context of the war, trying to look beyond the *ad hoc* commonplaces of war historiography to highlight the role played by Western powers in the centuries-old clash between Balkan nationalisms. Second, I have attempted to investigate, from a realist perspective, the strategic objectives that drove Western powers, led by the United States, to wage war on the Federal Republic of Yugoslavia. I have also tried to identify, at least approximately, the 'global' stakes in the political and military strategy of 'humanitarian intervention'. Furthermore, I have looked into the more strictly military aspects of the conflict to find clues about the evolution of warfare, the nature of which is rapidly changing under the pressure of technological advancements and globalization. Some, like Mary Kaldor and Régis Debray, have spoken, although with different nuances, of 'new warfare'. Ulrich Beck has gone so far as to formulate the notion of 'post-national war', while Edward Luttwak has proposed the cynically euphemistic formula of 'post-heroic war'.

A closely related subject is the effectiveness of international law and institutions in curbing violence and regulating the use of force by states. This is a crucial issue, since the powers that decided to wage the 'humanitarian war' meant to introduce – and party succeeded in introducing – radical innovations both in the sources of international law and in the standards of legitimacy for the use of force. (The countries that opposed the war – especially Russia, China and India – claimed that these innovations were serious violations of international law.) It would seem that the consensus of states, based on the principle of their 'equal sovereignty', tends to be the primary source of international legality no longer. The principle of equal sovereignty harks back to seventeenth-century Europe, to the Westphalia peace treaties, but it was confirmed in the twentieth century by a long series of covenants and treaties, including the Covenant of the League of Nations and, in substance, the United Nations Charter itself. Today it is replaced by categories such as 'world public opinion' and 'international ethics'. And these categories tend more and more often to coincide with the values and strategies of the major industrial powers of the planet, especially those of the Anglo-Saxon countries. The principle that lies at the core of the United Nations Charter, namely the need to safeguard peace and the consequent right of the international community to employ force to counter acts of 'aggression' threatening peace, is being replaced by the principle of the defence of human rights.

The Secretary-General of the United Nations himself, Kofi Annan, espoused the point of view of Western powers when he declared that in cases of 'systematic abuse and massive violation of human rights', humanitarian intervention can disregard the principle of the respect of the sovereignty of states and non-interference in their internal affairs. Thus, the universalist criterion of the defence of the fundamental rights of all human beings ought to supersede an antithetical criterion, namely the particularist principle of the sovereignty of national states and the inviolability of their frontiers. As we shall see, this trend raises some rather delicate issues. Such a universalist normative mutation does not seem compatible with the present structure of international institutions, especially that of the Security Council of the United Nations, dominated as it is by that extreme form of particularism represented by the veto power of its permanent members. Second, the doctrine of human rights, with its universalist claims, threatens to serve as a new ideology directed against the non-Western cultures of the planet in a perspective of 'Westernization of the world'. Third, the ethico-theological doctrine of *bellum iustum* (just war), a traditional apologetic instrument of Western wars, threatens to metamorphose into a 'humanitarian claim' according to which the use of force – and the killing of innocents – is compatible with the defence of human rights.

3

As the reader will see, I have paid special attention to the reactions of the non-Western world (especially Asia, and China in particular) against the new philosophy of 'humanitarian interference' and NATO's unprecedented aggressive projection. In my opinion, it is important to understand what effects the extraordinary display of power by the Atlantic Alliance in the Balkans may have on the political balance of the planet in the years to come. These effects will probably determine the future structure of international law, the role of the United Nations, and even the prospects for the permanent International Criminal Court, whose statute was approved in Rome in the summer of 1998.

Clearly, I could hardly neglect to deal with the subject of the future relations between NATO's new expansive and projective structure and the European Union, and, more generally, that of the compatibility between the United States' strategic unilateralism and the political, economic and military dynamics of the regional integration in course in Western and, especially, Eastern Europe. As we know, the European summit held in Helsinki in December 1999 accepted the application for membership in the EU of no fewer than twelve 'Oriental' countries, including Latvia, Lithuania, Slovakia, Romania, Bulgaria and, with some reservations, Turkey.

These premises will perhaps suffice to explain why my book does not offer a historical reconstruction of the war, a geopolitical analysis of the Balkan conflict, or an exegesis of diplomatic documents. At any rate, there is plenty of literature available on this subject. It is cited in the bibliography at the end of the book, together with a historical and political chronology furnishing a framework of reference for the reader. The pages containing a critique of cosmopolitan moralism, especially as articulated by Habermas, and 'judicial internationalism', which has led to the institution of the new international criminal courts, are meant as appendices to my main subject, which, again, is not a reconstruction of the war, but a reflection on its deep reasons, its nature and its 'global' impact.

I wish to thank Pier Paolo Portinaro, who amiably encouraged me to write this book, and Richard Bellamy, who urged me to publish it in English. Among the Italian and foreign friends with whom I have exchanged views in private encounters, electronic correspondence and, on occasion, heated journalistic disputes, I wish to remember with gratitude Norberto Bobbio, Antonio Cassese, Pietro Costa, Luigi Ferrajoli, Diana Johnstone, and Eugenio Ripepe.

Antonella Brillante assisted me in compiling the bibliography. Luca Baccelli, Letizia Gianformaggio and Emilio Santoro contributed useful criticism of the first draft of the text.

Florence, 24 March, 2000

Postscript

I learn just as the book has entered its production stages (May 2000) that the General Prosecutor of the International Criminal Tribunal for former Yugoslavia, Carla del Ponte, has informed the Security Council of the United Nations of her decision to archive as manifestly unfounded all accusations filed against NATO political and military authorities for violations committed in the bombing of the Yugoslav Republic. This decision confirms in full the doubts and worries I have expressed in this book concerning the political autonomy of the Hague Tribunal and, more generally, the function of international criminal jurisdiction. The Hague Tribunal has not hesitated to put international justice in the service of those powers on which it depends both politically and financially.

CHAPTER 1

Imperial Mapping and Balkan Nationalism

A Lesser Europe

Reconstructing the Balkan context of the 'humanitarian war' can help us to understand its reasons.[1] Such a reconstruction requires, first of all, an examination of the historical reasons why this war broke out in the Balkan peninsula rather than in some other region of the world, and, second, a clarification of the cultural, political and economic factors that made the Balkans the theatre of the 'new war'.

It may prove useful to start with a general consideration. The peoples of the Balkans have been regarded as culturally and politically 'European' at least since the first decades of the nineteenth century, when the major powers of Europe favoured their independence from the Ottoman Empire. Yet many of them share beliefs, linguistic features and customs derived from the eastern branch of the East–West schism. Orthodox iconography is still an essential component of Balkan identity, and a high percentage of Bosnians, the vast majority of Albanians and all the Sanzak people are Muslims. Today the Balkans are unquestionably perceived by Western culture as being a part of Europe, paradoxically by the very people who regarded it as inadmissible for something resembling the Holocaust to be re-enacted in the territories of former Yugoslavia in the form of 'ethnic cleansing' (this was one of the non-official motivations for NATO's military action against the Yugoslav Federation).

However, Westerners tend to look on the Balkans as somehow a lesser Europe, weak, peripheral and weighed down by a past it is unable to shuffle off. The main peoples inhabiting the region – Croats, Serbs, Romanians, Bulgarians, Bosnians, Albanians and Greeks – are certainly not culturally distinct from the peoples of Central Europe, as are, for example, the people of the Maghreb, the Berbers, or the Bedouin of Saudi Arabia. Still, their historical-political and cultural identity is very different from that of the French, British and Germans, as well the Italians. Western public opinion sees the Balkan peoples – except only for the Greeks – as afflicted with a kind of cultural primitivism, an ancestral coarseness, a provincial closed-mindedness. It is commonly thought that their elites have played only a marginal role in European intellectual life, and that their ruling classes have been cut off for too long from the vital streams of political democracy and economic freedom that have nourished Western civilization. Furthermore, the long interlude under communist regimes is believed to have aggravated this syndrome of isolation and backwardness.[2]

In a word, one could say that the Balkan peoples are, indeed, European, but not in the full sense of the term. They are near enough to the geopolitical fulcrum of Europe for all Europeans to be aware that their own historical destiny is interwoven with that of the Balkans. But they are also 'different' enough to be treated, if necessary, as domestic aliens. This attitude towards the Balkan peoples helps us to understand how it is that the West has chosen to place political and military exponents of former Yugoslavia under the penal jurisdiction of an international court nominated *ad hoc*, a treatment previously reserved only for Nazi criminals, and why the first international jail in history was built expressly for them. It also offers some clues as to why no anthropological aggression-inhibiting mechanism, no ethical or religious scruple, prevented the 'war from the sky' from placing the value of the life of the Serbs, Albanians and Roma on a scale far below that of US and European NATO soldiers.[3]

A second consideration: ever since the rapid expansion and subsequent centuries-long decline of the Ottoman Empire, the Balkan peninsula has been perceived by Europe not only as an area of constant political turbulence, but also as its least defended geopolitical quarter, the most vulnerable to possible aggression by enemies from outside. In the collective imagination of Europeans, today as well as yesterday, the Balkans are a desolate land, plagued by violence and full of danger. For decades their claim to fame was for having assassinated the archduke of Austria-Hungary, Franz Ferdinand, and his wife Sofia Chotek, setting off World War I. Both Otto von Bismarck's and Winston Churchill's disparaging comments about the Balkans are well known. A British prime minister, John Major, has gone so far as to say that the Yugoslavian peoples are 'incapable of learning'.[4] It is also well known that during the twentieth century, this European prejudice found its way into the political culture of the United States. One has only to think of the great popularity in the United States of journalist John Gunther's *Inside Europe*, written in the late 1930s. He denounced the fact that thousands of young Americans had died in a war provoked by one of 'these wretched and unhappy little countries in the Balkan peninsula' as 'an intolerable affront to the human and political nature'.[5]

A third consideration is called for, regarding the most common of the commonplaces in the political historiography of the Balkans. Balkan nationalism is claimed to be regressive and violent, at a far remove from the idea of nationhood in democratic Europe. It is rooted in an archaic logic of hatred, revenge and bloodshed. It is nourished by irrational symbolic representations and 'foundation myths'. According to an even more insidious stereotype, this perverse nationalism is thought to have given rise to an especially intolerant, aggressive and violent practice typical of the whole subcontinent, especially of the peoples of former Yugoslavia, namely 'ethnic cleansing', a term which today, in the language of Western media, designates the Balkan version of that most heinous of crimes, genocide.[6] Balkan countries are believed to gravitate, for historical reasons, towards the model of the 'ethnic state', practising a ruthless racial exclusiveness, while bringing tribal aggregations and, on occasion, criminal organizations into the political sphere.

Several authors, including some Balkan ones – from William Hagen to Mary Kaldor, Ismail Kadaré and Georges Prévélakis[7] – point to ethno-nationalist extremism as the endogenous cause of the Balkan troubles and construe the area as a sort of 'rogue continent'. Many of these authors believe that only an outside power – the European Union or the West – can save the Balkans from their final 'Balkanization'.

William Hagen, for example, claims that 'today's Balkan crises are rooted in the crippling dependence of all Balkan peoples on the ideology and psychology of expansionist nationalism'.[8] According to Hagen, the ethnic-nationalistic syndrome goes back to the Ottoman

Empire, whose political-administrative characteristics caused an 'extraordinary dispersion and intermixture of ethnic groups', a phenomenon also observable in other imperial regimes, such as India and tsarist Russia. The ethnic and religious minorities of the Ottoman Empire tended to organize at a local level, and each group enjoyed a sort of political and cultural extra-territoriality. By the end of the eighteenth century, as the crisis of the Ottoman Empire grew worse, European nationalism spread throughout the Balkans, inspiring Serbian, Greek, Romanian and Bulgarian struggles for independence. The victorious outcome of these struggles led to a devastating imposition, in the course of the nineteenth century, of the model of the nation-state – which the stronger ethnic groups imported from Europe and succeeded in implementing territorially – upon a broad, variegated array of cultural-ethnic minorities. It is out of this soil that the ultra-nationalist ideologies of 'Greater Serbia', 'Greater Albania' and 'Greater Greece' sprang up. These ideologies represent a transversal and cross-bred irredentism which, no longer being directed against the Turkish oppressor, fuels fratricidal wars in the name of an idolized 'national community'. According to Hagen, this explains not only the obsessive nationalism of the Balkan peoples (and the accompanying phenomenon of 'ethnic cleansing'), but also their total estrangement from the Western liberal democratic tradition, their innate readiness to violence and their authoritarianism.[9]

Mary Kaldor takes for granted that virulent nationalism and 'ethnic cleansing' have been constant features of the history of the Balkans for the past two centuries. Without going into a historical analysis, she discusses two alternative interpretations. The first is that Balkan nationalism, especially that of the Croatian, Serbian and Bosnian peoples, is atavistic, harking back to the dawn of their history. According to the second interpretation, contemporary nationalist ideology is merely the last attempt of desperate and corrupt elites to preserve their power after the crisis of the communist regimes.[10] Kaldor, committed to universalist and cosmopolitan ideals, maintains that what is at stake today in the Balkans is the 'values of civilization', threatened by tribalism and a ruinous 'politics of identity' that claims power on ethnic, racial or religious grounds. Following a pattern that is typical of 'Western globalists', Kaldor recommends that the international community use all the means at hand, including military force, against the irrationality of the new Balkan tribalism.[11]

Kadaré, the famous Albanian writer, believes that today it is 'urgent and fundamental' that the peoples of the Balkans be 'civilized and Europeanized'. And he adds:

> Europe has often ignored or scorned the Balkans. In the meanwhile, thick layers have deposited in the memory of the Balkan peoples. Isolated, separated from the European continent, these peoples have conceived all sorts of ghosts, myths and legends in which they have really believed, making them the basis of their nationalist ideologies. This explains why the Balkan peoples, instead of basking in the light of liberty, collaborating and working together to mend the disasters of the past, have often gone in the opposite direction, attacking one another in the name of the ghosts conjured up by their solitude.[12]

Georges Prévélakis had already expressed views like these in the early 1990s. Concluding an important essay on the culture and geopolitics of the Balkan peoples, he claims they are not capable, on their own, of restoring their unity and forsaking the road of nationalistic conflict for that of co-operation. Hence the urgent necessity for an outside power (Europe) to impose its 'cultural and political hegemony on the Balkans'.[13] Only by submitting to the process of European integration will the Balkan peoples be able to soothe the traumas of the past and overcome their centuries-old reciprocal mistrust. If Europe fails, adds Prévélakis, 'there is the risk that other world powers, first and foremost the United States, will intervene'.[14]

Imperial Mapping

Probably there is some truth in all the foregoing interpretations of Balkan nationalism, even in those animated by the haughtiest Eurocentric prejudice. It is certainly undeniable that nationalism is a very important element of Balkan tradition, nor can one underestimate the death and destruction caused by inter-ethnic conflicts in the region. Ethnic clashes, especially since the Balkan Wars of 1912–13 and the civil war of 1941, have been extremely bloody, with hundreds of thousands of victims. And it would be a mistake not to acknowledge that violence in the Balkans has reached very high levels of destructiveness and atrocity, although certainly not comparable with those reached on many occasions by other European peoples and the United States; one has only to think of the African slave trade, Nazi extermination camps, the bombing of German cities by the Allied forces, the atomic massacre of Hiroshima and Nagasaki, Vietnam.[15]

There is an element, however, that Eurocentric historiography has neglected, and that needs to be brought into focus: the role of the great European powers in the genesis and exacerbation of ethno-nationalism in the Balkans, the fragmentation of its political groups, the carving up of its territories and the subjugation of its states. Historical investigation cannot stop, as William Hagen does, with the Ottoman conquest, which was no more than a prelude. Other imperial powers played a major role in the 'Balkanization' of Danubian and South-Eastern Europe, first and foremost the Austro-Hungarian Empire and tsarist Russia, but also Great Britain, France and Germany, as well as Italy (and not just in the Fascist period).

After 1699, when the Balkan peoples finally managed to oust the Turks from Slavonia, Transylvania and other neighbouring territories, the advance of European states into the Balkans began. From then on, for nearly two centuries Turkish control of the region weakened progressively, until it was sharply curtailed at the Congress of Berlin in 1878 and lost altogether in the first two decades of the twentieth century as a consequence of the 'Balkan wars' and the treaties that followed them. In the first two decades of the eighteenth century, the Austrian Empire set foot in the Balkans, starting with the territories of the Croats, Serbs and Romanians. The Austrians were followed, with mixed fortune, by tsarist Russia. With the Treaty of San Stéfano (Yesilköy), also in 1878, Russia succeeded in forcing the Turks to accept the plan for a 'Greater Bulgaria' controlled by Russian diplomacy and the Russian army. Thus, Russia became the master of the Balkans and at last obtained an outlet on the Azov Sea and, thus, to the Black Sea and the Mediterranean.

On more than one occasion these two imperial powers, the Austrian Empire and Russia – sometimes joined by Great Britain and, later on, by France and Italy – sat at a table to split up the former Ottoman Empire among themselves. The same method was used in the decades following 1878 to carve up Africa and much of Asia. At the San Stéfano and Berlin congresses – the latter chaired by Bismarck in person – ethnographic maps provided by Balkan representatives were used for the first time.[16] But the 'Eastern

Question' was posed and answered by European powers according to the rules of imperial mapping; that is, they allotted conquered territories and drew state boundaries almost exclusively on the basis of strategic and economic considerations. Julius Andrássy, Austrian plenipotentiary at the Congress of Berlin, summarized the policies of European imperial powers by declaring that 'in all delimitations the decisions should in the first instance be based on geographical and strategical considerations, and only on ethnographical grounds if no other basis for decision could be found'.[17]

Doubtless the deep 'ethnic' roots of Balkan political entities do go back, as William Hagen maintains, to the Ottoman Empire. But this is hardly a valid polemical argument; rather, it is proof that the Ottoman Empire was not the oppressive, bloodthirsty regime it was made out to be in nineteenth-century Europe. Rather, it was a complex and sophisticated political formation, which apparently showed more religious tolerance than did many European countries. To non-Muslim subjects, the Ottoman state was a rather evanescent entity. In their everyday experience, they felt the presence of the *millet* – both a religious community and a decentralized administrative unit – more than that of the central state, whose sole function was to ensure order and security, the *pax ottomanica*. Within minority groups, cultural identity and a sense of collective membership were based on religion and language, with no specific connection to territory or state. This was a 'diasporic', non-territorial conception of nation, and was hence compatible with the universalism of Ottoman institutions.[18] It was only under the influence of European ideologies – liberalism, nationalism and later on, paradoxically, communism – that the ethnic-religious groups of the Balkans began to crystallize into states.[19] At this point, the 'imperial mapping' of the European powers came into play, with destabilizing consequences. As a result of their intervention, in the words of Prévélakis:

'Ethnic cleansing', up to then an expression of social tensions which in the Ottoman Empire took on ethnic characteristics, became a fundamental principle of Balkan geopolitics. Instead of waiting for European powers to make the territory of states coincide with the ethnic space, it was the ethnic space that had to be adapted to the territories claimed by each state. This approach was encouraged by the fact that in a vast intermediate zone national identities were not very clear and it was possible to influence local populations in one direction or the other.[20]

During the nineteenth century, Serbia, Greece, Romania and Bulgaria became independent states (Albania gained independence only in 1913). Relations among them were immediately marked by strong antagonism. In each case, the definition of boundaries under the influence of the great powers resulted in the 'nationalization' of territories inhabited by numerous ethnic and religious minorities, as well as the dominating ethnic group. The increasingly direct involvement of European powers in the management of conflicts did nothing but kindle hatred, fear and reciprocal mistrust. This also occurred when, following a well-oiled routine of the Holy Alliance, political and military interference was justified by appealing to the values of Christian peace or civilization.

Thus began the modern history of the Balkans; the processes leading to the dire events of the end of the millennium were set in motion. The Balkans were increasingly reduced to the role of a 'colonial periphery' or 'internal colony' of Europe. The main European powers used the Balkans as an outlet for their short-range, expansionistic aspirations, often in open conflict with each other. Each power, following the Westphalian logic of equilibrium, tried to control the Balkan space or prevent other powers from controlling it. In the nineteenth and the first half of the twentieth century, the Balkans were the crossroads of four imperial strategies: Russia's push towards the warm seas, Germany's *Drang nach Osten*, Great Britain's protection of sea routes and France's traditional presence in the Orient. To these was added, in the late 1930s, the expansionism of Fascist Italy and Nazi Germany, whose intervention in the Balkans had especially serious consequences, to the point where it can be regarded as one of the main historical preludes to the tragedies of the 1990s.

Finally, as Misha Glenny points out, it should not be forgotten that, along with nationalist and liberal ideas, Europe also exported its militarist ideology to the Balkans. The Serbs, Bulgarians and Turks (and, to a lesser degree, the Greeks and Romanians) looked up to Prussia's great military tradition as a model and sent their officers to train in German military academies, as well as in those of France, Great Britain and Russia. The armies that fought in the bloody 'Balkan wars' (1912–13) were financed by Western loans and armed by European companies such as Krupp, Škoda, Schneider-Creusot and Vickers. Representatives of these companies even took part in the wars as observers and drafted reports to be used as a basis for commercial advertisements for their weaponry.[21]

In sum, it can be argued that the ethnic tensions and nationalistic aggressiveness of the Balkan peoples received a decisive boost, not from the political-administrative structure of the Ottoman Empire or the struggle for freedom from its rule – on the contrary, in that struggle the people of the Balkans were often allied with one another – but from the policies of the European empires that carved up and fragmented their territories. Indeed, for a long time Ottoman diplomacy had managed, by skilfully exploiting the rivalries between European powers, to protect the Balkans from their designs of conquest. It is the creation, sponsored by the West, of small, weak, reciprocally hostile nation states,[22] that has turned the Balkans into a bloodstained land of war and conquest, an intricate geopolitical crossroads, and a source of international instability within increasingly vast scenarios; a 'powder keg of Europe' that threatens to become a powder keg of the world.

Serbian Nationalism: Diasporic Identity and Territorial State

According to Misha Glenny, the intervention of Italy and Germany in the Balkans had worse consequences for the region than any other event.[23] Between 1939 and 1941 the Italians and Germans managed to manipulate the most radical Balkan political fringes (the Croatian *ustaše* and the Macedonian revolutionaries) to subvert the political and military equilibrium of the territories of Yugoslavia in an attempt to seize control of the whole Balkan peninsula.

The conflict between Croats, Serbs and Bosnians exploded after 1941 with unheard-of violence, causing an estimated half a million victims among the Serbian population alone. This catastrophe was the direct consequence of Mussolini's and Hitler's decision to train, organize and arm the *ustaše* movement, founded in Italy in 1930 by the Catholic Fascist Ante Pavelić. The aim of this terrorist organization was to gain the independence of Croatia from the Kingdom of Yugoslavia and free the Croatian people from the hegemony of the Serbs.[24]

Thanks to the support of the Nazi-Fascist axis, the *ustaše* achieved their goal in April 1941. A Fascist government led by the *Duce* (*poglavnik*) Pavelić, was installed in Zagreb, and its jurisdiction was extended to include Bosnia-Herzegovina. The Franciscan order and the Catholic hierarchies led by Cardinal Alojzije Stepinac supported the new clerical-Fascist regime, which, in their eyes, had the merit of fighting abortion, pornography, freemasonry, communism, the 'schismatic' Orthodox Church and the Jewish community, all in one. As many as 150 military chaplains took part in campaigns for the physical elimination of the Orthodox Serbs and their religious leaders. These campaigns were followed, from 1942 onwards, by others for the forced mass conversion of the Serbian population to Catholicism.[25] In the meantime, Italy had conquered Albania, to which it annexed Kosovo and part of Macedonia, and started the invasion of Greece. In all the territories controlled directly or indirectly by the Germans and Italians, racial persecution was launched against Serbs, Jews and Roma. These atrocities left deep scars in the collective subconscious of the Yugoslavian peoples. An idea of the style of the Italian aggressors is provided by the following note of 17 July 1941, in the diary of Galeazzo Ciano, Italian Minister of Foreign Affairs:

> Mussolini, as usual, addresses the military in a rough tone, and says that he loves only one general – his name escapes me – who said to his soldiers in Albania: 'I have heard it said that you are good family men. This is fine at home, but not here. Here you will never be sufficiently thieves, murderers and rapists'.[26]

The breaking up of Yugoslavia, the mutilation of its national territory, German reprisals, and the atrocities inflicted by Croatian clerical Fascists on the Serb minorities of Slavonia and Krajina reawakened Serbian nationalism. Extremist movements sprang up in Serbia as well as Croatia. These movements rediscovered the Chetnik tradition and nursed the ideal of a 'Greater Serbia', which, like the analogous notions of 'Greater Albania' and 'Greater Greece', has little in common with the territorial expansionism of European totalitarian regimes. As Josip Krulić observes, the Serbs perceive their historical continuity with the Serbian Empire of the thirteenth and fourteenth centuries only through their identification with their autocephalous Orthodox church, which preserved their identity in the framework of the Ottoman institution of the *millet*, where religious unity coincided with administrative autonomy. Paul Garde stresses that the Serbs were the first people of the Yugoslavian region explicitly to found community membership on a religious basis.[27] It is their ethnic-religious identity that kept the Serbs from dispersing, as they would have if they had converted to Catholicism or Islam.

The goal of Serbian nationalism is essentially to restore the unity of the Serbian people, as a reaction against the imposing migrations which, from the early sixteenth century onwards, dispersed the Serbs over an area extending for over a thousand kilometres from north to south, from the upper course of the Sava to Kosovo.[28] Thus, following a typical pattern, the ideology of an identity based on the notion of 'Greater Serbia' sprang directly from the tension between the 'diasporic' dimension of the Serbian nation, on the one hand, and a territorial and state-oriented dimension inspired by Western models and dictated by the great European powers, on the other. Ever since its independence was acknowledged at the Congress of Berlin in 1878, Serbia has perceived itself as a small, poor country surrounded by enemies and forced to accept the statehood and territorial boundaries dictated by the European powers, although they do not correspond to its historical and 'diasporic' identity. Besides its historically rooted legitimacy – Kosovo is of fundamental importance – Serbia claims a religious and demographic legitimization: the territories settled by a majority of Orthodox Serbs, such as Krajina, Vojvodina and Banat, are thought to belong to Serbia. Although these claims have led to criminal violence against people and property, it would be a mere Enlightenment abstraction to ignore their deep historical and cultural roots.

Nationalism and Yugoslavism

From the last decades of the nineteenth century onwards, Serbian culture evolved in new and complex ways. A broader project of linguistic and cultural legitimization emerged alongside 'historical-diasporic' nationalist claims. This project gained favour especially in the periods immediately following the two world wars. Faced with an enormous loss of human life and political and economic isolation, the Serbs felt the need to create a larger and stronger state to allow them to resist pressure from Austria-Hungary and German expansionism, and later on from the two superpowers of the Cold War.

This plan was extremely controversial, since it roughly coincided with the 'Illyrian' ideal of the reunification of all the Slavs of the south – including the Slovenians and the Croats – based on the acknowledgement of their fundamental linguistic unity. It was also very risky, since it sought, in the name of linguistic unity and geopolitical contiguity, to wish away the religious diversity between Catholic Slavs and Orthodox Slavs – a diversity that today still represents one of the main fault lines in the European cultural space.[29] Under the influence of the studies of the foremost Serbian linguist, Vuk Karadžić, and later on of the geo-anthropological studies of Jovan Cvijic,[30] Belgrade political and intellectual elites tended to see themselves as the enlightened avant-garde of the Yugoslavian people; that is, of all the southern Slavs.

The Slovenians and Croatians had strong misgivings toward this policy, and the Habsburg Empire was hostile to the point of declaring a trade embargo against Serbia between 1906 and 1911. Nevertheless, this Yugoslavist ideology gained favour after World War I with the proclamation of a hereditary parliamentary monarchy headed by the Karageorgević dynasty. It was the defeat of Austria and the falling apart of the Habsburg empire that allowed this 'Kingdom of the Serbs, Croats and Slovenians' to arise. It lasted from 1918 to the civil war brought about by the intervention of Italy and Germany.

This experiment of national unity was renewed after World War II with the Federal Republic of Yugoslavia (1945–91), inspired initially by the Soviet model and led by Marshal Josip Broz Tito. Tito nursed the dream of a great federation of Yugoslavia, Bulgaria and Albania, in the framework of a general political vision centred on resistance against the great powers of central Europe and the renaissance of the Balkans. His plan, however, met with the immediate opposition of the Soviet Union (in accordance with the tsarist tradition), which used it as one of the reasons to justify the expulsion of Yugoslavia from the Cominform (1948).[31]

The Serbs played a prominent role in both of these 'Yugoslavian' experiences. Serbia's role in the Balkans was, in all aspects, analogous to that of Piedmont in the Italian Risorgimento. However, latent, corrosive ethnic tensions hung on, as we have seen, both during the monarchy and under Tito's communist federalism. During the federalist period, Croatia opposed Serbia's hegemonic ambitions. The Serbs were thought of as a less well-educated and less civilized people, far removed from European culture because of their Orthodox religion. Croatia regarded the powers allotted to the federal state as excessive, especially in the

economic and financial sphere, and barely tolerated Serb predominance in the army and secret services. But the Serbian nationalist
intelligentsia were frustrated, too. The ideal of Illyrian federalism,
although it did oppose the traditional policy of the European
powers, undermined the ideology of ethnic identity, and the Serbs
again felt dispersed and weak within the Yugoslav Federation.[32]

Marshal Tito's death in 1980 speeded up the involution of the
Yugoslav federalism by exposing and aggravating the economic and
financial crisis of the country. Yugoslavia's domestic economy
declined rapidly. The foreign debt reached $20 billion, a quarter of
the gross domestic product, and inflation galloped, rising to 2700
per cent a few years later. As a condition for renegotiating
Yugoslavia's debt, the World Bank and the International Monetary
Fund – both controlled by the Western powers – imposed
macroeconomic restructuring plans that made the country's
condition even worse. Public spending was cut, the population
became poorer, and the unemployment rate increased. Conflicts
arose between the federal government and the governments of the
federal republics (and autonomous provinces), and masses of workers
went on strike against the politics of the central government.

The rapid deterioration of economic and social conditions in the
Federation wore down the national spirit and feelings of political
loyalty. The pre-existing centrifugal tendencies became irresistible,
especially in Slovenia, Croatia and Macedonia, which were supported
by the European powers, especially Germany. Once again, Western
interference caused the break-up and disintegration of the Balkan
political body by fomenting disagreements rather than attempting
mediations. The Serbian population felt increasingly ill at ease, as a
document of the Serbian Academy of Science and Arts published in
Belgrade in 1986 dramatically bears out.[33] This text refurbishes and
carries to extremes the theme of Serbian nationalism in its classical
'historical-diasporic' formulation. It denounces the 'creeping
genocide' inflicted on the Serbs in the 'cradle of Serbian culture',
Kosovo. The famous speech delivered by Slobodan Milošević, newly
elected President of Serbia, before an immense crowd of Serbs on the
'Plain of Blackbirds', near Priština, on 28 June 1989, the six
hundredth anniversary of the battle of Kosovo Polje, was inspired by
this Serbian Academy document, although it did not cite it. Having
abandoned all reference to communist ideology, which in any case
had long been ineffective, Milošević espoused the theses of the most
uncompromising Serbian nationalists and firmly vindicated the

ethnic integrity of the Serbs of Kosovo. 'Nobody must thrash this people' is the sentence that gained him great popularity.[34]

In 1991, as the opposition movement of Kosovo's Albanian ethnic group against the Serbian authorities gathered strength and the latter's extremely harsh repressive retaliation began, Slovenia and Croatia, followed by Macedonia, unilaterally proclaimed their independence from the Yugoslav Federation. The leader of Croatia was the nationalist Franjo Tudjman, who had himself called *poglavnik* in memory of Ante Pavelić. Tudjman was supported by the Catholic clergy and financed by the Canadian Franciscan order. The independence of Croatia was promptly recognized by the German government and, with unprecedented rapidity, by the Vatican authorities, although it was easily foreseeable that this would provoke a response by the Serb minorities of Croatia and foment Serbian nationalism, thus accelerating the falling apart of the Yugoslav Federation. After Tito's death, German diplomacy, in line with its centuries-old tradition, worked constantly at undermining the unity of Yugoslavia and reducing the power of the Serbs. Germany's strategic objective was to extend its economic and cultural hegemony in both Eastern and South-Eastern Europe.

In October 1991 the Bosnian parliament voted for the region's independence, which the European Community promptly recognized. An immediate consequence was the outbreak of a war among the Serbs, Croats and Bosnian Muslims for the control of the territory of Bosnia-Herzegovina. This war caused the forced emigration of tens of thousands of Serbs, Croats and, in lesser numbers, Bosnian Muslims. Violence exploded in former Yugoslavia, including ethnic purges and deportations by all the main contenders. At the end of the war there were over 250,000 dead and over a million refugees.

The war in Bosnia saw the first intervention of NATO forces both in 'peacekeeping' actions by explicit mandate of the United Nations and, with the unspoken consent of the Security Council, in actual war actions against Serbian military posts. The final peace treaty was concluded in the military base of Dayton, Ohio, and solemnly signed in Paris in the presence of the president of the United States, Bill Clinton. The representative of the United Nations in former Yugoslavia, Kofi Annan, was not present at Dayton, not having been invited, whereas in Paris the Secretary-General of the United Nations, Boutros Boutros-Ghali, was one of the personalities invited to take part in the ceremony as spectators.

Once again, the peace agreement mandated the fragmentation of the Balkan territories and their control by NATO troops formally under the United Nations, but actually at the orders of the Western powers. Even the economy of the entire Bosnian region – which was given the juridical status of a state, the run-down, multi-ethnic Bosnian Federal Republic – eventually became entirely dependent on Western economic aid, partly controlled by international criminal organizations.[35]

The Three Claims of Humanitarian War

The Bosnian war brought a remarkable innovation into the history of Balkan wars, opening the way to the war over Kosovo. For the first time a Western, non-European power, the United States of America, stepped into the Balkan scene. Also for the first time, international institutions claiming to represent an impartial point of view and universal values, namely the Security Council and General Secretariat of the United Nations, worked side by side with the great Western powers, although the relationship was more often tense than symbiotic. Another important innovation was the creation of the International Criminal Tribunal for former Yugoslavia, instituted by the Security Council in 1993 and located in The Hague. Its task is to prosecute all those who have committed 'serious violations of international humanitarian law' within the boundaries of former Yugoslavia since January 1991. 'International humanitarian law' means the international defence of basic human rights and, hence, the repression of the more serious violations of these rights, such as genocide, crimes against humanity and war crimes, according to a model harking back to the Nuremberg Tribunal.[36]

Following a practice begun with the Gulf War,[37] the appeal to humanitarian motivations serves to legitimize not only the United Nations' repressive interventions, but also political interference or military intervention by other international organizations or agencies, including the G7 (or G8, with Russia) – the organization of the main economic powers of the planet – the Organization for Security and Co-operation in Europe (OSCE) and, above all, NATO. In the war in Bosnia, NATO played a primary political-military role, upstaging the organs of the United Nations. Furthermore, the US government adopted a policy of direct political and military interference. The president of the United States, Bill Clinton, promoted diplomatic initiatives and made political and military decisions with a wide margin of autonomy from all international organs and institutions.

Throughout the war over Kosovo, this contamination of universalism and particularism, ethical motivations and political decision-making, juridical impartiality and strategic hegemony, remained constant and much in evidence. From this point of view, one could argue that the war in Bosnia and the war for Kosovo are consecutive episodes of a single 'humanitarian war'. In both of them the humanitarian military intervention implied three fundamental claims. In the first place, present-day international institutions profess to oppose the particularism of the nationalist conflicts that are lacerating the Balkans with their institutional universalism, the universalism of the doctrine of the rights of man, and the 'thirdness' of international criminal jurisdiction. Second, certain Western powers or military organizations assert the legitimacy of their partisan use of force in the name of universal values such as the safeguarding of basic rights (and these 'particular' powers do not coincide with the organs specified by the Charter of the United Nations, and hence operate outside the protocol and procedures prescribed by international law). Finally, there is the claim that modern war – with all its disproportionate and indiscriminate destruction of human lives and possessions – can be used as an instrument of law to defend the rights of members of the human species recognized as subjects of the international legal system.

There are at least two other reasons why the war for Kosovo can be regarded not only as a continuation of the war in Bosnia, but also as a 'humanitarian' offshoot of the Balkan wars of the past century, especially those brought on by the intervention of Italy and Germany. In the first place, as in the case of the Croatian *ustaše* in 1941, the Western powers have taken advantage of nationalist extremism and acute ethnic tensions to intervene in the Balkans. Second, their intervention has once again imposed the logic of 'imperial mapping' – in this case, as we shall see in the next chapter, we are dealing with a 'global' hegemonic mapping – upon the history, culture and national identity of the Balkan peoples.

A Knife at the Back of Yugoslavia

NATO's 'humanitarian' intervention in the ethnic conflict between the Serbs and the Albanians of Kosovo occurred in the more general framework of tensions between Serbian and Albanian nationalism.[38] It is a well-known fact that the Albanians were the last people of the Balkans to develop nationalism, having managed to integrate better than any of the others into the administrative structure of the Ottoman Empire, to the point of embracing its religion and providing a large number of high officials to the Sublime Porte. The Albanians, unlike other Balkan peoples, did not fight for independence from the Ottoman Empire. They never aspired to anything more than an increase in autonomy.

The Albanian state was not established until the Peace of London in 1913, after the Balkan Wars were over. In the process of dividing up the territories conquered from the Turks among the Balkan states, the great European powers, headed by Austria-Hungary and Italy, decided to set up a new state under their protection, essentially for anti-Serb purposes. The result was, once again, a dramatic discrepancy between population distribution and state boundaries. About half of the Albanians were left outside the boundaries of the newly founded state, which included, on the other hand, non-Albanian minorities, mainly Greek. The area of present-day Kosovo was split up between Serbia and Montenegro. Thus arose the first tensions between Serbs and Albanians.[39]

The Serbs claimed Kosovo as the region where their ancient empires had been and where they had the main monuments of their religious culture. The memorandum sent by Serbia to the diplomatic conference held in London in 1913 states that 'Serbia and Montenegro would never consent to the assignment of Kosovo and Metohija, the holy land of the Serbian people from time immemorial, to another state'.[40]

As for the Albanians, ever since the foundation of the Prizren League in 1878, they have laid claim to Kosovo on the basis of equally sound and very down-to-earth demographic reasons: from the second half of the eighteenth century onwards, for nearly a century, Kosovo was the main destination of eastward-bound Albanian migration, and today the Albanians, owing to their high rate of population growth, are the majority ethnic group there, and their majority is getting bigger all the time.[41]

The clash between the historical legitimacy of Serbian nationalism and the 'diasporic' legitimacy of Albanian (and Kosovar-Albanian) nationalism fuelled an ethno-nationalistic tension with the typical features of Balkan conflicts. This controversy went on, with changing fortunes, throughout the twentieth century. It turned ugly in the 1980s, leading eventually to the civil war and the atrocities of 'ethnic cleansing' at the end of the 1990s. One of the most characteristic features of this process has been, of course, the role of the Western powers. Their interventions were both indirect and direct. The latter include the Italian and German invasion of Albania and, most recently, NATO's bombing of the Yugoslav Federation and the subsequent deployment of NATO troops in Kosovo.

It was under the Italian and German occupation of 1939–44 that the project of a 'Greater Albania' extending from Kosovo to Epirus was conceived, and this project had the explicit support of the Italians and the Germans, who meant to use it against Yugoslavia. Sergio Romano quotes an illuminating page of the diary of Galeazzo Ciano showing that in 1939 Kosovo was already a pawn in the game played by European diplomacy against Yugoslavia:

> The Kosovars [are] 850,000 Albanians, strong of body, firm in spirit, and enthusiastic about the idea of a Union with their Homeland. Apparently, the Serbians are terrified of them. Today one must ... chloroform the Yugoslavians. But later on one must adopt a politics of deep interest in Kosovo. This will help to keep alive in the Balkans an irredentist problem which will polarize the attention of the Albanians themselves and be *a knife at the back of Yugoslavia.*[42]

After World War II the federal entity governed by Marshal Tito eventually led, after the dismissal of Alexander Rancović, to a remarkable improvement in the relations between Serbs and Albanians. Ethnic tension eased, even in Kosovo, which in 1974 was recognized as an autonomous province with its own constitution and independent institutions. However, the breakdown of Yugoslavia after the death of Tito in 1980 rekindled the tensions, which flared up in an escalation that eventually led to the war. On the one hand, as we have seen, there was the crisis of the Yugoslav experience, fostered by the Western powers with the blessing of the Church of Rome. This crisis inflamed Serbian nationalism and allowed its most extreme representatives to prevail. The Kosovo question was exacerbated, Milošević's ultra-nationalist slogans won increasing support, and, with the connivance of the regime, paramilitary organizations such as Arkan's notorious 'Tigers' came to the fore.[43] In 1989 the government in Belgrade even went so far as to revoke Kosovo's political autonomy. From that moment onwards, it began to discriminate heavily against the Albanian minority, systematically and ruthlessly repressing the independence movement.

On the other hand, it was the West's support of the extremist fringes of Kosovar-Albanian irredentism which, after May 1997, made the civil war irreversible and increasingly bloody. The moderate and non-violent strategy for the liberation of the Kosovar-Albanian people was first marginalized and then defeated. However, it appeared clear that on several occasions almost all the Albanians were favourable to this strategy, notably in 1992, when they elected Ibrahim Rugova as president of the republic with 99 per cent of the vote and gave the majority in parliament to the Democratic League of Kosovo (DLK).[44] The rise, rapid growth and international success of the Kosovo Liberation Army (in Albanian, Ushtria Çlirimtare ë Kosovës, UÇK) is one of the crucial nodes for the understanding of the overall dynamics of the 'humanitarian war'.[45]

As Chris Hedges observes, the ideological roots of the UÇK are anti-democratic. Some of its leaders are followers of the Albanian extreme right-wing tradition, from the reactionary *kacak* (in conflict with the Serbs since the beginning of the twentieth century) to the Fascist militias which collaborated with the Italians, and the notorious Skanderbeg Division of volunteer Albanian SS troops, recruited by the Nazis to fight against Tito's partisans. From this standpoint there is clearly a remarkable ideological affinity between the UÇK and the Croatian *ustaše*. Then there is an 'Enverist' faction of the UÇK, which has taken the upper hand in recent years. It is made up of old Stalinists, once financed by the Albanian communist despot Enver Hoxha. The members of this faction fought against Tito's revisionism and for the annexation of Kosovo to Albania. Many of these leaders, including Hashim Thaci, were students at Priština University after 1974. Taking advantage of Kosovo's autonomous status, Priština University imported from Tiranë a large number of Marxist-Leninist texts printed under Hoxha's regime, as well as Albanian teachers. These two factions have in common an elementary form of political extremism, a tendency to employ violence (including terrorist attacks) and, above all, nationalistic fundamentalism. The strategy of the UÇK, however, is rather obscure. It is not even clear whether its final objective is the independence of Kosovo or its annexation to Albania.[46]

But the most delicate (and least-researched) subjects are the recruitment of the UÇK's militiamen, its financial resources, the sources of its weapons, and the political support it began to receive in 1997–8, culminating in its startling international legitimization at the summit of Rambouillet in February 1999. At the beginning of 1998, the UÇK, which had remained irrelevant throughout 1997, could count on at least 10,000 armed soldiers recruited among young Kosovars from the diaspora, especially from Switzerland and Germany, whose Kosovar communities number, respectively, 100,000 and 120,000 people. The network of the UÇK's money collectors is well developed, especially in Switzerland. The funds come in part from illegal trade – smuggling, drugs, prostitution – managed in Europe by powerful Albanian and Kosovar-Albanian groups.[47] But there are also important political and economic connections leading to Washington – more specifically, to the Albanian American Civil League (AACL), founded in 1986, and the National Albanian American Council (NAAC), founded in 1996, which represent the about 400,000 immigrant Albanians in the United States. These organizations were under the wing of leading personalities both in the Clinton administration and in the Republican Party. In Congress there is a strong pro-Kosovar lobby formed under the guidance of Senator Robert Dole.[48]

However, the decisive consideration is that, from autumn 1998 onwards, the United States, which had an office with diplomatic status and protection in Priština, began to display more and more explicitly its lack of esteem for Rugova and lack of confidence in the moderate strategy of the Democratic League of Kosovo. At the same time, the United States referred more and more often to the views of the leaders of the UÇK and made informal contact with them. Roberto Morozzo della Rocca writes:

Aside from the visible presence alongside the UÇK of former American diplomats as political consultants ... there are rumours and indiscretions, especially at Priština and Tirana, concerning an inflow of weapons and the presence of American instructors among the UÇK. Some European diplomacies note with misgiving the convergence between the Americans and the Albanian guerrillas. There is no doubt, at any rate, that the quick reorganisation of the guerrilla army in Kosovo is the fruit of an intelligent support providing materials and techniques that were previously not available to the UÇK.[49]

At the Rambouillet conference, convened in February 1999 by the 'Contact Group' as a reaction to the massacre of Raçak, it became evident that relations between the United States and the Kosovar guerrillas were very friendly. To quote Morozzo della Rocca again:

> The weeks of negotiations in the castle of Francis I brought the connection between the USA and the UÇK completely out in the open. It was the Americans who raised Hashim Thaci to the leadership of the Albanian delegation, in which Rugova, the president democratically elected by the Kosovars, had to take a back seat to this twenty-nine-year-old young man. Thaci obtained Albright's attention and the solicitude of Wesley Clark …... After the failure of the first phases of the negotiations, Thaci was invited to Washington, where the advantages of signing were patiently explained to him.[50]

Thus, in mid-March, when negotiations resumed in Paris, Hashim Thaci signed, because he knew very well that the 'knife at the back of Yugoslavia' was now ready to strike.

The 'Imperial Mapping' of Rambouillet

In Paris the UÇK accepted without hesitation the 'imperial map' drawn up at Rambouillet. American 'cartographers' had illustrated it to Hashim Thaci, both in its literal meaning and in its unexpressed intentions.[51] The United States had decided (and its European partners did not raise any objections) that Kosovo would be taken from Serbia, either by coercive diplomatic pressure or by force of arms. In fact, the troops had been ready for months, since the Atlantic Council's 'Activation Order' of October 13, 1998.

Unlike the Albanians, the Yugoslav Federation, by will of its president and parliament, refused to yield and sign. How can one explain such a refusal, which entailed a very high risk that the "Activation Order" would actually be carried out and NATO would launch a war that a small and isolated country like Yugoslavia could not possibly sustain? In what context did the authorities of Belgrade reach such a momentous decision?

From mid-January 1999 onwards, the violence and killings of the civil war in Kosovo had resumed, after a three-month suspension following the Holbrooke–Milošević agreement of October 1998. By signing that agreement, Milošević had assented to the idea that the Kosovo crisis should be considered an international question rather than purely an internal question of the Yugoslav Federation, or even a merely Balkan question. He had also consented to significant limitations of the sovereignty of Yugoslavia by admitting 2000 OSCE observers within the frontiers of Kosovo, allowing part of Kosovo to be patrolled by armoured vehicles provided by the OSCE countries, and agreeing to let NATO planes monitor the skies of southern Yugoslavia. Moreover, he had withdrawn the bulk of the Serbian security troops from Kosovo and finally made the 'education agreement' with Rugova effective by giving the main buildings of the Priština campus back to the Albanians.[52] However, in spite of Milošević's initial concessions, however partial and ambiguous, and his tentative, touch-and-go acceptance of negotiations with the democratic representatives of the Kosovar resistance, the Yugoslavian request that the 'activation order' imparted by the Atlantic Council to NATO be cancelled was not granted.[53]

From this moment onwards, a feeling of deep frustration began to circulate once again in Belgrade, and nationalistic extremism gathered strength. The withdrawal of the police forces had entailed the *de facto* loss of Yugoslavia's sovereignty over almost all of Kosovo, which was now in the hands of the UÇK. The Kosovar-Albanian militia, encouraged by NATO's standing threat to use force against Yugoslavia, became increasingly aggressive.[54] For Serbian nationalists, this was the most humiliating defeat after the uninterrupted series of political and military reverses suffered by Serbia during the 1990s. The Serbs had been driven out of Krajina, where they had lived for at least four centuries, in the largest ethnic cleansing operation of the war.[55] They had been defeated in Bosnia and had been forced to bow to the harsh conditions of the *pax americana* of Dayton, including the jurisdiction of the Hague Tribunal, which they felt, probably rightly, was directed mainly against themselves. They had been driven out of eastern Slavonia, which had been inhabited by a majority of Serbs and was now definitively in the hands of the Croats. In Montenegro, the only republic that had agreed to remain federated with Belgrade after the break-up of Tito's Yugoslavia, the number and influence of anti-Belgrade autonomists was growing, and now they were pushing for a total break. In addition, at least 700,000 Serbian refugees from

Croatia and Bosnia were gathered on Serbian soil, with virtually no assistance.

Not only had the historical-diasporic idea of a Serbian nation been totally defeated, but the thwarting of Serbia's national aspirations was compounded by the complete failure of the Yugoslavian project. Partly because of the economic sanctions,[36] Serbia was now reduced to a small, poor, weak country surrounded by hostile countries, themselves small, weak and poor, but supported by great powers. Slovenia and Croatia were assisted by Germany; Bosnia survived under what amounted to a protectorate of the United States; Hungary had just entered NATO; Albania, too, was firmly under the control of Western powers, especially the United States and Italy; Macedonia was ready to apply for membership of NATO; and Bulgaria was bound by increasingly strong economic ties to Turkey, a true oriental bulwark of NATO.[57] The only traditionally friendly power, Russia, was economically and financially weak, and dependent on institutions such as the International Monetary Fund, dominated by the United States. Hence, its diplomacy could not help yielding, in substance, to NATO's actions. Moreover, it was engaged in the brutal repression of a small country in the Caucasus, Chechnya, also struggling for national autonomy.

What did the 'cartographers' of Rambouillet really want from Milošević? What punishment did they intend to inflict on Serbia for the massacre at Račak, which NATO had seized upon as proof of the failure of diplomatic mediation and the uselessness of the OSCE observers? What they were actually demanding was Serbia's total surrender of Kosovo, barely dissimulated by the notion of a temporary regime of autonomy under the protectorate of the United Nations (actually of NATO). They were also demanding a further, humiliating limitation of the territorial sovereignty of Serbia. A 'military chapter', presented by General Wesley Clark as non-negotiable, was appended to the draft of the proposed agreement, where one reads: 'NATO personnel shall enjoy, together with their vehicles, vessels, aircraft and equipment, free and unrestricted passage and unimpeded access throughout the FRY [Federal Republic of Yugoslavia]'.[58] This amounts to a right to armed interference not limited to the region of Kosovo, but extending to the entire territory of Serbia, Vojvodina and Montenegro. It is further specified that:

NATO shall be exempted from duties, taxes and other charges and inspections including providing inventories or other routine customs documentation, for personnel, vehicles, vessels, aircraft, equipment, supplies and provisions entering, exiting, or transiting the territory of the FRY.[59]

The military 'cartographers' of Rambouillet, as even Henry Kissinger admitted,[60] could not possibly be unaware that their 'imperial mapping' was an intolerable diktat. For Milošević and Serbia, to accept would have meant nothing less than political suicide and an unconditional surrender. It would have meant accepting NATO as a military occupation force. Of course Milošević could not accept, particularly because of the nature of his power, his extremely nationalistic ideology, and the structure of his regime, which was only formally democratic, being actually founded on military force, and in many ways corrupt and despotic. However, all this aside, had Serbia accepted, it would have been denying its own history, culture, identity and national dignity.[61]

On the evening of 24 March with no previous authorization by the Security Council of the United Nations, NATO started bombing the Republic of Yugoslavia. The 'humanitarian war', with its thousands of Serbian victims, its bloody purges, and the forced exodus of hundreds of thousands of Kosovar-Albanians, went on uninterruptedly for 78 days, during which period about 1000 allied planes completed over 10,000 attack missions, and over 23,000 missiles and bombs were launched, without counting tens of thousands of depleted uranium shells.

Notes

1. It is not my purpose here to carry out an exhaustive historical and geopolitical analysis. On the history of the Balkans and Eastern Europe, I refer the reader to works such as B. Jelavich, *History of the Balkans*, 2 vols. Cambridge: Cambridge University Press, 1983; D. Kitsikis, *L'Empire ottoman*. Paris: Presses Universitaires de France, 1985; A. Corm, *L'Europe et l'Orient. De la balkanisation à la libanisation.* Paris: La Découverte, 1989; G. Castellan, *Histoire des Balkans, XIV–XX siècle.* Paris: Fayard, 1991; F. Conte, *Gli slavi. Le civiltà dell'Europa occidentale e orientale.* Turin: Einaudi, 1991; C. Cvijic, *Remaking the Balkans.* London: Pinter, 1991; A. Graziosi, *Dai Balcani agli Urali. L'Europa continentale nella storia contemporanea.* Rome: Donzelli, 1999; N. Janigro, *L'esplosione*

delle nazioni: le guerre balcaniche di fine secolo. Milan: Feltrinelli, 1999. Janigro's book, besides being very interesting, contains a useful annotated bibliography (on pp. 204–12).

2. An opinion often presented as an indisputable truth, e.g. by Antonio Calabrò in his essay 'Le responsabilità dell'Europa', in E. Berselli, A. Calabrò, C. Joan, P. Matvejevic, A. Negri, M.C. Platero, S. Silvestri and D. Siniscalso, *La pace e la guerra. I Balcani in cerca di un futuro.* Milan: Il Sole 24 Ore, 1999, pp. 15–16.

3. I am referring here to the particular character of the 'war from the sky', which allowed NATO forces to conclude the war with virtually no casualties, but having caused a high number of innocent victims among the population of Yugoslavia. For a critical examination of this aspect, see R. A. Falk, 'Reflections on the war: postmodern warfare leads to severe abuses of the community that is supposed to be rescued', *The Nation*, 28 June 1999; R. A. Falk, 'Kosovo, world order, and the future of international law', *American Journal of International Law*, 93(4) (1999), 855–6. Michel Walzer also expressed doubts ('L'idea di guerra giusta non va abbandonata', in U. Beck, N. Bobbio, *et al.*, *L'ultima crociata? Ragioni e torti di una guerra giusta.* Rome: Libri di Reset, 1999, pp. 51–7), followed by Giancarlo Bosetti ('I lati oscuri della guerra umanitaria', *ibid.*, pp. 5-15).

4. M. Glenny, *The Balkans, 1804-1999: Nationalism, War and the Great Powers*. London: Granta Books, 1999, p. 141.

5. J. Gunther, *Inside Europe*. New York: Harper, 1938, p. 102.

6. On the notion of ethnic cleansing (*etnicko ciscenje* in Serbo-Croat), see M. Roux, 'Le "nettoyage ethnique": théorie et pratique', in S. Cordellier and E. Poisson (eds), *Nations et nationalismes*. Paris: La Découverte, 1995; M. Grmek, M. Gjidara and N. Simac, *Le 'Nettoyage ethnique'*. Paris: Fayard, 1993; G. Prévélakis, *Les Balkans. Cultures et géopolitique*. Paris: Nathan, 1994, pp. 163–9.

7. See G. Prévélakis, *Les Balkans*; W. Hagen, 'The Balkans' lethal nationalism', *Foreign Affairs*, 78(4) (1999), 52–62; M. Kaldor, *New and Old Wars, Organised Violence in a Global Era*. Cambridge: Polity Press, 1999; I. Kadarè, *Le Monde*, 5 April 1999. See also Calabrò, 'Le responsabilità dell'Europa', pp. 7–28.

8. Hagen, 'The Balkans' lethal nationalism', p. 52.

9. *Ibid.*, pp. 52–4.

10. Kaldor, *New and Old Wars*, pp. 40–8.

11. *Ibid.*, *passim*. On the ideology of 'Western globalists', see H. Bull, *The Anarchical Society*. London: Macmillan, 1977.

12. I. Kadaré, *Le Monde*, 5 April 1999, quoted in Calabrò, 'Le responsabilità dell'Europa', p. 15.

13. Prévélakis, *Les Balkans*, pp. 181–3.

14. *Ibid.*, p. 185.

15. For a vivid report on the atrocities committed during wars in the twentieth century, see the following manual, edited by two US journalists, R. Gutman and D. Rieff: *Crimes of War*, New York: W. W. Norton, 1999. Gutman and Rieff, however, are over-indulgent with the war crimes committed by Western powers, especially the United States.

16. Prévélakis, *Les Balkans*, pp. 127–33.

17. Glenny, *The Balkans,* p. 140.

18. Prévélakis, *Les Balkans*, pp. 97–103. On the theme in general, see B. Badie, *L'État importé. L'Occidentalisation de l'ordre politique.* Paris: Fayard, 1992; B. Badie, *La Fin des territoires. Essai sur le désordre international et l'utilité sociale du respect.* Paris: Fayard, 1995.

19. Prévélakis, *Les Balkans*, pp. 99–101. According to Prévélakis, the distinction between the cultural, religious and diasporic idea of 'nation', typical of Balkanian Eastern Europe, and the Western idea of 'nation', based on the notions of territory and state, is of fundamental importance to the understanding of the 'Eastern question', both yesterday and today. Many of the ethnic and territorial problems of the Balkans, which today one tends to attribute, superficially, to the primitive character of Balkan nationalism, actually derive from the transformation of diasporic nations into territorial nations.

20. *Ibid.*, pp. 131–3.

21. Glenny, *The Balkans*, p. 143.

22. See I. Bibó, *A Kelet-európai Kisállamok nyomorúsága*, Budapest: Új Magyaroszág, 1946; Italian translation. *Miseria dei piccoli Stati dell'Europa orientale.* Bologna: Il Mulino, 1994.

23. Glenny, *The Balkans*, p. 144; M. Glenny, *The Fall of Yugoslavia.* London: Penguin, 1992.

24. See P. Iuso, *Il fascismo e gli ustascia, 1929–1941. Il separatismo croato in Italia.* Rome: Gangemi, 1998; J. W. Borejsza, *Il fascismo e l'Europa orientale. Dalla propaganda all'aggressione*, Rome and Bari: Laterza, 1981.

25. See M. A. Rivelli, *L'arcivescovo del genocidio.* Milan: Kaos Edizioni, 1999, and G. Lerner's comment, 'Il mistero di Stepinac', *La Repubblica*, 19 November 1999, p. 13. Lerner reminds his readers that on Sunday, 4 April 1941, Cardinal Stepinac had the Te Deum sung in all the churches of Croatia in thanks for the birth of the independent Croatian state in the shadow of the Nazi–Fascist bayonets. As is well known, in 1998, during a pastoral visit to Croatia, the present Pope (John Paul II) took part in the rite for the beatification of Stepinac.

26. G. Ciano, *Diario 1939–43*, vol. 2. Milan: Rizzoli, 1963, p. 63.

27. See P. Garde, *Vie et mort de la Yugoslavie.* Paris: Fayard, 1992.

28. See J. Krulić, 'La percezione dello stato-nazione da parte dei croati, dei "musulmani" bosniaci e dei serbi', in S. Cordellier and E. Poisson (eds), *Nazioni e nazionalismi* (translation of *Nations et nationalismes*). Trieste: Asterios, 1999 pp. 127–32.

29. Prévélakis, *Les Balkans*, pp. 133–9.

30. The importance of Jovan Cvijic's works on the geomorphology and political geography of the Balkans is well known. See J. Cvijic, *La Péninsule balcanique*. Paris: Colin, 1918, and cf. Prévélakis, *Les Balkans*, p. 135.

31. See S. Romano, 'Serbia e Kosovo', in M. Cabona (ed.), *'Ditolo a Sparta'. Serbia ed Europa contro l'aggressione della Nato*. Genoa: Graphos, 1999, pp. 188–97.

32. Krulic, 'La percezione dello stato-nazione', pp. 118–19; Prévélakis, *Les Balkans*, pp. 137–9; Hagen, 'The Balkans' lethal nationalism', p. 56. Hagen regards Marshal Tito's dismissal of Minister of the Interior Alexander Ranković, an intransigent Serbian nationalist, as a symptom of growing inter-ethnic tensions within the Yugoslav Federation.

33. The text appeared in September 1986 in the Belgrade newspaper *Večernje Novosti*, and was partially disavowed by the Academy, which called it 'a draft of a document, not meant for publication'; cf. T. Benedikter, *Il dramma del Kosovo. Dall'origine del conflitto tra serbi e albanesi agli scontri di oggi*. Rome: Datanews, 1998, pp. 70–4; Janigro, *L'esplosione delle nazioni*, pp. 83–7.

34. Benedikter, *Il dramma del Kosovo*, pp. 21–4, 71–2; G. Scotto and E. Arielli, *La guerra del Kosovo*. Rome: Editori Riuniti, 1999, pp. 42–2.

35. See R. J. Smith, 'In Bosnia, free enterprise has gotten way out of hand', *International Herald Tribune*, 27 December 1999.

36. On the notion of 'international humanitarian law', see J. Gardam (ed.), *Humanitarian Law*. Aldershot: Ashgate, 1999; S. R. Ratner and J. S. Abrams, *Accountability for Human Rights Atrocities in International Law: Beyond the Nuremberg Legacy*. Oxford: Oxford University Press, 1999.

37. On this point, I refer the reader to my *Cosmopolis: Prospects for World Government*. Cambridge: Polity Press, 1997, pp. xii–iv, 23, 43. In the postscript to this edition of the book I dedicate some pages to a reflection on the war in Bosnia.

38. On the history of Albania and Kosovo, see A. Pipa and R. Sami, *Studies on Kosova*. New York: Columbia University Press, 1984; R. Morozzo della Rocca, *Nazione e religione in Albania*. Bologna: Il Mulino, 1990; M. Dogo, *Kosovo. Albanesi e serbi: le radici del conflitto*. Cosenza: Marco Editore, 1992; Benedikter, *Il dramma del Kosovo*; M. Vickers and J. Pettifer, *Albania: From Anarchy to a Balkan Identity*. London: Hurst, 1997; N. Malcolm, *Kosovo: A Short History*, New York: New York University Press, 1998; M. Vickers, *Between Serb and Albanian: A History of Kosovo*. New York: Columbia University Press, 1998.

39. See G. de Rapper, 'Che cosa significa essere albanese', *Limes*, 3 (1998), 49–62.

40. Benedikter, *Il dramma del Kosovo*, p. 33; see also M. Roux, 'Di chi è il Kosovo? Cento anni di conflitti', *Limes*, 3 (1998), 31–48; A. Konomi,

'Albania e Kosovo possono unirsi?', *Limes*, 3 (1998), 71–88; R. Morozzo della Rocca, 'Kosovo. Le ragioni di una crisi', *Limes*, 3 (1998), 89–100.

41. On the demographic aspects of the crisis in Kosovo, see D. T. Batakovic, 'Progetti serbi di spartizione', *Limes*, 3 (1998), 153–69. Batakovic argues, among other things, that the demographic growth of the Albanians threatens to make them the majority ethnic group in Serbia within a few decades.

42. My emphasis. Cf. S. Romano, 'Serbia e Kosovo', p. 195.

43. On the criminal careers of characters such as Zeljko Raznatović (nicknamed Arkan), Asanin Darko, Cedomir Mihailović and, more generally, on the far-reaching network of Serbian and Albanian mafias, which are interconnected and collaborate with other European criminal groups, including the Italian mafia, see. J. Peleman, 'Gli Stati-mafia: dietro le quinte dei regimi balcanici', *Limes*, supplement to no. 1 of 1999, pp. 59–72.

44. On the initial successes and eventual failure of the project for the emancipation of Kosovo through democratic and non-violent means – a project endorsed by the Democratic League of the People (LDK) led by Ibrahim Rugova – see R. Morozzo della Rocca, 'La via verso la guerra', in *Limes*, supplement to no. 1 of 1999, pp. 11–26; Benedikter, *Il dramma del Kosovo*, pp. 97–103. On European non-governmental organizations' generous but ineffective attempts to prevent the war in Kosovo, see A. L'Abate, *Kosovo: una guerra annunciata*. Molfetta: La Meridiana, 1999.

45. On the history of the UÇK, see C. Hedges, 'Kosovo's next masters?', *Foreign Affairs*, 78(3) (1999), 24–42; A. Nativi, 'Tecniche per un massacro', *Limes*, supplement to no. 1 of 1999, pp. 35–42; A. Konomi, 'Che cosa vogliono i kosovari', *Limes*, supplement to no. 1 of 1999, pp. 49–58; Benedikter, *Il dramma del Kosovo*, pp. 113–15.

46. Hedges, 'Kosovo's next masters?', pp. 26–8; A. Konomi, 'I Balcani secondo gli albanesi', interview with B. Mahmuti, *Limes*, 3 (1998), 123–6.

47. Today, the drug syndicates of the Kosovar-Albanians are regarded as the most powerful and violent in Europe. In 1996 about 800 Albanians and Kosovars were arrested for heroin dealing in Germany alone. In Switzerland there are 2000 Albanians and Kosovars in prison for the same reason (Peleman, 'Gli Stati-mafia, pp. 66–8).

48. Vickers and Pettifer, *Albania*, pp. 175ff.; P. Mastrolilli, 'La lobby albanese in America', *Limes*, 3 (1998), 287–90. Moreover, the UÇK has supporters among the sizeable Albanian minority in western Macedonia; it is from them that it obtains its supplies of automatic weapons plundered from Albanian barracks in 1997 (Benedikter, *Il dramma del Kosovo*, pp. 114–15).

49. Morozzo della Rocca, 'La via verso la guerra', p. 23.

50. *Ibid.*, p. 25.

51. The English text of the Interim Agreement for Peace and Self-

Government in Kosovo (23 February 1999), patterned after the Dayton agreement and used as the reference text for the Rambouillet negotiations, is reproduced in 'Dieci documenti sul Kosovo', *Rivista di studi politici internazionali*, 66(3) (1999), 378–81. The full English text can be consulted at the following Web address: <http://www.monde-diplomatique.fr>. On the conference of Rambouillet in general, see G. Scotto and E. Arielli, *La guerra del Kosovo: anatomia di un'escalation*. Rome: Editori Riuniti, 1999.

52. On the agreement on education between Milošević and Rugova in September 1996, see Morozzo della Rocca, 'La via verso la guerra', pp. 20–1. On the scarce effectiveness and final failure of the OSCE mission, see Ulisse, 'Come gli americani hanno sabotato la missione dell'Osce', *Limes*, supplement to no. 1 of 1999, pp. 113–21.

53. F. Fubini, 'Il bacio di Madeleine, ovvero come (non) negoziammo a Rambouillet', *Limes*, 2 (1999), 19–20; M. Calvo-Platero, 'Le tentazioni di una superpotenza', in E. Berselli *et al.* (eds), *La pace e la guerra*, pp. 131–6.

54. M. Zucconi, 'Crisi del Kosovo. L'occidente industriale contro la Serbia', in *Guerra e pace in Kosovo*, Quaderni Forum, 12 (2) (1998), 14; Morozzo della Rocca, 'La via verso la guerra', p. 22; Fubini, 'Il bacio di Madeleine', p. 20.

55. G. Scotti, *Croazia, Operazione Tempesta. La liberazione della Krajina e il genocidio del popolo serbo*. Rome: Gamberetti, 1996. On pp. 10–11 Scotti claims that the Croatian militias' attack against the Serbs was assisted by NATO planes, which bombed the radars of Knin, capital of Krajina.

56. On the effects of the economic sanctions repeatedly decreed against Yugoslavia, see J. Müller and K. Müller, 'Sanctions of mass destruction', *Foreign Affairs*, 78(3) (1999), 43–53; R. Becker, 'Il ruolo delle sanzioni nella distruzione della Jugoslavia', in T. Di Francesco (ed.), *La Nato nei Balcani*. Rome: Editori Riuniti, 1999, pp. 3–26.

57. E. Di Nolfo, 'Cosa si muove oltre il Kosovo?', *Diorama letterario*, 225 (1999), 5–8.

58. Art. 8 of appendix B to chapter 7 of the Interim Agreement for Peace and Self-Government in Kosovo.

59. Art. 9 of appendix B to chapter 7 of the Interim Agreement for Peace and Self-government in Kosovo; on this subject, cf. D. Caccamo, 'Kosovo: vincitori e vinti', *Rivista di studi politici internazionali*, 66(3) (1999), p. 370; Fubini, 'Il bacio di Madeleine', pp. 24–30.

60. See H. Kissinger, 'US intervention in Kosovo is a mistake', *Boston Globe*, 1 March 1999; H. Kissinger, 'Nato must consider ground troops if Serbia rejects terms', *Newsweek*, 5 April 1999; H. Kissinger, 'New world disorder', *Newsweek*, 31 May 1999.

61. 'One will have to understand', writes Georges Prévélakis, 'the values of these peoples coming from a hostile environment and characterized by a

particular sense of honour, an almost suicidal behaviour in the face of superior odds, expressing their rejection of a cruel destiny and a strong sense of life and death' (*Les Balkans*, p. 185).

CHAPTER 2

Why the War Was Fought

An Intelligent War

Why did the United States and its European allies decide to wage war on the Federal Republic of Yugoslavia? What meanings can plausibly be attributed to the alleged 'humanitarian war'? What was actually at stake in the war, and what kind of war was it?

It is not easy to answer these questions. It would be easier if the humanitarian motivation – the international community's moral duty to put a stop to a serious violation of human rights – could be unhesitatingly accepted, among the wide range of explanatory hypotheses so far put forward, as the 'true', or at least the main, reason for the war. Since the answer, in my opinion, is not that simple and transparent, I shall begin by discussing the humanitarian motivation and then turn to the main alternative hypotheses.

In dealing with this question I shall take for granted that the war for Kosovo was an 'intelligent' war; that is, that it involved a large investment of cognitive resources, specialist know-how and informatics technology, as well as an elaborate and sophisticated strategy that the United States had begun developing, as I shall try to show, as far back as the early 1990s. Hence, I will not give much credit to the notion entertained by Eric Hobsbawm and, in Italy, by Lucio Caracciolo that the war was just a mistake, a sloppily planned initiative, or, as was also argued, that it was 'absurd' and 'purposeless'.[1] Nor will I subscribe to the thesis circulating in some areas of left-wing political culture that it was a 'preventive' and, so to speak, 'apocalyptic' war, in response to a serious and imminent risk of a collapse of the hegemony of the United States, which found itself, it is claimed, unable to control the economic and financial complexity of globalization processes by non-violent means. There is no doubt that the international situation is far from stable. There is always the lurking danger of a sudden economic and financial, and hence political and military, catastrophe. The gaps in economic and 'human' development are tending to widen, producing explosive tensions. However, since the fall of communism the American superpower has proved quite capable of keeping crisis factors under control, thanks in part to its nuclear supremacy and to the fact that no strategic alternatives seem to exist; no political force, Europe least of all, appears capable of standing up to US hegemony.[2]

Whoever Invokes Humanity Is Trying to Cheat

The willingness to give credit to humanitarian motivations, in this as in other cases, obviously depends on the philosophical perspective from which one looks at war. Those who espouse the doctrine of *bellum iustum* or the precepts of military ethics in the Anglo-Saxon tradition – I am thinking, for example, of Michael Walzer – are much readier to accept humanitarian motivations than those who, like the present writer, hold with political realism. From the realist perspective, the sincerity of the ideological convictions of individual political or military decision-makers is irrelevant. It is important, instead, to grasp to what extent ethical motivations can play a role of persuasion in a war. From this point of view, to qualify a war as 'humanitarian intervention' is a typical ploy for self-legitimization by those who wage that war. As such, it is part and parcel of war itself, an instrument of military strategy in the strict sense, used to obtain victory over the enemy.

Every war takes a large investment of human, political and economic resources, and can have very negative consequences not only for the citizens of the losing side, but for the winners as well. Because of its human costs and very high risks, war, more than any other initiative, demands an ideal justification and the emotional consensus of the masses. Humanitarian motivations are a way of ensuring this consensus, whatever the reasons and objectives of the war itself.

From the point of view of Western powers, an appeal to humanitarian motives was probably the most suitable way to deal with international political turbulence after the fall of the Soviet empire and the end of the bipolar world. Today, civil wars spawned by ethnic or religious contrasts provide occasions for military intervention much more frequently than wars between states or groups of states. The traditional motivations for the military interventionism of Western powers – defence of Christianity, keeping the peace, promotion of civilization – have become obsolete. Moreover, as politics and communications became increasingly globalized, the universalizing of humanitarian motivations is an effective rhetorical instrument; it allows one to set 'world public opinion' and 'universal ethics' against the deviant law-unto-itself of a single state or political regime.

'Wer Menschheit sagt, will betrügen' ('whoever invokes humanity is trying to cheat'), wrote Carl Schmitt seventy years ago, paraphrasing a maxim by Proudhon. One need not accept Schmitt's radical anti-humanism to mistrust those who use the word 'humanity' in the context of a war. They most likely use it to morally degrade their foe, singling him out as an 'enemy of humankind', and to justify their own *in*humanity in dealing with him.[3] The argument that the war one is 'regrettably' forced to wage is imposed by the moral imperative of putting a stop to 'crimes against humanity' that one's foe is committing – crimes that modern mass media are able to picture in vivid colours – answers the traditional need to legitimize one's war as *bellum iustum* and stigmatize one's foe as *iniustus hostis* (the unjust enemy). In fact, the ethical-theological doctrine of 'just war' was formulated way back in the Middle Ages and has been consistently employed ever since precisely to this end.[4]

Apart from these general considerations, in the case of the war for Kosovo there are important circumstances of fact that call for scepticism concerning the motives and objectives of the humanitarian war. Leading Western political exponents, from Tony Blair to Massimo D'Alema, from Madeleine Albright to President Bill Clinton himself, occasionally let slip some eloquent admissions. They admitted that besides humanitarian reasons, the war had to do with the security, economic prosperity and international prestige of their countries.[5] Blair's words about the new internationalism inaugurated by NATO's humanitarian interference are exemplary in their moralistic ambiguity and neo-colonial overtones:

Now we need to build a new system. Today our actions are guided by a subtle blend of our own interests and ethical purposes, to defend values we cherish. If we are able to affirm and spread the values of liberty and rule of law, of human rights and open society, this is also in our interest. Spreading our values makes us more secure.[6]

The declarations of the US Secretary of State, Madeleine Albright, are no less illuminating:

Upholding human rights is not merely a new form of international solidarity. It is indispensable for our security and well-being, because governments which trample on the rights of their citizens sooner or later end up by no longer respecting even the rights of others. Regimes which spread insecurity by oppressing their minorities also offer shelter to terrorists, deal in drugs, or secretly prepare weapons of mass destruction.[7]

The US government repeatedly declared that it saw Kosovo, much more than Bosnia-Herzegovina, as a geopolitical space of fundamental strategic interest for American national security. This was stressed, for example, in the famous 'Christmas message'; that is, President George Bush's explicit intimation to the Yugoslav government on 24 December 1992. It is equally well known that in 1994 President Clinton had the new Secretary of State, Lawrence Eagleburger, send a short telegram to the US ambassador in Belgrade with instructions to read it personally to Milošević. The telegram read: 'In case of a conflict in Kosovo caused by a Serb action, the United States will be ready to use military force against the Serbs in Kosovo and against Serbia itself.'[8]

But what makes the Western powers' humanitarian rhetoric sound false is their unreliability in representing the horrors of 'ethnic cleansing'. Western media imputed them unilaterally to Serbian militias and held the Belgrade government politically (and legally) responsible for them. However, even the massacre at Raçak, branded as the emblem of Serbian barbarity, is far from being a well-documented and incontrovertible 'fact'. The reader probably remembers that, on the day following the discovery of the massacre, the American leader of the OSCE mission, William Walker, publicly defined it, after lengthy telephone consultations with the Department of State, as a 'crime against humanity', and unhesitatingly blamed it upon the Serbian army and police. The emotional shock wave caused by these declarations induced the countries of the 'Contact Group' to call the Rambouillet conference, opening the way to NATO's military intervention. As of today, many doubts, which the Finnish investigation committee has been unable to resolve, still remain as to the responsibility for the massacre, the actual course of the events leading to it, and even the identity of many of the victims. Some people think it was a massacre of defenceless civilians by the Serbian police; for others it was the result of shoot-outs during UÇK ambuscades against Serbian patrols (as some Italian OSCE observers confirmed), later construed as a heinous and appalling crime for propagandistic purposes.[9]

The lugubrious tally of the losses suffered by the Kosovar-Albanian community during the civil war turned out to be equally unreliable. While one should not underestimate the gravity of the massacres that the Serbs are responsible for, the accusation of genocide brought against them should be seen as an instrument of war, just like the humanitarian justification for the war. In the year before NATO's attack, the victims of the civil war did not number more than 2000. Today this datum, corroborated by the Council for the Defence of Human Rights and Liberty in Priština,[10] is generally accepted. It is sufficient to give the lie both to the statements by US Defense Secretary William Cohen, who on 16 May 1999 denounced the killing of 100,000 Kosovar-Albanians, and to NATO's official estimate of 10,000 victims.

On the basis of investigations carried out in Kosovo after the end of the war by NATO troops and teams of specialists sent over from the United States and Great Britain to assist the Hague Tribunal, it is realistic to estimate the total number of victims of armed engagements in the Kosovo area, in the year before NATO's intervention and during its intervention, at 4000–5000, mostly of Albanian ethnic origin. Nowhere in Kosovo was any trace found of the notorious 'mass graves' of the type discovered in Bosnia-Herzegovina after the conclusion of the war.[11] Thus, one cannot speak of genocide. It was not even an especially bloody civil war if one compares it, for example, with other conflicts in the Mediterranean area, notably the civil war in Algeria, where in the same length of time no fewer than 100,000 civilians were slaughtered.

If there is any merit at all in the foregoing remarks, it can be concluded that humanitarian motivations, whatever the degree of sincerity of those who appealed to them, cannot explain the war for

Kosovo, being themselves an element of that war – an element which calls in its turn for an explanation, as do many other aspects of this conflict.

A War Against Europe?

A hypothesis that was put forward as an alternative to humanitarian motivations to explain NATO's attack against the Yugoslav Federation is that it was conceived by the United States as a move against Europe's process of integration. It is argued that the main reason for the war lay in the United States' will to subordinate – militarily, politically and economically – the countries of united Europe, whose process of integration was beginning to threaten US predominance. This thesis, endorsed mainly by European authors, was laid out with special thoroughness by Alain de Benoist and Charles Champetier.[12]

According to de Benoist, the main objective of the American superpower was to make it clear to the Europeans that they could never have dealt with the Balkan question without Washington's intervention. That is why the United States intended to create, by force of arms, a new Iron Curtain between Western Europe and the Orthodox Slav world, including Russia.

Another objective of the United States, claims de Benoist, was to create a permanent protectorate in the territory between Kosovo and Albania, a strategic area of the Balkans. This would have allowed the United States to play the role of policeman of the Balkans and the Mediterranean, holding Yugoslavia in a vice between Eastern European countries presently integrated into NATO (Poland, the Czech Republic and Hungary) and Muslim countries or countries with strong connections to the Muslim world (Albania, Bulgaria and Turkey). Finally, the United States meant to encourage the formation of Islamic enclaves (Bosnia, the future 'Greater Albania') in South-Central Europe to accentuate divisions within the continent and make up for its support of Israel in the eyes of European Muslims' Arab allies.[13]

As for Champetier, in his essay 'Una guerra contro l'Europa' ('A war against Europe') he argues that one of the main reasons for the United States' decision to go to war was that it wished to 'divide Europe'. The American superpower intervened to remove an obstacle – the Yugoslav Federation – that thwarted its plans for political and military occupation of the whole territory extending from the Baltic to the Adriatic and the Eastern Mediterranean. This area is, currently or potentially, controlled by NATO, with the sole exception of Yugoslavia, a country with a long tradition of independence, 'non-aligned' ever since the time of Tito, and even today leaning more towards Moscow – or, at the most, Paris – than towards Berlin, London or Washington. In the plans of the United States (here Champetier's analysis converges with de Benoist's), the territorial continuity of NATO countries is to become a new Iron Curtain splitting Europe in two. The United States, a maritime power just like Great Britain, is haunted by the same spectre that obsessed the British during the Balkan wars and whenever they have dealt with the 'Eastern Question', namely the risk of the emergence of a continental power in Eurasia. Thus, the war for Kosovo is part of a plan to separate West-Central Europe, which is naturally inclined to accept the US protectorate, from Eastern Europe and the Orthodox Slav world – first and foremost Russia – which the United States intends to drive back eastwards within Asian boundaries.[14]

According to Champetier's 'anti-European' interpretation, the war for Kosovo is the most recent phase – the Atlantic phase – of the 'Eastern Question'; that is, a continuation of the Balkan wars sparked or kindled by Western powers during the twentieth century. Once again the Balkans have been the object of a competitive carve-up among great powers, this time with the United States joining in alongside the West European countries.

Champetier's interpretation is intriguing. It is borne out by the fact that, as I argue in the previous chapter, NATO's military intervention refurbished political and diplomatic practices that had long been characteristic of the European powers' involvement in the Balkans. Nor must one underestimate the fact that the local effects of this new intervention are strongly reminiscent of those of the traditional Balkan wars; that is, exacerbation of tensions between diasporic nations and territorial states, mass exoduses of autochthonous populations, disruption of the Yugoslav political body, and overall impoverishment, as well as military, political and economic dependence of the Balkan countries on the protectorate of the Western powers. Moreover, tensions did appear within the Atlantic Alliance, and they are capable of being interpreted as the sign of potential antagonism between the United States' strategic unilateralism and continental Europe's aspiration to a certain degree of military and political autonomy. This emerged, in spite of much reticence and ambiguity, in the months immediately following the war.[15]

All this can hardly be gainsaid and provides very significant elements for an overall interpretation of the causes and objectives of the Western powers' 'humanitarian' intervention. However, it is far from an exhaustive explanation. Other investigations into the strategic labyrinth of the war are called for. The reasons that led European imperial powers to take an interest in the 'Eastern Question' were quite clear. For centuries, the Balkans have been one of the main playgrounds for the European powers' games of equilibrium. As we have seen, the strategic interests of tsarist Russia, the southward expansion of Germany, Great Britain's mastery of the seas, and French colonialism all came to a head in the Balkans. But the sophisticated strategy of the United States, the only planetary superpower left after the Cold War, transcends the geopolitical boundaries of the 'Eastern Question'. The same can be said of NATO and of every other direct and indirect protagonist of the 'humanitarian war', including India and China, which opposed the war even though they were not directly involved in the geopolitical sphere of the 'Balkan question'.

Thus, to understand the overall strategy of the war for Kosovo, one must reinterpret the 'Eastern Question' within a much larger framework and see the Balkans as a board where a game in which world hegemony is at stake has been played for the first time, and will probably continue to be played in the years to come.

A War for the Control of 'Corridors'?

Another important thesis stresses the economic implications of the war against the commonplace that in the Balkans, unlike the Persian Gulf, the United States cannot be accused of having stepped in to gain control over local economic resources, extend its market outlets, or seize opportunities to compete economically with Europe.

First of all, it has been argued that it was in the United States' overall interest to make the Balkans as unstable as possible. This instability would effectively thwart the development of a unified European economy by increasing emigration from the Balkans to Europe, hindering European investment, paralysing tourist flows, and encouraging smuggling and illegal trade. In a word, it would produce turbulence that Europe – and the euro financial system – could hardly cope with without the United States' hegemonic tutelage. Indeed, with hindsight, there is no denying that the war has had negative effects on the economic and financial stability of the European Union.

Other authors, using arguments that were once a monopoly of Marxist analyses, lay stress on the economic interests of the powerful US arms industry. They argue that the United States' intervention in the Balkans, besides stimulating the arms market, has contributed to making NATO an irresistible military centre of gravity for the countries of former Socialist Europe. It is well known that every time a new country joins the Atlantic Alliance, the US arms industry reaps profits. Furthermore, when Eastern European countries come into NATO, they are also integrated into the Southeast European Co-operation Initiative, an economic partnership controlled by the Trade and Development Agency, and competing with the European Union and the expansion of the euro economic and financial area.[16]

But the main issue is control of the so-called 'corridors' connecting the Caspian Sea and Caucasus with the Mediterranean, the Balkans and Southern Europe. Europeans and Americans, in competition with Russia and Iran, consider these corridors of vital importance; it is through them that the immense oil reserves of the Caspian Sea and Caucasus are to be piped to the industrialized countries. It is estimated that the hydrocarbon reserves of that area are equal, or even superior, to those of the Persian Gulf. Kazakhstan alone is believed to possess oil reserves of over 9 billion barrels, with a potential daily yield of 700,000 barrels. This explains the interest of US oil companies, such as Chevron, in the Transcaucasian region, and the fact that Turkey and the Balkans are regarded as crucial transit areas between that region's oilfields and Mediterranean Europe.[17]

These 'corridors' will play a decisive role in shaping the future geo-economy of the whole Eurasian continent. The delicate issue is to establish what course is to be followed by the 'oil routes' leading from Turkmenistan (a great producer of black gold) and Azerbaijan beyond the ports of the Black Sea, the Bosporus and the Dardanelles. The United States is determined to have the pipelines run through secure territories; that is, through dependent, controllable countries (whether Muslim or not), excluding other states. Hence its increasing diplomatic interest in Turkey, which it regards as a valuable oriental bulwark of NATO. Europe, in its turn, running counter to its cultural identity and democratic bent, has pledged to admit Turkey into the Union by 2004. The United States, of course, wants to make sure that the pipelines skirt Iran and especially Russia, and tends to adopt a competitive attitude towards Europe.[18]

In this context, the 'Corridor 8' project, financed by the International Monetary Fund, the European Union and France, has gained special prominence. This plan calls for an east–west route from the Bulgarian Black Sea coast through Macedonia and southern Albania to the ports of Durrës and Vlorë. It involves the creation along this route – which, as Luca Rastello observes, was laid open by the heroin trade from Turkey – of a highway, a high-speed railway and, above all, the longest pipeline in European history.[19]

The strategic importance of projects such as this for Western economies came out clearly at the OSCE summit of 18–19 November 1999. On the one hand, Western leaders, including Clinton and D'Alema, spoke very harshly against the Russian government, represented there by Yeltsin in person. They censured Russian repression of the rebellion in Chechnya and reasserted the right of (Western) states to interfere wherever human rights were at stake. On the other hand, Clinton determinedly fostered and managed to conclude a political and commercial agreement, from which Russia was excluded, to build a pipeline over 1700 kilometres long from Baku, the capital of Azerbaijan, to the Turkish port of Ceyhan in the Gulf of İskenderun on the Mediterranean Sea. This pipeline will have a potential daily yield of over a million barrels of petrol, and a major gas pipeline will run alongside it. Turkmenistan, Azerbaijan, Georgia and Turkey, as well as major US corporations, will take part in its construction, while the territories of Russia and Iran will be skirted.[20]

So it is that the Turkish–Balkan area plays a role as crucial as that of the Middle East, albeit less direct, in the international strategy to secure energy sources. Major industrial powers, first and foremost the United States, have always shown themselves ready to use force to guarantee safe transportation and avoid shortages or excessive cost hikes. Hence, realistically, one cannot rule out that economic considerations – especially competition for the control of 'corridors' – weighed heavily on the Western powers' decision to start the 'humanitarian war'.

Hegemonic Federalism?

A third interpretation, which deserves careful consideration, focuses on the world hierarchy of power and wealth presided over by the United States. After the collapse of the Soviet Union and the break-up of the Warsaw Pact, the United States is the only war (or peace) lord left on the planet. The war for Kosovo can tentatively be read in the light of the American superpower's guiding political and economic strategies.

From this standpoint, strategic analyses by American commentators such as Zbigniew Brzezinski, Richard Haas and Samuel Huntington are especially interesting. Even if they are not specifically interpretations of the war for Kosovo or of other conflicts involving the United States, they are nevertheless theoretical studies addressed to the administration of the United States itself and are authoritative and representative enough to provide a sound basis for reasonable guesses as to what led the United States to launch the 'humanitarian war'. Indeed, all of these authors take for granted that the United States must necessarily and inevitably be the supreme world power and that this role calls for the use of force.

In Zbigniew Brzezinski's opinion, the Balkans are an area of crucial importance in the United States' hegemonic perspective. As some strategic studies of the early 1990s had already pointed out, the Balkans, no less than the Middle East, are a 'crisis arc'.[21] They are an area where, to use the tectonic metaphor employed by Huntington, the 'fault lines' between Western Christianity, the Orthodox Slav world and Islam overlap and cause friction. The Balkan peninsula lies at the edge both of the geopolitical void opened by the collapse of the Soviet Union and of the vast Caucasian and Transcaucasian area, a major scenario in the worldwide competition for energy resources. Now that the era of regional empires has come to a close, the United States must be aware of its absolute supremacy and its inevitable function of governing the destiny of the world. Hence, it must keep watch lest an enemy should arise on the Eurasian continent. This is why the European security system should 'fully coincide with the American one' to make Europe the American bridgehead on the Eurasian continent, and why it is necessary to set aside any 'dogmatic multilateralism' that could jeopardize the hegemonic stability of a unipolar world.[22]

According to Richard Haas, the United States should develop a network of planetary connections – both by using the many already operative international regimes and institutions, and by promoting new interactions – to avoid any risk of losing the great advantages gained by winning the Cold War. The American superpower should resist the temptation to exercise its hegemony in a hierarchical and unilateral way, which would be dangerous in a world that is complex, turbulent and too loosely structured. The American objective should be to promote democracy, respect human rights, and favour the market economy through forms of intervention that may also be military, but should always remain essentially co-operative and be decided upon within the international community. It would be a matter of recruiting willing partners each time, while the undecided or reluctant should be nudged in appropriate ways.[23] In other words, Haas proposes the model of a 'global sheriff' who knows how to use his power in an intelligent and flexible way, as in the Gulf War, when the American superpower obtained the military co-operation of a large, heterogeneous coalition of states, including many Islamic countries. This co-operation might take place in the complex and dynamic system of relations connecting the United States to NATO and the European Union or, more specifically, to the United States' traditional partners, to new members of NATO and to new members of the European Union. The United States should do the same in Central and South America as well, and especially in the Balkans, the Middle East and South-East and North-West Asia.

Brzezinski's and Haas's arguments resurface in Huntington's essay 'The lonely superpower', which appeared in *Foreign Affairs* during the war for Kosovo.[24] Huntington argues that since the end of bipolarism the global structure of power has become peculiar. Although there is only one 'superpower', this does not mean that the world is 'unipolar'. Other great powers coexist with the American superpower, albeit on a lower, regional level: Germany and France in Europe, Russia in the Eurasian area, China and Japan in the Pacific area, India and Iran in Southern Asia, Brazil in Latin America, South Africa and Nigeria in Africa. The American superpower must take account of the regional hegemonies of these powers. In handling important international questions, it is necessary each time to obtain the consent of a certain number of regional powers.[25] Huntington recognizes that the United States is the only state enjoying an absolute superiority in all the main functional sectors – economic, military, diplomatic, ideological, technological, cultural – and capable of promoting its interests all over the world. But this hybrid 'uni-multipolar' situation threatens to cause serious tensions. The American superpower is tempted to act as if the world were perfectly unipolar, while the great regional powers push for a less imperfect multipolarism and feel threatened by the United States' tendency to impose its 'global hegemony'. Huntington claims that during the 1990s the United States tried, or gave the impression of trying, to carry out operations such as the following:

> [to] pressure other countries to adopt American values and practices regarding human rights and democracy; prevent other countries from acquiring military capabilities that could counter American conventional superiority; enforce American law extraterritorially in other societies; grade countries according to their adherence to American standards on human rights, drugs, terrorism, nuclear proliferation, missile proliferation, and now religious freedom; apply sanctions against countries that do not meet American standards on these issues; promote American corporate interests under the slogans of free trade and open markets; shape World Bank and International Monetary Fund policies to serve those same corporate interests; intervene in local conflicts in which it has relatively little interest; bludgeon other countries to adopt economic policies and social policies that will benefit American economic interests; promote American arms sales abroad while attempting to prevent comparable sales by other countries; force out one United Nations secretary-general and dictate the appointment of his successor; expand NATO initially to include Poland, Hungary and the Czech Republic and no one else; undertake military action against Iraq and later maintain harsh economic sanctions against the regime; and categorise certain countries as 'rogue states', excluding them from global institutions because they refuse to kowtow to American wishes.[26]

This long list denouncing the United States' hegemonic unilateralism is used by Huntington to recommend, in partial disagreement with Haas, a sort of multilaterally hegemonic practice. Sub-regional powers should be involved each time as partners in the United States' actions to minimize conflict while promoting American interests.[27] Thus, small and middle-sized powers would no longer have any reason to be mistrustful of the 'global sheriff', who today is perceived as a threat to their autonomy and prosperity and accused of 'financial imperialism' and 'cultural colonialism'.

The theoretical models of Brzezinski, Haas and Huntington do not merely highlight the dynamics of, and the alternatives within, the global hegemonism that the American superpower is 'forced' to put into practice. They also indicate one of the probable reasons why the United States counts on the close military co-operation of European countries within the 'new NATO' for its control of the Eurasian continent. During the 1990s, NATO, shedding its original role as a defensive military alliance, became a supranational institution within which the United States is experimenting with the model of 'hegemonic federalism',[28] a strategic concept that can provide us with another important clue as to the reasons for, and the characteristics and objectives of, the 'humanitarian war'.

An Atlantic Alliance for Eurasian Hegemony?

One of the main keys to understanding the general strategic reasons for the war for Kosovo can be found in that complex process whereby, during the 1990s, NATO evolved into something that could be called a 'supranational hegemonic regime', using the term 'regime' as in Stephen Krasner and Robert Keohane's theory of 'international regimes'.[29] A further key to understanding the global strategy underlying this transformation can be found in US administration documents, which, from the early 1990s onwards, while the Gulf War was being planned, have brought into focus the notions of 'new world order' and 'global security'.

The Atlantic Alliance was formed immediately after World War II for defensive purposes. The United States and Europe joined forces against the Soviet threat, aggregating democratic countries, as well as some dictatorial ones such as Portugal, Turkey and Greece that wanted the protection of NATO's nuclear umbrella. Of course, NATO's supreme command and top posts were firmly held in hand by the United States.

This defensive military structure risked seeming useless after the collapse of the Soviet Union and the dismantling of the Warsaw Pact. In a no longer bipolar world, the transatlantic sodality guaranteeing the United States' presence in Europe had to be founded on a new basis. Its mighty military apparatus had to be given new goals. This new Atlanticism had to reflect a renewed strategy, projective rather than defensive, expansive rather than just reactive, dynamic and flexible instead of static and rigid. And the theme of security must not be limited to the military; it had to take in the political and economic domain, partly for the purpose of controlling the dismantling of the Soviet empire.[30]

With these objectives in mind, at NATO's Rome Summit in November 1991 the United States, showing remarkably quick reflexes, presented the 'new strategic concept of the Alliance'. The United States argued that after the tension between East and West had come to an end, threats against peace and stability were coming primarily from the Third World in the form of the proliferation of nuclear weapons, cut-offs of energy supplies necessary for the industrialized world, acts of terrorism and sabotage, and ethnic and territorial conflicts. In the conclusive declaration of the Rome Summit there is a first hint of NATO's new inclination to overstep the geographic limits of the military jurisdiction defined in its statute, and reference is made to the Alliance's duty to take the 'global context' into account.[31]

The road was opened for NATO to announce in June 1992 that it was at the disposal of the United Nations and the CSCE (today OSCE) for a peace-keeping intervention in former Yugoslavia. This was an out-of-area, non-defensive intervention that violated not only Articles 5 and 6 of NATO's statute but also the provisions in Chapter 4 of the United Nations Charter. According to this chapter, a military intervention that is not strictly defensive cannot be turned over to a regional organization, especially if that organization is not under the direction or control of the Security Council.[32] Nevertheless, the offer was accepted, and during the period 1993-5 NATO interventions in former Yugoslavia began, and soon turned into political and military actions with the authorization or tacit consent of the United Nations and of the CSCE (OSCE).

By repeatedly stretching or openly violating both its statute and the United Nations Charter, NATO became the self-appointed 'right-hand man' of the United Nations. It demanded full command over the troops deployed in the Balkans. This was especially evident during Operation Deliberate Force in August 1995. The situation eventually drifted into blatant international anarchy when NATO was granted judicial functions as well. The International Criminal Tribunal for the former Yugoslavia, created in the meantime by the Security Council, was authorized to regularly employ NATO troops stationed in former Yugoslavia (IFOR, SFOR, KFOR) as a judicial police force to prosecute and arrest individuals incriminated by the tribunal.

The last stage in this institutional metamorphosis was reached at the NATO summit in Washington, held in April 1999, on the occasion of the 50th anniversary of the foundation of the Atlantic Alliance. While the war for Kosovo was already under way, the 1991 'new strategic concept' was reformulated to assert, in the broadest terms, NATO's right to intervene in cases not provided for by Article 5 of its statute (i.e. outside of its legal and geographic limits) to guarantee respect of human rights, democracy, individual freedom and rule of law. NATO also reaffirmed its aim to expand eastwards. It was stated that the admission of three new members – Poland, the Czech Republic and Hungary – was part of a project for the gradual and selective incorporation into NATO of European countries formerly under Soviet hegemony and members of the Warsaw Pact, including the Baltic republics, Ukraine, Slovakia and several Balkan countries (Romania, Bulgaria, Macedonia, Albania). At least two Eurasian countries, Georgia and Azerbaijan, were chosen as future bridgeheads in the Caucasian region, although they were not explicitly mentioned. Having cast to the winds all diplomatic caution towards Russia (even though a mutual co-operation agreement with Russia was also planned), NATO resolutely proceeded to lay economic, political and military siege to the former superpower, as part of a plan to extend United States-dominated 'hegemonic stability' to the whole Euro-Atlantic space.[33]

Finally – and this was the most significant innovation – in the conclusive statement of the Washington Summit, entitled *An Alliance for the 21st Century*, the customary reference to NATO's obligation to respect the United Nations charter was dropped. The United Nations is mentioned at the end of the list of organizations which NATO intends to co-operate with to deal with the problems in the Balkans, and it is put on a par with multilateral organisms lacking legal universality such as the WEU, the European Union and the OSCE.[34] This, as Stefano Silvestri observes, was a nebulous and ambiguous way to ratify the intervention against the Yugoslav Federation a posteriori, while asserting NATO's readiness to operate out-of-area even without the leave of the Security Council.[35]

In the meantime, Assistant Secretary of State Strobe Talbott, anticipating the conclusions of the NATO summit, and implicitly announcing NATO's attack against the Yugoslav Federation, declared:

We expect NATO and its members will continue to be guided by their obligations under the United Nations Charter and the Helsinki Final Act. At the same time, we must be careful not to subordinate NATO to any other international body or compromise the integrity of its command structure. We will try to act in concert with other organisations and with respect for their principles and purposes. But the Alliance must reserve the right and the freedom to act when its members, by consent, deem it necessary.[36]

Thus, NATO's intervention against the Yugoslav Federation on 24 March 1999 is not to be seen as an 'absolute exception', as some European NATO members tried to argue. Through one of its foremost authorities, and following the directions of the US Senate, the US government asserted that it considered NATO a supranational institution that could use force legitimately without depending on any other authority or institution. In this way, the United States did not merely violate international law *de facto*, as it had repeatedly done in the past; it was now declaring itself, and the military alliance it dominated, to be *legibus solutum* (above the law). At the same time it was investing itself with the role of arbiter both of peoples' right to self-determination and of the sovereignty of states.[37] Through NATO the hegemonic will of the United States has taken on the form of an aspiration to wield absolute planetary authority, subject neither to the consensus of other members of the international community nor to the rules and principles of the United Nations Charter and general international law.

A War for Global 'Hegemonic Stability'

Up to this point, after arguing that humanitarian motivations cannot credibly explain the war for Kosovo, I have discussed four 'realistic' interpretations of the war: the war as an epilogue to the 'Eastern Question', by which the United States meant to reaffirm its political and military superiority in Europe; the war as an economic conflict for the control of Balkan 'corridors' connecting Europe to the Caucasian and Caspian area; the war as an occasion to test NATO as the instrument of a new 'hegemonic federalism'; and finally, the war as a projection of Atlantic hegemony over the whole Eurasian region.

Each of these four interpretations is, in my opinion, an important contribution to our understanding of the 'humanitarian war'. Furthermore, taking them in order, each interpretation offers, so to speak, a higher degree of reliability than the previous one. In my opinion, interpretations of the war are the more persuasive the more they expand the interpretative scenario of the 'humanitarian war' and introduce theoretical categories drawn from a holistic approach to international relations. In fact, I intend to argue that one cannot understand what is at stake in an armed conflict involving the leading world powers (and hence, the reasons and objectives of the conflict) without analysing the long-term dynamics of 'global power'.

My thesis holds to the tenets of international political realism, especially as developed by 'neo-realist' authors such as George Modelski, Robert Gilpin and Robert Keohane.[38] According to this perspective, no geopolitical analysis can produce reliable results unless it takes into account the overall framework of power relations. And this is all the more true today in the face of the powerful processes of globalization of the economy, the media, finance and transportation, at the start of the third millennium.

This realist approach requires a study of the conflicting forces and mechanisms leading to a concentration or, conversely, a dissemination of international power – a power that war reapportions in different quotas to various international players in a complex and risky game of allocation and dislocation. Long-term dynamics show a tendency for world powers to take on the role of guarantors of international peace and order; that is, of a specific hierarchic stratification of power ensuring, in Robert Keohane's words, the 'hegemonic stability' of the international system.[39] Small and middle-sized powers (especially the latter) try instead to break up consolidated hierarchies in a quest for new alliances and a more favourable balance of power.

When the political, economic and military foundations of 'hegemonic stability' are threatened, it is inevitable that major powers turn to the use of force. Only for exceptional and short periods of time is stability assured by the 'regular' functioning of global markets, as claimed by a neo-liberal ideology that is increasingly contradicted by the turbulence of financial markets and the overbearing power of the major corporations. As some US analysts have remarked, in the present-day scenario of globalization the need for permanent political vigilance and prompt military intervention arises in underdeveloped areas, where instability is favoured by the growing, albeit inhomogeneous, relative impoverishment of many countries. Some areas, such as sub-Saharan Africa, are in absolute poverty as a result of an utter collapse of the means of production.

Hence, hegemonic powers have no choice, under penalty of losing their hegemonic position, but to react to the phenomena of fragmentation and delegitimization of the international *status quo*, which are linked above all to technological, economic and military changes. The use of force is indispensable to remodel and stabilize new forms of hierarchical concentration of international power and experiment with new institutions and legal systems to legitimize them.[40]

From this point of view, there is a remarkable historical continuity that is worth dwelling upon. During the past two centuries, the most stable hegemonic systems have been the result of major conflicts – the 'world wars' – and the winning nations became the hegemonic powers of each post-war period. After the end of each conflict, the winners engaged in ambitious plans for 'stable and universal peace' in an attempt to crystallize the *status quo* of international relations. From the early decades of the nineteenth century onwards, the countries that came out of 'world' conflicts on the winning side have always engaged in such projects: after the Napoleonic wars the Holy Alliance was formed, after World War I there was the League of Nations (under the impulse of Wilsonian 'idealism'), and World War II was followed by the foundation of the United Nations at the behest of the United States, Great Britain and the Soviet Union.

I intend to argue that something similar occurred at the end of the Cold War. After 1989 the United States, emerging from the Cold War as the only 'superpower' capable of playing a primary strategic role, conceived the grandiose project of a 'new world order' founded on the notion of 'global security'.[41] Under the presidency of the Republican George Bush, Sr, a legion of economists, political scientists, strategists, military analysts and Department of State officials set to work.[42] The result was a very authoritative doctrine which today still provides the guidelines for the main political choices of the US government and offers a key to understanding its foreign policy and military interventions, from the Gulf War to Somalia, from the war in Bosnia to the war for Kosovo.

The fall of the Soviet empire and the end of the Cold War, it is argued, have opened a new era, finally free of the threat of nuclear terror. The United States now has a chance to establish a peaceful and just international system founded on the values of liberty and democracy, and on the 'rule of law'. Although the world is increasingly interdependent and no longer torn asunder by ideological conflicts, threats against peace have not abated; they have merely spread out over a broader area. Hence, the new world order must be founded on a 'global' security system taking account of the growing economic, technological and electronic interdependence of the world – a system requiring close co-operation among the countries of the three great industrial areas of the planet (North America, Europe and Japan) under the political and military leadership of the United States.

It is also argued that the most serious threats against collective security come from the Third World. Growing economic competition between developing countries, the explosion of nationalism, religious intolerance, inter-racial hatred, demographic pressure, climatic variations and the consequent environmental disasters are certainly going to pose a threat to the security of the international community, and especially to the interests of industrialized countries.[43] The latter are further threatened by international political terrorism and the proliferation of biological, chemical and nuclear weapons.

This strategic vision had two fundamental implications. The first was that the organization of a global security system required a radical reforming of NATO (as well as WEU and CSCE). NATO's traditional geographical limits must be furthered to allow the alliance to deal with threats to security in other geopolitical quadrants. The second implication was that industrial powers needed to shelve the old principle of non-interference in the internal affairs of sovereign states. It was their right and duty to have recourse to 'humanitarian intervention' wherever they deemed it necessary to put an end to internal crises in individual countries if these crises appeared to go against Western interests and values.

During the 1990s, the Democrat president Bill Clinton espoused this doctrine in full, abiding by the guidelines set by his Republican predecessor. He sought to downplay the United Nations by insistently refusing to place the United States' 'humanitarian interventions' under its control, and striving to impose the political and military structure of NATO as the only operational 'international police' during the war in Bosnia. The same doctrine inspired the United States' resolve, in 1999, to promote the 'humanitarian' intervention for Kosovo on its own, ignoring the decisions of the Security Council. The reason for this is clear. The veto power held by the five permanent members of the Security Council places the United States and the Russian Federation (and China) on a par. This parity reflected the hierarchical structure of international relations after the end of World War II, a structure which the end of the Cold War, however, has subverted. Hence, the Security Council of the United Nations is an organism in which the distribution of power is too broad – too 'democratic', one might say – and hence does not reflect the actual concentration of international power in the hands of the American superpower and its closest allies. To promote global hegemonic stability, the United States must subvert the 'old' international institutions and the legal order on which they are founded. It needs to experiment with new paths for the ethical and legal legitimization of the use of force in search for a doctrine of *ius ad bellum* more suited to present circumstances.

A Technologico-Military Execution

If what I have maintained so far is at all useful for an understanding of the reasons and purposes of the war for Kosovo, then it may also help to clarify the 'nature' of that war. It is common opinion that from the technical and military point of view the 'humanitarian war' was a 'new war', very far removed from the classical paradigm of a 'modern' war between sovereign states, as described by Karl von Clausewitz. The expression 'new war' was employed, for example, by Mary Kaldor to refer to the Balkan conflicts of the 1990s. They were rooted, she argues, in tensions between a cosmopolitan culture founded on the values of inclusion, universalism and multi-culturalism, and a politics of identity based on ethnical and national particularism.[44]

Ulrich Beck, too, expressed his conviction that the war for Kosovo was 'new', in the sense of being the forerunner of the wars of the global era. It is a type of war that can no longer be understood in terms of the classic von Clausewitz doctrine, because it was not waged between enemy states or in the name of a national interest. Rather, it was a 'post-national' war, featuring an unprecedented mix of ethics and global politics, humanitarian generosity and imperialist reasoning. During the war for Kosovo the classic distinctions between peace and war, domestic politics and foreign politics, attack and defence, law and abuse, civilization and barbarity, were toppled one after the other. Beck argues that the neo-realist view of the war, which rejects the humanitarian motivation and explains the conflict solely in terms of the economic and geopolitical interests of the United States, distorts reality:

> It is incapable of understanding globalization's new game of power [...] and is unable to realize to what degree the politics of human rights is becoming a civil religion, the United States' true credo. [...] The outbreak of the war in Kosovo has brought a new aspect into the spotlight: we are witnessing the birth of a post-national politics of military humanism, the politics of transnational powers that intervene to impose the respect for human rights beyond national borders.[45]

Neither Régis Debray nor Alain de Benoist agrees with Beck's idea that the ambiguities of 'military humanism' make the war for Kosovo a conflict whose 'dialectic' nature introduces us to the 'new modernity' of globalization. Both, however, assign great importance to the ethical motivations of the war. Debrais stresses that the war for Kosovo has marked a moral and legal regression by bringing back the old idea that war can be used to promote universal values against an antagonist branded as an 'enemy of the human race'. Thus, the 'humanitarian war' reintroduces the archaic theological model of 'just war' in its Wilsonian version: 'moral idealism plus technological superiority plus Tomahawk missiles'.[46]

Alain de Benoist, updating a famous statement by Carl Schmitt, argues that the war for Kosovo heralds the end of nations:

> It is the war of the triumph of that globalization which, as Carl Schmitt prophetically announced, is achieved through the polarity between economy (the great world market) and morals (the rights of man), the two prongs of the tongs that are tightening around the politics of states and the sovereignty of peoples.[47]

It is de Benoist's opinion that the 'humanitarian war' was, on the one hand, a neo-liberal war fought for the cause of globalizing markets. On the other hand, it was a typical 'ideological' war, fought not merely to defeat the enemy but to annihilate him as the embodiment of evil, injustice and the negation of law. The antagonist is first and foremost 'guilty' and must be subjected to the justice of the winners. From this point of view, the humanitarian motivation and the incrimination of Milošević by the Hague Tribunal have a precedent in the Treaty of Versailles, which, at the end of World War II, denounced Kaiser Wilhelm II of Hohenzollern as a war criminal and demanded his incrimination and condemnation.[48]

While these last comments do highlight some significant and innovative features of the 'humanitarian war', in my opinion they fail to focus on its most important aspect, namely that the hegemonic objectives and global scope of the war were reflected in its operative characteristics; that is, the overwhelming technologico-military superiority of one side over the other. It is precisely the dramatic gap in military potential between the two sides that defines the nature of this war (and links it to the Gulf War). On one side we have the most powerful military alliance in history, on the other a small, poor and politically isolated country whose armed forces are unable to put up more than a weak defence. This inequality is reflected in the disproportion between the losses on the two sides, which was even greater than in the Gulf War. There were thousands of casualties on one side, especially among civilians, while the attackers did not suffer a single loss. Some have spoken of a 'Hiroshima model', alluding to the fact that this was more of a 'military execution', whose outcome was beyond doubt, than a war.

The most striking aspect of NATO's military supremacy was the technological sophistication of its weapon systems. That is why labels such as 'computer war', 'space war' and 'war from the sky' were coined, alluding to the extensive network of satellite monitors and the telematic espionage that were a permanent electronic counterpoint to the war,[49] and to the fact that this war, for the first time in history, ignored the territorial dimension.

It was especially at the insistence of the United States, which held out for a long time against the idea of a ground intervention, that the 'humanitarian war' remained a 'war from the sky'. The success of this strategy – a personal decision of the president of the United States, even against the opinion of the highest authorities of NATO and authoritative partners like Great Britain – has shown that the great powers of the world can guarantee the international order without having to undertake a territorial invasion of the country under attack. We can expect that in the future they will be able to exercise the function of guaranteeing global order without risking the loss of human (Western) lives, a risk that would be ethically intolerable from the point of view of Western public opinion. The United States is presently designing completely automated, pilotless aircraft that will be able to reach any point of the planet taking off from US bases. They are destined to replace the powerful, very expensive B2 Spirit bombers (each one costs over $2 billion, more or less the gross national product of Albania) used against the Yugoslav Federation.[50] Thus, in the near future 'global security' will take on a new meaning: new military technologies will give an absolute 'robotic' security to the great power that takes on the task of maintaining global order by sending missiles or dropping bombs in any corner of the earth.

Notes

1. In an interview with Giancarlo Bosetti, Eric Hobsbawm argues that the war had 'no specific purposes' and brought 'no advantages' to Western powers (E. J. Hobsbawm, 'Guerra umanitaria? No, è solo un pasticcio', in U. Beck, N. Bobbio et al., L'ultima crociata?, Ragioni e torti di una guerra giusta. Rome: Libri di Reset, pp. 58–67). This is also the thesis of Lucio Caracciolo (cf. his editorial 'Il club dei suicidi', Limes, supplement to no. 1 of 1999, pp. 5–10), who has nevertheless given an important contribution to the analysis of the conflict in the Balkans. An opposite view is put forward by I. Mortellaro in I signori della guerra. La Nato verso il XXI secolo, Rome: Manifestolibri, 1999, pp. 32–40, 115.
2. Much has been written in the West on the theme of economic globalization and its dangers. I shall limit myself to referring the reader to K. Ohmae, The End of the Nation State: The Rise of Regional Economics, New York: Free Press, 1995; P. Q. Hirst and G. Thompson, Globalization in Question: The International Economy and the Possibilities of Governance, Cambridge: Polity Press, 1996; Ulrich Beck, Was ist Globalisierung?, Frankfurt am Main: Suhrkamp, 1997. See also my discussion with Ulrich Beck, 'Tutto il bene e tutto il male di Cosmopolis', Reset, 55 (1999), 71–80.
3. 'When a state fights its enemy in the name of mankind, its war is not a war by mankind. It is a war in which this state tries to appropriate a universal concept to identify with it at its opponent's expense. Analogously, one can use the concepts of peace, justice, progress, or civilization, to claim them as one's own and deny them to one's enemy. The term "humanity" is especially well suited for imperialistic expansions and, in its ethical and humanitarian form, is a specific vehicle for economic imperialism. A maxim by Proudhon, albeit with a necessary modification, applies in this case: "Whoever invokes humanity

is trying to cheat." ... All this is merely a manifestation of the terrible pretension that the human nature of the enemy must be denied, that he must be declared *hors-la-loi* and *hors-l'humanité*, and war hence must be carried to a point of extreme inhumanity' (C. Schmitt, *Begriff des Politischen*, Berlin and Grunewald: Walther Rothschild, 1928). On this theme, cf. J. Habermas, 'Kants Idee des ewigen Friedens – aus dem historischen Abstand von 200 Jahren', *Kritische Justiz*, 28(3) (1995), 293–319.

4. On the theme of 'just war', see my *I signori della pace*. Rome: Carocci, 1998, pp. 25–32, 71–83, 102–6, 143–5.

5. President Clinton declared that military intervention was not only the right thing to do, but also 'the smart thing to do', decidedly in the national interest of the United States (quoted by R. Menotti, 'Che cosa resta della Nato', *Limes*, supplement to no. 1, 1999, p. 128). In his turn, Massimo D'Alema claimed Italy's status of a great power, which it had earned for good by loyally taking part in the war (M. D'Alema, *Kosovo. Gli italiani e la guerra*, interview with F. Rampini. Milan: Mondadori, 1999, pp. 53–4).

6. T. Blair, 'Doctrine of international community', *Chicago Tribune*, 22 April 1999, quoted in I. Mortellaro, *I signori della guerra*, p. 15. In less refined language, NATO Secretary-General Javier Solana peremptorily declared that with the war 'Europe intended to maintain its ethical greatness' (from an interview with P. Buongiorno, *Panorama*, 29 April 1999); cf. also F. Giovannini, 'La demonizzazione dell'avversario', in M. Cabona (ed.), *'Ditelo a Sparta'. Serbia ed Europa contro l'aggressione della Nato*. Genoa: Graphos, 1999, p. 125.

7. M. Albright, 'Menschenrechte und Außenpolitik', *Amerika-Dienst*, 25 (1998), 8, quoted in U. Beck, 'Il soldato Ryan e l'era delle guerre post-nazionali', in Beck *et al.*, *L'ultima crociata?*, p. 69.

8. M. Calvo-Platero, 'Le tentazioni di una superpotenza', E. Berselli, A. Calabrò, C. Jean, P. Matveyevic, A. Negri, M. C. Platero, S. Silvestri and D. Siniscalco (eds), *La Pace e la guerra. I Balcani in cerca di un futuro*. Milan: Il Sole 24 Ore, 1999, pp. 126–7.

9. R. Morozzo della Rocca, 'La via verso la guerra', *Limes*, supplement to no. 1 of 1999, pp. 24–5; Ulisse, 'Come gli americani hanno sabotato la missione dell'Osce', *Limes*, supplement to no. 1 of 1999, p. 118; 'A year later, the mystery still endures' is the opening sentence of an article by E. Rosaspina, 'Raçak, la "collina dei martiri" senza giustizia', *Corriere della Sera*, 16 January 2000.

10. According to report no. 8 (Summer–Autumn 1998), from January to October 1998, Kosovar-Albanian victims numbered 1291; see A. Lodovisi, 'La grande dissipazione', *Guerre e pace*, 7(60) (1999), 14. R. Debray, in his famous *Letter to Chirac*, wrote, 'I remind you, President, that in 1998 1,700 Albanian guerrillas, 180 policemen and 120 Serbian

soldiers were killed. The UÇK kidnapped 380 people, 103 of whom it set free, while the others are dead or missing, sometimes after being tortured. Among them were two reporters and fourteen workers' (R. Debray, *Croire, voir, faire*, Paris: Éditions Odile Jacob, 1999).

11. On this point, cf. Lodovisi, 'La grande dissipazione', pp. 14–18; Morozzo della Rocca, 'La via verso la guerra', pp. 24–6. See also the following newspaper articles: G. Rampoldi, 'Kosovo, le fosse dell'orrore che fanno paura all'Occidente', *La Repubblica*, 13 November 1999; T. Di Francesco, 'Kosovo, le prime indagini', *Il Manifesto*, 11 November 1999; S. Cingolani, 'In Kosovo violenze, non crimini contro l'umanità', *Corriere della Sera*, 7 January 2000.

12. A. de Benoist, 'Cronache di guerra', in Cabona (ed.), *'Ditelo a Sparta'*, pp. 56–8; C. Champetier, 'Una guerra contro l'Europa', *Diorama letterario*, 20(9) (1999), 10–14. See also M. Dufourt, 'La Francia senza Europa', *Limes*, 8(2) (1999), 103–8.

13. De Benoist, 'Cronache di guerra', pp. 56–7.

14. Champetier, 'Una guerra contro l'Europa', p. 14.

15. See C. R. Whitney, 'Europe's mobile force: an uncertain factor for U.S. strategists', *International Herald Tribune*, 13 December 1999; W. Drozdiak, 'Europe force plan draws a U.S. caution on Nato', *International Herald Tribune*, 16 December 1999.

16. Champetier, 'Una guerra contro l'Europa', p. 14.

17. A. Negri, 'Alle radici della violenza', in Bersalli *et al.*, *La pace e la guerra,* pp. 53–6; E. Di Nolfo, 'Cosa si muove oltre il Kosovo?', *Diorama letterario* 225 (1999), 103–4; S. D. Gervasi, *La strategia della Nato dopo il crollo dell'URSS e la guerra in Jugoslavia*. Rome: Aginform, 1996.

18. See S. Finardi, 'Sporchi di oro nero', *Il Manifesto*, 14 April 1999.

19. See L. Rastello, 'Corridoio 8, la strada dell'oro nero', *Il Manifesto*, 27 March 1999. Other important routes are 'Corridor 5', which should connect the port of Ancona with that of Ploce, in Bosnia, and from there reach Hungary; and 'Corridor 10', which should reach the Greek port of Salonika from Germany and Austria, through Zagreb, Belgrade and Skopje (cf. Negri, 'Alle radici della violenza', pp. 54–5).

20. See J. Perlez, 'Key pipeline deal at risk', *International Herald Tribune*, 22 November, 1999; A. Ferrari, 'Lo sdegno dello Zar, aggirato dal gasdotto', *Corriere della Sera*, 19 November 1999.

21. See R. D. Asmus, R. L. Kluger and F. S. Larrabee, 'Building a new NATO', *Foreign Affairs*, 72(5) (1993), 28–40.

22. See Z. Brzezinski, *The Grand Chessboard*. New York: Basic Books, 1997; on this subject see also Mortellaro, *I signori della guerra*, pp. 89–130.

23. See R. N. Haass, *The Reluctant Sheriff: The United States after the Cold War*. New York: Council of Foreign Relations, 1997; R. N. Haass, 'What to do with American primacy', *Foreign Affairs*, 78(5) (1999) 37–49.

24. See S. P. Huntington, 'The lonely superpower', *Foreign Affairs*, 78(2) (1999), 35–49.

25. *Ibid.*, p. 36.

26. *Ibid.*, p. 37.

27. *Ibid.*, pp. 48–9.

28. See D. P. Calleo, 'Nato: ricostruzione o scioglimento?', in S. Romano (ed.), *L'impero riluttante. Gli Stati Uniti nella società internazionale dopo il 1989*. Bologna: Il Mulino, 1992; cf. also Mortellaro, *I signori della guerra*, pp. 111–27.

29. The notion of 'international regimes' was introduced in 1975 by John G. Ruggie in his 'International responses to technology: concepts and trends', *International Organisation*, 29(3) (1975), 557–84. For its 'neo-realist' reformulation, see R. O. Keohane, 'The demand for international regimes', in S. D. Krasner (ed.), *International Regimes*. Ithaca, NY: Cornell University Press, 1983, pp. 141–71.

30. See E. Grove (ed.), *Global Security: North American, European and Japanese Interdependence in the 1990s*. London: Brassey's, 1991.

31. Literature on NATO and its most recent transformations is abundant. See, besides previously quoted relevant literature, the following essays: H. Scheer, 'L'irresistibile ascesa della Nato', in T. Di Francesco (ed.), *La Nato nei Balcani*. Rome: Editori Riuniti, 1999; L. Sorel, 'Il nuovo atlantismo contro l'Europa', *Diorama letterario*, 20(5) (1999), 26–9; M. Tarchi, 'La guerra della Nato e le vecchie appartenenze', in Cabona (ed.), '*Ditelo a Sparta*', pp. 213–20; S. Silvestri, 'Nato, la sfida delle incertezze', in Berselli *et al.*, *La pace e la guerra*, pp. 97–116; Menotti, 'Che cosa resta della Nato', pp. 123–34; A. Cagiati, 'La nuova Alleanza Atlantica', *Rivista di studi politici internazionali*, 66(3) (1999), 339–47. See also fascicle 4, 1999 of *Limes*, mainly devoted to the theme of the transformation of NATO and Italy's role in it, with contributions by F. Fubini, A. Desiderio, C. Pelanda, F. Mini, R. Menotti, A. Nativi and others.

32. B. Conforti, *Le Nazioni Unite*, Padua: Cedam, 1979, pp. 205–8; B. Simma, 'NATO, the United Nations and the use of force: legal aspects', *European Journal of International Law*, 10(1) (1999), 10; C. Pinelli, 'Sul fondamento degli interventi armati a fini umanitari', in G. Cotturri (ed.), *Guerra – individuo*. Milan: Angeli, 1999, pp. 86–90; U. Villani, 'La guerra del Kosovo: una guerra umanitaria o un crimine internazionale?', *Volontari e Terzo Mondo*, 1–2 (1999), 30. Villani stresses that NATO is not only a 'partial', but also *not an impartial* organization, born as a military alliance against the Soviet Union and the countries of socialist Europe. An opposite view is held by M. Spinedi ('Uso della forza da parte della Nato in Jugoslavia e diritto internazionale', in *Guerra e pace in Kosovo*, Quaderni Forum, 12(2) (1998), 27).

33. Silvestri, 'Nato, la sfida delle incertezze', pp. 98–103.

34. See the integral text of the statement in *Rivista di studi politici internazionali*, 66(3) (1999), 348–60. The United Nations is mentioned at point 17 on, p. 354.

35. Silvestri, 'Nato, la sfida delle incertezze', p. 101.

36. Talbott, *Address*, Bonn, 4 February 1999, quoted by Simma in 'NATO, the United Nations and the use of Force', p. 15; Talbott spoke in similar terms in London on 10 March 1999, in his address to the Royal United Services Institute, 'A new NATO for a new era'.

37. Menotti, 'Che cosa resta della Nato', p. 132.

38. See G. Modelski, 'Long cycles of world leadership', in W. R. Thompson (ed.), *Contending Approaches to World System Analysis*. Beverly Hills, Calif.: Sage Publications, 1983; R. Gilpin, *War and Change in World Politics*. Cambridge: Cambridge University Press, 1981; R. O. Keohane, *Neorealism and Its Critics*. New York: Columbia University Press, 1986. On political realism in general, see P. P. Portinaro, *Il realismo politico*. Rome and Bari: Laterza, 1999.

39. See Keohane, *Neorealism and Its Critics*, *passim*.

40. W. R. Thompson, *On Global War: Historical-Structural Approaches to World Politics*. Columbia University of South Carolina Press, 1988, p. 5; R. Väyrynen, 'Global power dynamics and collective violence', in R. Väyrynen, D. Senghaas and C. Schmidt (eds), *The Quest for Peace*. London: Sage, 1987, pp. 81ff.; I. Clark, *The Hierarchy of States*. Cambridge: Cambridge University Press, 1989.

41. In August 1990, in a speech delivered at Aspen, Colorado, the president of the United States, George Bush – as Woodrow Wilson had done with his 'Fourteen points' in 1918 and Franklin D. Roosevelt and Winston Churchill with the Atlantic Charter in 1941 – set the guidelines for a new project for world order. This project was later to be perfected with the directive *National Security Strategy of the United States* and, at the beginning of 1992, with the document *Defense Planning Guidance*, drawn up by a staff of Department of State and Ministry of Defense officials under the presidency of the Subsecretary of Defense, Paul Wolfowitz. This document was published by the *New York Times* on 8 March 1992. Cf. my *Cosmopolis. La prospettiva del governo mondiale*. Milan: Feltrinelli, 1995, pp. 39–44; D. Gallo, 'Il "Nuovo Ordine Internazionale" fra predominio degli Stati Uniti, debolezza dell'ONU e militarizzazione delle istituzioni europee', in U. Allegretti, M. Dinucci and D. Gallo, *La strategia dell'impero*, San Domenico di Fiesole: ECP, 1992, pp. 68–98.

42. See, among many others, P. Wolfowitz, 'An American perspective', in E. Grove (ed.), *Global Security: North American, European and Japanese Interdependence in the 1990s*, London: Brassey's, 1991, pp. 19–28; R. Art, 'A defensible defense: America's grand strategy after the Cold War', *International Security*, 15(1) (1991), 5–53; J. L. Gaddis, 'Toward the post-Cold War world', *Foreign Affairs*, 70(2) (1991), 102–22; T. G. Weiss

(ed.), *Collective Security in a Changing World*, Boulder, Colo.: Lynne Rienner, 1993; R. F. Helms II and R.H. Dorff (eds), *The Persian Gulf Crisis: Power in the Post-Cold War World*, Westport, Conn.: Praeger, 1993.

43. M. Wörner, 'Global security: the challenge for NATO', in Grove, *Global Security*, pp 100-51

44. M. Kaldor, *New and Old Wars: Organized Violence in a Global Era*, Cambridge: Polity Press, 1999, *passim*.

45. Beck, 'Il soldato Ryan', pp. 68–9; U. Beck, 'Der militärische Euro. Humanismus und europäische Identität', *Suddeutsche Zeitung*, 10 April 1999; U. Beck, 'Der militärische Pazifismus. Über den postnationalen Krieg', *Suddeutsche Zeitung*, 19 April 1999.

46. Debray, *Croire, voir, faire*, pp. 17ff.

47. De Benoist, 'Cronache di guerra', p. 64. For a profound philosophical reflection on the relationship between war and politics, see C. Galli, 'Guerra e politica: modelli d'interpretazione', *Ragion pratica*, 8(14) (2000), 163–95; on the relationship between national sovereignty and globalization, see A. Loretoni, 'Uno sguardo critico dentro la globalizzazione', in B. Henry (ed.), *Mondi globali. Integrazione, identità, confini*. Pisa: Ets, 2000.

48. A. de Benoist, 'Ripensare la guerra', *Trasgressioni*, 14(1) (1999), 3–27.

49. On the informatic aspects of the war, and especially electronic espionage, see L. Mainoldi, 'Spiarsi fra alleati: la Nato nella rete anglo-americana', *Limes*, 2 (1999), 151–66.

50. On the military costs of the war, see Lodovisi, 'La grande dissipazione', pp. 16–18.

CHAPTER 3

A War against Law

Law Will Follow

In the eyes of a large part of Western public opinion, influenced by the mass media, the war for Kosovo was a success for international ethics and justice.[1] It reaffirmed the primary responsibilities of the international community in the face of a paralysis of the Security Council of the United Nations, blocked by Russia's and China's vetoes. Europe and the United States had a moral, even more than a legal, right to prevent a revival of the horrible crimes of World War II – mass deportation, rape, terrorism, genocide – in former Yugoslavia. The civilized world could not remain inert in the face of the threat of a new edition of the Holocaust. Human rights must be considered *ius cogens*; that is, rights that are valid and enforceable in every corner of the globe, certainly in Europe. After Nuremberg, the Universal Declaration of Human Rights and the various Geneva conventions, no other meaning can possibly be attached to the expression 'international humanitarian law'.

Many authoritative Western jurists, theorists of law, political scientists, philosophers and politicians have stood behind this 'humanitarian' interpretation of the war. Their aim has been to lay down some ethical and juridical principles having general validity; that is, going well beyond the specific event of the war. The humanitarian goal, they maintain, must prevail over the old principle of non-interference in the 'internal affairs' of a sovereign state, going back to the peace treaties of Westphalia. In cases of emergency the international community must authorize the repression of crimes against humanity and an immediate defence of basic rights, even if this means violating the sovereignty of legitimate governments.

It has been argued that in cases where positive law is inadequate and international institutions prove powerless, a superior normative level, ethics, comes into play, imposing the duty to intervene by force of arms outside or even against the explicit provisions of law. Only thus, it is claimed, in the absence of an international legislator and criminal jurisdiction, is it possible to establish a new customary law updating what is now an obsolete international legal system that needs to be thoroughly reformulated. Michael Glennon wrote: 'If power is used to do justice, law will follow'.[2]

In the era of globalization, it is argued, 'international humanitarian law' must reach far beyond its traditional function of giving economic and sanitary assistance to populations under extreme circumstances. It needs to incorporate the whole discipline that was once called 'international war law' or *ius in bello*. Even modern wars, including ethnic-national conflicts, can be fought in barbarous or civilized ways. One of the fundamental tasks of international law should be precisely to draw a clear line between barbarity and civilization in war. Basic rights, especially those of non-belligerents, should be respected even during a war, especially a civil war. Therefore, there is a need for international judiciary organisms endowed with the power to sanction the worst violations of these rights.[3]

These are all major legal and ethical issues that the war for Kosovo has helped to put on the international community's agenda. These issues deserve to be discussed even by those who do not lend credence to the 'humanitarian motivation' for the use of force, especially in the case of the war for Kosovo. It is a matter of investigating the function and purposes of present international institutions and weighing the impact the 'humanitarian war' has had on the international legal system. Will the new international law be, as Habermas hopes, 'cosmopolitan', that is, founded on universal citizenship and a universal defence of human rights? What relationship will be established between the new cosmopolitan order, the right of a people to self-determination, and the sovereignty of states? Will all the civilizations and cultures of the planet have to bow to the doctrine of human rights? Will war be a morally and legally suitable instrument with which to promote these rights? And will international law courts be able to serve the same purpose?

From the standpoint of both political and legal realism it is not a matter of formally and naively summoning states, especially the great powers, to a strict observance of international law. Nor can one expect, with Kant and Kelsen, that law alone will bring about international peace and justice. The point is rather to test, first of all, the capability of international institutions and law to favour a legal ritualizing of conflict between and within states, and hence some kind of limitation of its more destructive forms; and second, to show that jurists and theorists of international ethics tend to interpret – and often confuse – legal norms and moral imperatives in accord with their own political and ideological inclinations, according to theoretical modes that Kelsen would have regarded as highly 'impure'.

The Subversion of International Law

There were important precedents in the 1990s for the humanitarian motivation used by NATO to justify its war against the Federal Republic of Yugoslavia, notably the United States' and Great Britain's interventions to limit Iraq's territorial sovereignty after the end of the Gulf War, the intervention of Western powers in Somalia and Rwanda, and especially NATO's military actions in former Yugoslavia during the war in Bosnia.

The official motivation for all these military initiatives was the priority of humanitarian reasons over the principle of non-interference in the domestic jurisdiction of nation-states; that is, the principle of the inviolability of their sovereignty. The highest international institutions, the Security Council and General Secretariat of the United Nations in the first place, seconded this line *de facto* by raising no objections. It has hence been argued that within the international community there is currently a trend to legitimize 'humanitarian interference', even in its military forms. Current 'international humanitarian law' allegedly provides, by custom, for the Security Council's power to authorize any state (or alliance among states) to undertake an armed intervention within the political and territorial jurisdiction of another state, once it has been ascertained that serious violations of human rights are taking place in that state.

Other authors argue against the existence of a customary norm which, departing from the Charter of the United Nations, authorizes the use of force in situations of humanitarian emergency. Such a customary norm would have to arise from a uniform practice of states and a general conviction that this practice is legal. But the behaviour of the international community in applying sanctions is far from uniform. In some cases, for example that of Somalia, there was an armed intervention, while in others (such as Chechnya) a non-violent intervention was deemed sufficient, and in others still, such as Turkey's brutal repression of its Kurdish minority, there was practically no reaction.[4] Moreover, even simple humanitarian assistance (sending food, medicine, civilian personnel, etc.) is normally undertaken with the consent of the state benefiting from this assistance. Such consent is also required in the case of peacekeeping operations, with which humanitarian military interventions have been sometimes rather arbitrarily equated, notably during the war in Bosnia-Herzegovina.[5]

However, there is a specific legal aspect that sets the war for Kosovo apart from previous humanitarian military interventions, marking it even more explicitly as a breach of international law. In previous cases, countries promoting military interventions had sought to justify their decision by appealing to international law and soliciting and in one way or another obtaining a posteriori the approval of the Security Council of the United Nations. In the case of the war for Kosovo, NATO instead first threatened to use force and then actually did so without even beginning to go through the formalities required to obtain an authorization from the Security Council. Nor did it try to obtain some form of approval once the war had started. The political authorities of NATO did not even appeal to three resolutions of the Security Council (those of 31 March, 23 September and 24 October 1998) that might have offered at least a pretext, however weak, to justify their recourse to force without an explicit mandate from the Council.[6] They did not even propose stretching interpretation of Article 51 of the United Nations Charter, which refers to the right to self-defence, as the North Atlantic Parliamentary Assembly itself had proposed in November 1998 in its Resolution on Recasting Euro-Atlantic Security.[7] This document even went so far as to argue, as Bruno Simma disapprovingly stresses, that for NATO the inherent right of individual or collective self-defence, enshrined in Article 51 of the United Nations Charter, must extend to defence of common interests and values, including when the latter are threatened by humanitarian catastrophes, crimes against humanity, and war crimes.[8]

NATO has simply ignored the provisions of the United Nations Charter, implying that they did not reflect the functions that great powers – especially the United States – today have the right and the duty to take upon themselves to guarantee international order and the respect of human rights. Moreover, as we have seen, during the war, front-rank exponents of the US government, such as Assistant Secretary of State Strobe Talbott, declared that NATO claimed the prerogative to use force independently of any other international institution. In this case, too, the way had been opened by the Resolution of November 1998 of the North Atlantic Parliamentary Assembly, where it was declared that NATO needed 'to seek to ensure the widest international legitimacy for non-Article 5 [out-of-area] missions and also to stand ready to act should the United Nations Security Council be prevented from discharging its purposes of maintaining international peace and security'.[9]

All this leads to the conclusion that the Atlantic Council's threat to use force against the Yugoslav Federation, contained in the 'activation order' of October 1998, is in open conflict with Article 2 of the United Nations Charter, which prohibits not only the use of force against the territorial integrity and political independence of a state, but also *the threat* to use force. Moreover, the 'activation order' violates Article 52 of the 1969 Vienna Convention on the Law of Treaties, which forbids threatening to use force to induce a state to subscribe to an international agreement.[10]

It is thus still more the case that the aerial and missile attacks against Serbia, Kosovo and Montenegro, the North Atlantic Parliamentary Assembly's Resolution on Recasting Euro-Atlantic Security, and Strobe Talbott's declaration claiming NATO's full military autonomy are in open contradiction with the United Nations Charter and general international law.

As is well known, the United Nations Charter provides for the use of force of arms only in one case: when the Security Council, having ascertained the existence of a threat against peace, or an act of aggression, deems it necessary to use force, under its direction and control, to re-establish international security (Articles 39 and 42).

In other words, the United Nations Charter places the legitimate use of military force strictly in the hands of the Security Council, denying it to individual nation-states.

The only exception to this general rule is the right of 'self-defence' of a state that is attacked by another state or group of states. In this case, the attacked state can legitimately employ force to withstand the attack, while waiting for the Security Council to take the necessary measures to restore peace and international order (Article 51). By 'aggression', the United Nations Charter, abandoning the traditional doctrine of *bellum iustum*, means simply the use of military force. In other words, the aggressor is the state that first employs, or threatens to employ, force, whatever the reason invoked by its political authorities to justify this behaviour. This is a norm of 'general international law'; that is, it belongs to those rules and principles of international law that the international community regards as *ius cogens*, meaning that they are binding for all its members and do not depend on mere bilateral or multilateral agreements.[11]

As authoritative jurists such as Antonio Cassese, Jonathan Charney and Bruno Simma have argued, neither the rule nor the exception applies in the case of NATO's military attack against the Yugoslav Federation: the Security Council issued no authorization to use force under its control, nor did NATO intervene to defend some of its members against an outside aggressor.[12] Cassese spelled this out:

> The breach of the United Nations Charter occurring in this instance cannot be termed minor. The action of NATO countries departs radically from the Charter system for collective security, which hinges on a rule (a collective enforcement action authorized by the Security Council) and an exception (self-defence). There is no gainsaying that the Charter system has been transgressed, in that a group of states has deliberately resorted to armed action against a sovereign state without being authorized to do so by the Security Council.[13]

And he added:

> In the present instance, the member states of NATO have not put forward any legal justification based on the United Nations Charter. At most, they have emphasized that the

Security Council had already defined the situation in Kosovo as a 'threat to the peace'. Even cursory consideration of the Charter system shows however that this argument does not constitute *per se* a legal ground for initiating an armed attack against a sovereign state.[14]

Thus, the armed attack against the Federal Republic of Yugoslavia, a sovereign state and a member of the United Nations, was a pure and simple act of aggression, a most serious breach of current international law, against which the Security Council had the duty to intervene on the authority of Articles 2, 39, 41 and 42 of the United Nations Charter, using military force, if necessary, to assist the state attacked.

Finally, it should be observed that from the normative point of view, the declarations of the political authorities of the United States and NATO, claiming an unconditional *ius ad bellum* (right to resort to force) for themselves in the present and future, represent, if possible, an even more serious act of subversion of general international law than the aggression itself. By reasserting the principle that war is a sovereign prerogative of states and an instrument for the solution of international conflicts, these declarations reject an essential aspect of the evolution of modern international law.[15]

Towards a Widespread Legitimizing of War

In the face of this blatant subversion of international law, the United Nations reacted in a very weak and totally ineffectual fashion. The resolution condemning NATO's military intervention submitted by Russia, India and Belarus to the Security Council was rejected first of all by the Western powers' veto. Only three members out of fifteen – Russia, China and Namibia – dared to oppose the will of the Western powers. Thus, governments representing over two-thirds of the world population did not find any instrument of 'international democracy' to express their dissent adequately.

The Secretary-General of the United Nations, Kofi Annan, remained silent for some time. When he finally spoke up, it was to align himself with the position of the United States, justifying NATO's military intervention without a mandate from the Security Council in response to a state of necessity. The use of force was a lesser evil compared to the inertia of the international community in the face of a risk of genocide. Instead of appealing to the United Nations' institutional prerogatives granting it an absolute mono-poly over the legitimate international use of force, Kofi Annan harped on the priority of the protection of human rights and the declining role of nation-states in the era of globalization.[16]

As to the Hague Court of Justice, the supreme judicial organ of the United Nations, it lacks binding jurisdiction. Inevitably, this court declared itself incompetent to judge the complaint lodged by the Yugoslav Federation against the ten NATO countries involved in the attack.[17] The International Criminal Tribunal for former Yugoslavia did not intervene either, being equally incompetent to judge the legitimacy of a NATO military attack, since its competence regards the behaviour of the parties at war in the territory of former Yugoslavia (*ius in bello*), not the reasons for which they began to fight (*ius ad bellum*).

The doctrinal considerations of scholars of international law who made public statements about the war for Kosovo deserve close attention. Michael Glennon, for example, justified NATO's 'illegal' intervention by claiming that it was inspired by an ideal of justice to which it was well worth sacrificing, with no regrets, the anti-interventionist principles mummified in that archaic temple of international law, the Charter of the United Nations. But, at the same time, he cautioned against allowing the new humanitarian interventionism to follow a logic of case-by-case improvisation. In so doing, one would run the risk of merely introducing a greater degree of tolerance towards the use of military force. To obtain a stable consensus and a certain international legitimacy, the United States and NATO cannot limit themselves to undertaking military interventions whenever they believe them to be just, violating current international law each time. While they should not give up their new interventionism, they should at the same time promote a new legal system with new general norms providing for the use of force by international institutions every time the safeguarding of human rights demands it.[18] It is clear that Glennon intends here to state his divergence from the theses upheld by President Clinton and, in blunter terms, by the Secretary of State, Madeleine Albright:

> As to the use of force, Kosovo teaches us what we should have known anyway. It is true, force is sometimes necessary to face evil and protect our interests, but, as before the Kosovo war, it is not wise to formulate generalizing hypotheses to establish

how and when to recur to the use of force. In case of future crises, the sum of past experiences will find specific factors, characteristic of a specific place or time, on the other pan of the scales.[19]

An opposite thesis to Glennon's, which only seemed to converge with the United States administration's anti-normative orientation, was upheld by Bruno Simma in an essay I have already cited several times here. Commenting on NATO's 'activation order' and echoing opinions circulating within the German political establishment, Simma worries lest the military intervention threatened by NATO establish a precedent giving rise to a stable political and legal practice. Like the Californian Glennon, the Bavarian Simma accepts the moral reasons for the attack and approves it unconditionally. 'NATO has done a rather convincing job,' he writes, so that 'only a thin red line separates NATO's action on Kosovo from international legality.' But this case must be considered exceptional, justified by very special circumstances that led to an *ad hoc* decision. If instead, Simma argues, the Atlantic Alliance intended to turn this exception into a rule, regarding its violation of the United Nations Charter as a strategic programme, this could have a devastating effect on the whole collective security structure outlined in the Charter itself. Other countries, under the most diverse circumstances, could appeal to the precedent of the war for Kosovo and the possibility of NATO engaging in similar actions in the future. The recourse to unlawful practices must be considered an *extrema ratio* (last resort), and the subordination of NATO to the principles of the United Nations Charter must remain an intangible normative core which no innovative reinterpretation of the NATO statute must undermine.[20]

Like Glennon and Simma, Antonio Cassese believes that NATO has violated the United Nations Charter and, like Glennon and Simma, he proclaims his support of the 'important moral values' that motivated and, in his opinion, justified NATO's intervention. But, unlike Glennon and Simma, while vigorously stressing that NATO has committed a serious violation of the United Nations Charter, Cassese seems to believe that it was not a crime from the point of view of general international law, and hence that the state that was the victim of the aggression deserves no solidarity or reparation. Milošević is wrong, Cassese claims, in arguing that NATO's war against his country is 'illegitimate'. Rather, this war is proof that 'a new international legitimization of the use of force is in the making'.[21] In other words, he argues that there is a normative trend within the international community to legitimize the use of force even without a previous mandate of the Security Council when it is a matter of putting an end to serious violations of human rights. From this perspective, argues Cassese, NATO's military intervention was legitimate on the legal, as well as the ethical and humanitarian, plane.

Cassese also maintains that it is unwise to hope, like Simma and other German jurists, that the illegal intervention of NATO will remain an isolated case. It would be an illusion to expect a return to the traditional principles regulating the use of force outlined in the United Nations Charter. Such an attitude would be conservative, as well as ineffective. International law, argues Cassese, in agreement with Glennon and Charney, needs to be updated.[22]

The jurist's task is not to oppose the present 'humanitarian trend' but to specify the conditions under which this trend can give rise to a positive legal regime providing for new possibilities for the legitimate use of force, while placing it, at the same time, under general rules. In other words, taking an opposite stance to Simma's, Cassese argues that the exception must become the rule. He lists six conditions under which, in the future, the use of force for humanitarian reasons by a group of states, even without the authorization of the Security Council, should become totally legitimate. These conditions are deduced from the case of the war for Kosovo, and hence are consistent with Cassese's legitimizing of the NATO attack against the Yugoslav Republic from the legal as well as the moral point of view.[23]

One could object to Cassese, however, that his new rules of humanitarian war cannot be used to legitimize NATO's attack against the Yugoslav Republic a posteriori, unless one intends to apply the maxim *ex iniuria oritur ius* (from the crime arises the law). A maxim, as Norberto Bobbio has observed, representing an utter negation of the international rule of law.[24] The very fact that Cassese's rules are elements of a newly formulated doctrine means that they were not in force before the war and there was no customary trend within the international community to legitimize the use of force for humanitarian reasons without a mandate from the Security Council.[25] (In fact, as I have argued above, it is far from demonstrated that there was a customary trend to legitimize the use of force for humanitarian reasons even *with* an authorization of the Security Council.) Indeed, Cassese himself, as we have seen, vigorously stresses that the attitude of NATO authorities towards the Security Council was without precedent.

Furthermore, unless one chooses to identify the international community with the nineteen NATO countries that waged war on Yugoslavia, one cannot ignore the opposition of countries of great international prominence such as Russia, India and China. Nor does it seem right to underestimate the question of the subjects to which Cassese would entrust the coercive tutelage of human rights, namely military alliances between or clustered around great powers. These powers are far from being impartial actors; they normally disregard procedures and tend to take little account of universal moral values in their decisions[26] – not to mention that Cassese's rules would mean, today, assigning *de facto* to NATO and, through it, the United States the power of imposing upon the rest of the world the Western conception of democracy, rule of law and individual rights.

Moreover, there is no factual evidence that NATO's illegal intervention has inaugurated, as an indirect normative effect, an international legal custom in the sense indicated by Cassese. If one can speak of a trend in act, it goes in the direction feared by Simma and welcomed by Albright and, in substance, by Glennon and Charney as well; that is, a trend towards the end of the United Nations' monopoly over the legitimate use of force. Instead, groups of states or individual states – especially those equipped with nuclear weapons – arrogate the right to use military force in defence of collective interests, or rather, what each state construes as 'collective interests'. As Marina Spinedi observed, we are returning to the situation preceding the foundation of the League of Nations and the United Nations in the past century, with the concomitant danger that an increasing number of international actors, both public and 'private', Western and Eastern, will claim the legitimate right to wage war.[27] This trend threatens to be seconded, whether consciously or not, by Western jurists who, for ethical, ethical cum legal, or merely legal reasons, have approved NATO's intervention against Yugoslavia, while admitting at the same time that it was totally against the United Nations Charter.

The Heights of Morality

To legitimize the 'humanitarian war', the above-mentioned jurists ventured *in munere alieno* (in a realm where they are laymen); that is, they abandoned the terrain of positive law to climb to a higher normative plane, that of international ethics. Even Cassese, while attempting to play the trump card of customary law, lays stress on the 'moral values' that Western powers meant to safeguard by force of arms. These jurists' references to ethics, however, tend to be generic; they are limited essentially to claiming the normative superiority of humanitarian intentions as against the provisions of international law. In spite of the fact that many delicate moral questions remained open, these jurists' meta-legal option is not backed by an analytical discourse on morals, or a reflection on the ethical principles and rules that are supposed to replace or integrate those of positive law judged to be inadequate.

One wonders, first of all, whether in a time of 'polytheism of values' an international ethics can exist consisting of a single body of principles and rules of conduct, or whether in this domain, too, one should take a pluralist and relativist stance. It may also be necessary to decide whether in a military context one should espouse what Weber called the ethics of 'convictions', or prefer instead an ethics of 'responsibility', centred more on the concrete effects of 'moral' acts than on the good intentions of their performers. In other words, is it morally legitimate to kill innocents to prevent or stop a massacre? Who has the *moral* authority – not the mere political or military power – to decide? Is the killing of innocent people morally acceptable, under the sole condition that it not be intentional but merely an expected 'collateral damage' by military actions (the 'law of double effect')? By what parameters can one gauge the acceptable proportion between *willed* and merely *foreseen* effects? In sum, these jurists' recourse to ethical arguments has essentially served the purpose of loosening the links of international law by circumventing the provisions that subject the use of force to conditions and procedures agreed upon by the international community.

Surprisingly, there were also respected Western legal scholars and philosophers who made this sort of summary use of ethics to provide a meta-legal legitimization of NATO's 'humanitarian war'.[28] Michael Walzer, for example, argued that the obligation to use force of arms to put a stop to crimes, like 'ethnic cleansing', that are 'an insult to human conscience' is what 'moral philosophers call an "imperfect duty" '. This means, he claimed, that no one in particular had the moral obligation to intervene against the Yugoslav Federation, but all had the right to do so, especially neighbouring states, or an alliance between neighbouring states. NATO, however, was a morally ideal choice, being 'the most appropriate military instrument in the case of Kosovo, considering the role European powers have played for centuries in the Balkans'.[29] In sum, when international diplomacy is unable to put a stop to heinous crimes such as ethnic cleansing, 'military intervention is always justified'; in spite of the doubts expressed by Norberto Bobbio, such intervention is always a 'just war', even when it is a unilateral intervention disregarding the United Nations Charter. The United Nations, Walzer claimed, has proved incapable of establishing something even vaguely resembling a global rule of law. It lacks a common will, and its normative acts are so ineffective that they cannot even be regarded as legally binding.[30] Thus, as he had already done in his well-known *Just and Unjust Wars*, the leading theorist of the doctrine of 'just war' used military ethics to sustain the legitimacy of war. Once again his main objective would seem to be that of doing away with the limitations with which, over the centuries, modern international law has tried to curb the right of the strongest, albeit with serious flaws and a very limited effectiveness.[31] His ethical militarism is akin to Edward Luttwak's military cynicism in its radical scepticism towards international law and institutions, lack of interest in peacekeeping interventions, and faith in the virtuous physiology of war.[32]

Jürgen Habermas comes to quite similar conclusions, although in the framework of a complex, fine-tuned ethical and philosophical discussion. In an essay entitled 'Bestialität und Humanität' – which paraphrases and strives to confute the famous Carl Schmitt aphorism quoted earlier – the most authoritative contemporary German philosopher takes a stand in favour of NATO's 'humanitarian war'.[33] He begins by exalting its 'surgical precision' and systematic effort to spare the civilian population, which make it something far removed from the twentieth-century model of 'total war' and lends it a 'high degree of legitimacy'. Second, he denies that the NATO war was waged for 'reasons of state':

> A hermeneutics of suspicion can draw very little from the attack upon Yugoslavia. ... Neither what is imputed to the United States (viz a will to guarantee and expand its sphere of influence), nor the motivation attributed to NATO (a search for a new role), nor what is blamed on the 'European fortress' (a preventive defence against waves of refugees), can explain the decision to engage in such a grave, risky, and costly intervention.[34]

It is more plausible, argues Habermas, to see the war as an attempt to change international law by asserting the right to universal citizenship. Through this war, the 'legal pacifism'[35] of the German Red–Green coalition (as well as the 'legal pacifism' of NATO) did not merely pursue the objective of putting an end to 'murderous ethnic nationalism' and imposing peace in the Balkans; in line with a cosmopolitan philosophy going from Kant to Kelsen, it strove to transcend existing international law and metamorphose it into a fully legal universal system.

Thus, NATO's war against the Yugoslav Federation should not be judged in terms of existing international law, according to which it is obviously an interference in the internal affairs of a sovereign state and a violation of the prohibition to use military force. It should be viewed, instead, from the ethical perspective of Kantian and Kelsenian 'legal pacifism', as a 'pacifying mission which made use of arms, but did so with the consensus of the international community, albeit without a mandate from the United Nations'.[36] According to this interpretation, the war for Kosovo is a decisive step forwards on the road from classical international law to cosmopolitan law, a road that will soon lead us to truly effective international institutions, such as an international Court of Justice endowed with binding jurisdiction, and a General Assembly of the United Nations composed not only of representatives of governments but also of direct representatives of the citizens of each state.

And here is the central argument of Habermas's ethical and philosophical summation: until the cosmopolitan metamorphosis of international institutions is completed, as long as human rights remain weakly institutionalized at the global level,

> the borderline between law and morals will be inevitably blurred, as it was, in fact, in the war for Kosovo. Faced with a blocked Security Council, NATO could not help appealing to the moral validity of international law, i.e. to norms which are not actually applied and upheld within the international community. The sub-institutionalization of the right to universal citizenship finds expression in a gap between the legitimacy of peacekeeping interventions and their effectiveness. ... NATO has been able to successfully oppose the Yugoslav government precisely because it acted without a legitimization it would certainly have been denied by the Security Council.[37]

Confronted with a feeble institutionalization of universal law, an interventionist policy aimed at the defence of human rights – NATO's policy – 'is forced to anticipate the future cosmopolitan condition while attempting at the same time to promote it'.[38] Of course, Habermas admits, there can be doubts over some aspects of the war, and NATO's self-investiture cannot become a rule. However, 'victims cannot be left to their torturers'. The Yugoslavs' terrorist abuse of state power turned a classical civil war into carefully planned mass murder. Death, terror and deportation, writes Habermas, had already been afflicted on about 300,000 Kosovars in the years preceding the beginning of the aerial raids. In the absence of alternative solutions, democratic countries were obliged to offer succour as legitimized by universal ethics.[39]

Thus, like Walzer, Habermas superimposes universal ethics on positive international law. But, unlike Walzer, who never specified in his works what he meant by 'moral principles' and what their normative foundation might be,[40] Habermas does not hesitate to identify international ethics with a specific German philosophical tradition, going from Kant's *Zum ewigen Frieden (Perpetual Peace)* to Kelsen's 'legal pacifism' and the radicalization of Kantian cosmopolitanism which Habermas himself has been advocating for some years.[41] Nor does he balk at lending NATO's political and military leadership the motivations and ends of his own personal cosmopolitan philosophy and theory of the moral universality of human rights. As a premise to all this, Habermas accepts the most extreme version of the information diffused by Western mass media on the genocide in course in Kosovo before NATO's intervention.

One cannot help remarking that Habermas's ethical and philosophical reflection has the pretension of being founded on the ruins of international positive law and international institutions. Like Walzer, Habermas dismisses these institutions as normatively and politically evanescent but makes no attempt to analyse the reasons for their weakness. His view of the war is moralistic, rejecting as pure 'exegesis from suspicion' all interpretations of US motivations that do not ground them in Wilsonian idealism rooted in the American pragmatic tradition.[42] Finally, one should not overlook the conflict between cosmopolitan universality and a strong 'ethnocentric' polarity in Habermas's theoretical perspective. This leads him to identify Western public opinion as the 'international community' and keeps him from perceiving, beyond the horizon of his noble Kantian utopia, the diversity, estrangement and increasing hostility of other cultures, civilizations and governments – not just India and China, but Russia as well – which have judged NATO's 'humanitarian generosity' with sarcasm. Maybe one should address the same appeal to Habermas that German pacifists – as he himself mentions – addressed to their government; that is, to 'descend from the heights of morality'.[43] To do so would mean, in Habermas' case, to stop using the principles of Kantian ethics once again to legitimise what is a hegemonic war waged by Western powers.

The Destiny of the United Nations

Habermas can certainly be accused, as he has been by Karl Otto Hondrich and others, of having justified the atrocities, destruction and dangers of war in abstract moral terms.[44] But, setting aside all possible ethical or political criticism, the theoretical interest of Habermas's reflection cannot be denied, especially that of his attempt to interpret the war against the Yugoslav Republic within the perspective of cosmopolitan law and universal citizenship. In my opinion, Habermas has analysed in depth some major legal and political issues raised by what I have called the 'claims' of humanitarian war. These issues remain controversial and still open.

The first issue is what is to become of the United Nations. Secretary General Kofi Annan has stated that, thanks to the experience in Kosovo (and East Timor), the United Nations has come to life again, invested with a new, extremely important function, namely the international safeguarding of human rights, alongside its traditional peacekeeping function.[45] This is an optimistic declaration which some have interpreted as evidence of the present United Nations Secretary-General's 'limited sovereignty'. Indeed, it is generally felt that the war for Kosovo speeded up the decline of the United Nations' authority and role, a process that had started in the early 1990s and has since been fostered, with strategic consistency, especially by the United States.

Today more than ever, the United Nations appears weak, dependent, not credible, and oppressed by a financial crisis partially caused by the United States, which, along with other countries, does not pay the substantial quotas it owes.[46] The Security Council – there is little sense today in taking the General Assembly into account – looks more and more like an empty box that great powers can fill freely with whatever contents happen to suit their political strategies. When they find it convenient, they can even leave the box empty, ignoring, as in the case of the war for Kosovo, the competence of the United Nations' leading organs, and entrusting the functions that the United Nations Charter assigns to the Security Council to a military organization representing a specific party – the 'new NATO'.

It is easily foreseeable that in the years to come the decisional powers of the whole organization of the United Nations will be reduced to the present level of those of the General Assembly, which, as is known, is only entitled to discuss issues and vote 'recommendations'. The 'humanitarian war' has further weakened the United Nations, having deprived it of what was by far its most significant function, namely the faculty to determine and control the international use of force, and relegated it to a humiliating role of rubber-stamping protocols drafted elsewhere. The 'humanitarian war' has weakened the United Nations especially because it has driven it up a blind alley, although few seem to have realized this so far.[47]

Habermas and upholders of 'legal pacifism' such as Robert Falk, David Held and Norberto Bobbio have always insisted on the need to strengthen the United Nations, entrusting it with the task of 'institutionalizing' the universal protection of human rights by laying the foundations for the development of 'cosmopolitan law'. They have solicited the creation of institutional apparatuses and a legal system in which individuals, as well as states, are represented and protected as subjects of international law. In the perspective of 'legal pacifism', the doctrine of human rights has as its fundamental corollary the attribution of the subjectivity of international law to all the inhabitants of the planet as an original right that all individuals are entitled to 'as human beings'. A legally binding protection *erga omnes* (enforced as a duty by the international community) of human rights cannot be guaranteed, they contend, by judicial organisms with non-binding or merely *ad hoc* jurisdictions, like the tribunals for former Yugoslavia and Rwanda; it is necessary, as Hans Kelsen was the first to propose, to establish a permanent tribunal with universal jurisdiction.[48]

However, the upholders of Kantian cosmopolitan law do not seem to grasp that this 'universalist claim' is not enforceable within the framework of current international institutions. Indeed, its enforcement is problematic even within the structures of the international criminal tribunals set up by the Security Council in the 1990s. The hoped-for judicial independence and impartiality of these tribunals is not easily practicable. One can hardly lay enough stress on the structural constraints that keep the United Nations from becoming an institution capable of operating, or at least tending to operate, on the basis of the general interest and universal values.[49] Besides this, there is the even more irksome issue of turning the United Nations into a more broadly representative organization (on the basis of what rules of representation?),[50] or at least into one less removed from the model of 'rule of law'.

The theorists of 'legal pacifism' seem to forget that international institutions and legal system are all founded on the consent of states and – with some traumatic exceptions, probably bound to become more frequent in the years to come – on their sovereignty. The war for Kosovo has revealed the incompatibility between the principle of guaranteeing peace among nation-states (which involves respect for each state's particularity) and the universality of the doctrine of human rights as a new justification for the use of force.

In the war for Kosovo, some great powers took upon themselves the prerogative of using force of arms to uphold values they claim are universal; this brought to a head the conflict between the particular 'interests' and 'values' of each state, on the one hand, and the (pretended) universality of the doctrine of human rights and its ethical premises, on the other. The Security Council was paralysed by the clash between conflicting particular interests, to all of which the institution as such attributed full legitimacy. The United Nations is founded on the representation of nation-states, each with its own particularity, and not the representation of the 'citizens of the world'. Moreover, it is marked by an extreme particularism in the discrimination between permanent and non-permanent members of the Security Council and, even more, in the attribution of veto power to the permanent members, that is, the five great powers that won World War II. International protection of human rights and the whole cosmopolitan ideal inevitably require interference in the internal affairs of states; hence, they are incompatible not only with the principle of self-determination of peoples and the sovereignty of states, but even more with the decisional structure of current international institutions.

Hence the dilemma that has driven the United Nations into a blind alley and that Kofi Annan's optimistic declarations have attempted to exorcise. To universalize the United Nations according to the model of 'legal pacifism' is to destroy it. On the other hand, to preserve its structural particularism – especially the veto power of the permanent members of the Security Council – would be to relegate the United Nations to the margins of the international arena once and for all, since this particularism clashes with the global scope of the hegemonic strategies (and matching ideologies) of the Western powers – first and foremost the United States – which are no longer willing to submit to the veto of non-Western powers. In the face of this alternative, one thing is clear: that legitimizing 'humanitarian war' is no way to strengthen existing international institutions, much less to promote an increasing institutionalization of human rights within these same institutions. It rather threatens to make the international order regress to a 'primitive' level, to use Kelsen's theoretical legal vocabulary.[51] 'Humanitarian war' reassigns to states an indiscriminate *ius ad bellum*, voids the 'pacifying' functions of international law, and even casts discredit on the cosmopolitan ideal of universal citizenship.

The Universality of Human Rights

A second theoretical issue brought to the forefront once again by the war for Kosovo is the Western claim that human rights are universal and hence are applicable, by coercion if necessary, all over the world. It goes almost without saying that the fate of the international legal system hangs on this claim. If it were accepted, the structure and sources of current international law would have to undergo radical change to yield, as we have seen, to 'cosmopolitan law'; that is, a legal system no longer anchored, as Groz puts it, in the sovereignty of states, but founded on the universality of human rights and the acknowledgement that all members of the human species are legal and political subjects. An intrinsic logic draws the doctrine of human rights towards the perspective of 'universal citizenship', a legal system with no territorial or cultural boundaries, guaranteeing, in terms of an absolute formal equality, the rights of all individuals as rational beings and moral persons.[52] It is significant that the first article of the Universal Declaration of Human Rights of 1948 states that all human beings, being born free and equal, and endowed with conscience and reason, are duty-bound to have a brotherly attitude towards one another. This philosophy of international relations openly contrasts with Groz's and Hobbes's paradigm of 'international society' as a society of states whose relations may well be competitive and conflictual, as well as co-operative.[53]

From a strictly legal point of view, the issue of the universality of human rights coincides with that of the normative value to be granted to the Universal Declaration of 1948. According to some jurists, it is *ius erga omnes* which, under certain conditions, may also be applied coercively.[54] According to others, the document voted by the United Nations Assembly lacks the formal prerequisites of a legal text. Kelsen was among the first to argue that the doctrine of human rights contained in the Universal Declaration cannot be regarded as legally binding, since the organ that approved it lacks legislative powers, the formulation of the text is not imperative, and, finally, the text lacks 'secondary norms' providing for sanctions.[55]

At any rate, the universality of human rights is a controversial issue, especially in the philosophy of international law. The dispute here does not concern the meaning of the doctrine of the rights of man in Western political and legal history; it is unquestionable that this doctrine is one of the most significant legacies of the great European tradition of liberalism and democracy. The problem has to do with the relationship between the individualist philosophy underlying this doctrine, on the one hand, and the wide spectrum of civilizations and cultures whose values are not those of Europeans, on the other. One has only to think of the countries of South-East and North-East Asia, prevalently Confucian in culture, as well as those of sub-Saharan Africa and, of course, the Islamic world.

In this respect, the polemic that livened up the second United Nations Conference on human rights, held in Vienna in 1993, is illuminating. At Vienna, two opposite conceptions faced one another. On one side was the Western doctrine of the universality and indivisibility of human rights. On the other, there were the theses of many countries of Latin America and Asia arguing that in the protection of human rights priority must be given to economic and social development, the struggle against poverty, and freeing Third World countries from the burden of foreign debt. These countries also accused Western countries of using the ideology of humanitarian interventionism to impose their economic supremacy, political system and world-view on the rest of humankind.

A recent polemic, launched especially by Singapore, Malaysia and China, is equally emblematic. This polemic, which led to the 'Declaration of Bangkok' in 1993, opposed 'Asian values' to the West's tendency to impose its own ethical and political values – as well as its science, technology, industry, and bureaucracy – upon Oriental cultures.[56] Today, the ruling classes of a growing number of South-Eastern Asian countries are striving to reassert their political and cultural identity on the basis of values such as order, social harmony, respect for authority, and family. In this perspective, the West is perceived as a place where community values decline under the attack of a boundless individualism that claims rights but admits no duties. Even the doctrine of human rights is accused of being founded on an individualistic and liberal philosophy that clashes with the community-oriented, anti-formalistic ethos of the Asian traditions, also shared by traditional African and American cultures.

Thus, it is clear that the universality of human rights cannot be taken for granted. Their universality could be affirmed only on the basis of a philosophical 'foundation' offering cogent arguments for the inherence of human rights in human nature (or human rationality) as such, independently of the particular European cultural context that gave rise to the discourse on human rights. Habermas has denied that the doctrine of human rights is so dependent on the Western model of rationality that it cannot be proposed to all human beings without running the risk of cultural imperialism. He believes that the theory of fundamental rights reflects a nucleus of moral intuitions common to the major universalist religions of the planet. It 'conforms to the normative substance of the great prophetic doctrines and metaphysical interpretations that came to the fore in universal history'.[57]

According to Habermas, one could even speak of a pragmatic universality of the theory of human rights. This pragmatic univer-sality resides, he claims, in the fact that its normative standards reflect a need felt by all cultures; that is, the need to answer the challenges of modernity and a growing social complexity. Accordingly, he regards modern Western law, with its norms which, although coercive, guarantee individual freedom, as a technically universal normative apparatus, not the expression of a particular cultural tradition.

One might object to Habermas – and to many other upholders of the universality of human rights – that the rule of law and the doctrine of individual rights arose in a context of political conflict and legal and philosophical particularism, a particularism that present-day Western philosophies of law do not seem to have got beyond.[58] One could also object, as Bobbio has argued in *L'età dei diritti*, that it is impossible to lay a philosophical foundation for a corpus of normative propositions weighed down by major deontic antinomies, first and foremost between the right to freedom and private property and the right to social equality.[59]

Furthermore, the protection of human rights can hardly be regarded as a technical implication of legal formalism made necessary by the process of 'modernization'. In spite of Ulrich Beck's recent theses,[60] the notion of modernity itself is deeply rooted in Western philosophical, political and ethical traditions. It is inconceivable outside of the liberal tradition, with its individualism, the ethical rationalism of its anthropology, its idea of progress and, last but not least, its religious agnosticism.

Thus, the universality of the rights of man is a rationalistic postulate that lacks theoretical confirmation and is also rightly viewed with misgivings by non-Western cultures. Over twenty years ago Hedley Bull argued, with remarkable foresight, that the Western ideology of humanitarian intervention in defence of human rights was a direct offshoot of the missionary and colonizing tradition of the West, with its roots in the early nineteenth century, the period of US intervention in Cuba and European intervention in the Ottoman Empire.[61]

Humanität, Bestialität

A further issue is the 'claim' that modern war can be used as a legal instrument to defend human rights. Some authors fear that humanitarian interference could be, as Carl Schmitt would have argued, still another incarnation of the doctrine of just war: an intolerable ethical and legal swindle, or, at best, an irresponsible self-delusion.

Habermas does not neglect this problem. After stressing NATO's efforts to spare human lives and praising the surgical precision of its aerial attacks, he suddenly seems to be struck by an afterthought. He expresses doubts concerning the consistency of the bombings with the humanitarian ends which NATO claimed to pursue. He wonders whether one could have spared more human lives, for example by announcing the bombing of the Belgrade television station half an hour in advance. And whether one could have avoided the massive destruction of bridges and non-military structures in a country already seriously damaged by the embargo. All this suffering, writes Habermas, weighs on our conscience: 'every child who dies as he's trying to escape jars our nerves'. Habermas is even grazed by the doubt lest Carl Schmitt's contemptuous anti-humanist formula – *Humanität, Bestialität* – might be tragically true: 'our deepest source of worry is the nagging doubt that it is "legal pacifism" itself which is in the wrong'.[62]

Habermas's doubt deserves to become certainty – and not merely a moral certainty, but a juridical and political conviction. On this point, 'legal pacifism' is certainly 'in the wrong', since its exponents, beginning from its founding father, Hans Kelsen, espouse the theory of 'just war' in a context allegedly inspired by pacifism. It is Kelsen who invented not only the formula 'peace through law' – the title of his renowned essay of 1944, which has become the slogan of 'legal pacifism' – but also the notion that war can be viewed as a 'legal sanction' when used in response to a violation of international law.[63] In this case, Kelsen argues, the state using force is vested with penal functions by an implicit authorization of the international legal community. Kelsen concedes that the practical applicability of his theory is controversial in the absence of a superior, neutral authority empowered to qualify acts of war as crimes or sanctions. He also bows to the equally serious objection that only a state that is stronger than the state to be sanctioned can use war as an instrument of coercion. But this does not stop the formalist and Kantian pacifist Kelsen from posing – supreme paradox – the ethical doctrine of 'just war' as the condition for the legal legitimacy of the international system.[64]

The thesis that I believe should be upheld against Kelsen's and Habermas's 'legal pacifism' is that modern war can in no way and in no case be viewed as a 'legal sanction'.[65] A realist philosophy of international law should reject the doctrine of 'just war' in all its versions, whether in its traditional ethical and theological formulation or one of its legal variants, as in Kelsen's case.

If, as I believe, the primary function of law, and of international law in particular, is to submit the wielding of power to general rules and, hence, to standards of proportion, discrimination and restraint in the use of force, it follows that in the nuclear age war must be considered incompatible with law, *legibus solutum* (outside the law). Bobbio himself, while siding with 'legal pacifism', has put forward this very thesis in direct polemic against modern advocates of the doctrine of *bellum iustum*. Modern warfare, he wrote, has put itself beyond any possible criterion of justification or legalization. It is as uncontrolled and uncontrollable by law as an earthquake or a storm. Bobbio argues that, after having been regarded as a means to enforce law (by the theory of 'just war') and then as a possible object of legal regulation (by the evolution of *ius in bello*), today war is, once again, the antithesis of law.[66]

Modern war, fought with nuclear weapons (or quasi-nuclear ones, as in the Gulf War in 1991 and, to a certain extent, the war for Kosovo as well), is incommensurable with the categories of ethics and law. By nature its function is to destroy – without bounds, discrimination or restraint – the lives, possessions and rights of thousands, or hundreds of thousands, of human beings, without any evaluation of their responsible behaviour. Seen as a legal sanction, war is substantially the meting out of a collective capital punishment on the basis of a presumed criminal responsibility of the whole staff of the military organization of the state that is being sanctioned, from the generals down to the last private. Besides, in spite of their claim to 'surgical precision' – regularly disproved – military sanctions today indiscriminately strike both those responsible for the acts judged as criminal and a great number of people who have no part at all in military decisions and operations, and may even be victims of the totalitarian power of the political elite that provoked the war in the first place.

Thus, in its destructive consequences modern war is hardly distinguishable from international terrorism, if by terrorism we mean the use of force against innocent victims to cause panic. One could use arguments akin to Kelsen's to propose a theory of 'just terrorism' as an international legal sanction and argue that a terrorist attack may be a legally valid act. In fact, modern war is refractory, exactly like terrorism, to the application of any rule whatsoever, whether legal or moral. That is, unless one accepts as a moral justification the notion of 'objective responsibility', which Kelsen has tried to revive to legitimize his theory of war as 'legal sanction'. But it is a theory that runs counter to a basic principle of modern criminal law: the personal nature of criminal responsibility.

In the case of the war for Kosovo, in particular, the life of thousands of citizens of the Yugoslav Federation was sacrificed simply because they objectively belonged to a state whose regime the attackers wanted to overthrow. This regime, moreover, was accused of being despotic and totalitarian; if so, its citizens could not share the political and moral responsibility for its acts. Thus, the war for Kosovo has proved incompatible with international law, just as it would be incompatible with the laws of a constitutional state to mount a police operation during which, to catch or kill a criminal barricaded in a quarter of a town, one decided to bomb it, killing a large number of residents together with the criminal. In a legal system based on the rule of law, such 'humanitarian actions' would be prevented by force, their authors incriminated, and severe penalties inflicted upon them if these actions brought about the death, mutilation, or wounding of hundreds of innocent persons or the destruction of their possessions as 'collateral' (but avoidable and predictable) effects.

One of the general conclusions that one can draw from all this is that war cannot be used as a legal instrument by international institutions charged with peacekeeping or the defence of human rights, not even by the United Nations, especially if one intends to redirect these institutions to the new objective of defending human rights. In the past few decades there has been a growing tendency to 'farm out' the use of force to great powers, independently of the direction and control of the Security Council. Luigi Condorelli has argued that the Security Council has been issuing what are simply modern equivalents of privateering commissions; that is, blank authorizations for states interested in using force. Such a practice not only violates the United Nations Charter but subverts the most elementary principles of the rule of law, according to which the operative techniques of public security forces must be based on profoundly different criteria from those of terrorism (for example, the life of citizens and the life of law-enforcers should be given equal value).

These arguments are all the more persuasive when they are contrasted *ad hoc* with those of the advocates of the universal legal cogency of human rights and international legal subjectivity of individuals. We are faced here with an insoluble aporia. To claim that all individuals are subject to international law and hence entitled to inviolable and inalienable rights means acknowledging, in the first place, their right to life, established by Article 3 of the Universal Declaration. Second, it means, again on the authority of the Universal Declaration, acknowledging their basic rights of habeas corpus: nobody can be submitted to hostile treatment undermining his or her physical integrity, freedom, emotional attachments, or possessions, unless his or her infringement of criminal law can be ascertained. And this ascertainment demands that judicial action be carried out in a fair and public debate, before an independent and impartial court. Finally, Article 7 of the Universal Declaration acknowledges the right of all human beings to equal treatment before the law.

The legitimizing of 'humanitarian aggression' by the advocates of 'legal pacifism' – and by the political and military leadership of NATO – is a self-contradictory negation of all these principles. The 'humanitarian war' meted out a death sentence 'from the sky' to thousands of Yugoslav citizens without any attempt to investigate their personal responsibilities. The war also violated the principle of equal treatment before the law, since the defence of human rights in former Yugoslavia has followed two mutually incompatible approaches. The Hague Tribunal wields its repressive power in the name of legal values, while following procedures based on the principle of constitutional law that nobody can be punished unless he or she has been judged responsible for crimes committed personally and knowingly. Furthermore, the Hague Tribunal does not contemplate the death penalty among its sanctions. However, only a small minority of citizens of former Yugoslavia, mostly members of the political and military leadership, have been subjected to this judicial action, which is formally respectful of some important principles of the rule of law. Thousands of private citizens, instead, were treated in a very different way. They were bombed, often with cluster bombs or depleted-uranium projectiles. If that were not enough, the 'war from the sky' placed their lives below those of Western soldiers. Thus, it can be argued that thousands of Serbs, Montenegrins, Roma and also Kosovar-Albanians were brutally denied acknowledgement not only of their status as subjects of the international legal system but of their human nature itself. *Humanität, Bestialität*.

Notes

1. The effects of media on world public opinion have been stressed especially by A. Pizzorno, 'Caro Habermas, l'autoinvestitura della NATO non basta', in U. Beck, N. Bobbio *et al.*, *L'ultima crociata? Ragione e torti di una guerra giusta*. Rome: Libri di Reset, 1999, pp. 91–2, and M. Tarchi, 'La guerra della Nato e le vecchie appartenenze', in M. Cabona (ed.), *'Ditelo a Sparta'. Serbia ed Europa contro l'aggressione della Nato*. Genoa: Graphos, 1999, pp. 213–18. On this subject, see especially

J. Toschi Marazzani Visconti, 'Milosevic visto da vicino', *Limes*, supplement to no. 1 (1999), 27–34. The latter essay affirms that the public relations company Ruder & Finn has been working since 1991 for the Croatian and Bosnian governments and the Kosovar-Albanians to promote anti-Serb interests (after its offers had been rejected by Milošević). Its director, James Harf, vaunted his professional activity in the following terms: 'We were able to equate Serbs to Nazis in public opinion ... We are professionals. We have got a job to do and we do it' (*ibid.*, p. 31).

2. 'The higher, grander goal that has eluded humanity for centuries – the ideal of justice backed by power – should not be abandoned. If power is used to do justice, law will follow', see M. J. Glennon, 'The new interventionism: the search for a just international law', *Foreign Affairs*, 78(3) (1999), 7. Similar positions are expressed by L. Henkin, 'Kosovo and the law of "humanitarian intervention"', *American Journal of International Law*, 93(4) (1999), 824–8.

3. A humanitarian ideology upheld by R. Gutman and D. Rieff, editors of *Crimes of War* (New York: W. W. Norton, 1999).

4. C. Pinelli, 'Sul fondamento degli interventi armati a fini umanitari', in G. Cotturri (ed.), *Guerra–individuo*. Milan: Angeli, 1999, pp. 88–90; P. Picone, 'Interventi delle Nazioni Unite e obblighi erga omnes', in P. Picone (ed.), *Interventi delle Nazioni Unite*. Padua: Cedam, 1995, p. 544; F. Lattanzi, *Assistenza umanitaria e interventi di umanità*. Turin: Giappichelli, 1997, p. 80; E. Garzón Valdés, 'Guerra e diritti umani', *Ragion pratica*, 713 (1999), 25–49; P. De Sena, 'Uso della forza a fini umanitari, intervento in Jugoslavia e diritto internazionale', *Ragion pratica*, 713 (1999), 141–65. On this subject in general see P. de Senarclens, *L'Humanitaire en catastrophe*. Paris: Presses de Sciences Po, 1999.

5. Pinelli, 'Sul fondamento degli interventi, p. 88; U. Villani, 'La guerra del Kosovo: una guerra umanitaria o un crimine internazionale?', in G. Cotturri (ed.), *Guerra–individuo*. Milan: Angeli, 1999, pp. 30–1.

6. These three resolutions (no. 1160 of 31 March 1998, no. 1199 of 23 September 1998, no. 1203 of October 24, 1998), approved with the abstention of China, and – on the last of them – of Russia as well, condemned the Serbian police for using excessive force and the UÇK for acts of terrorism, and invited the parties to reach a political solution. The resolution of 23 September mentioned the risk of a 'humanitarian catastrophe', and those of 23 September and 24 October stressed the existence of a 'danger for peace and security in the region'. The original texts of the three resolutions can be consulted at the United Nations' Internet site: <http://www.un.org/peace/kosovo/98sc1160.htm>; <http://www.un.org/peace/kosovo/98sc1199.htm>;<http://www.un. org/peace/kosovo/98sc1203.htm>.

7. B. Simma, 'NATO, the UN and the use of force: legal aspects', *European Journal of International Law*, 10(1) (1999), 16.

8. Quoted in Simma, 'NATO, the UN and the use of force', pp. 15–16.

9. Simma, 'NATO, the UN and the use of force', p. 16.

10. *Ibid.*, p. 3. 'NATO's logic at the time was to show Milosevic a loaded gun to induce him to negotiate', wrote the Italian prime minister, Massimo D'Alema, with a realism revealing scarce awareness of the norms of international law (M. D'Alema, *Kosovo. Gli italiani e la guerra.* Milan: Mondadori, 1999, p. 12).

11. 'In the contemporary international law, as codified in the 1969 Vienna Convention on the Law of Treaties (Articles 53 and 64), the prohibition enunciated in Article 2(4) of the Charter is part of *jus cogens*, i.e., it is accepted and acknowledged by the international community of states as a whole as a norm from which no derogation is permitted' (Simma, 'NATO, the UN and the use of force', p. 3). It can be added that according to the International Court of Justice (sentence of 1986 on the Nicaragua case, paragraphs 187–90, 267–8), the prohibition against using force is part and parcel of international customary law, and violations of human rights do not justify armed actions by foreign states to put an end to them (cf. M. Spinedi, 'Uso della forza da parte della Nato in Jugoslavia e diritto internazionale', in *Guerra e pace in Kosovo*, Quaderni Forum, 12(2) (1998), 23, 26–7).

12. A. Cassese, '*Ex iniuria ius oritur*: are we moving towards international legitimation of forcible humanitarian countermeasures in the world community?', *European Journal of International Law*, 10(1) (1999), 23–5; J. I. Charney, 'Anticipatory humanitarian intervention in Kosovo', *American Journal of International Law*, 93(4) (1999), 834ff.; Simma, 'NATO, the UN and the use of force', pp. 1–6; A. Cassese, 'A follow-up: forcible humanitarian countermeasures and *opinio necessitatis*', *European Journal of International Law*, 10(4) (1999), 791–9. For a critical assessment of NATO's intervention, see C. M. Chinkin, 'Kosovo: a "good" or "bad" war?', *American Journal of International Law*, 93(4) (1999), 841–7.

13. Cassese, '*Ex iniuria ius oritur*', p. 24.

14. *Ibid.*

15. It has also been convincingly argued that NATO's military attack against the Yugoslav Federation violated the statute of NATO itself, as well as the Constitutions of several of the NATO countries taking part in its military operations, notably those of Italy, Spain and Germany. See L. Ferrajoli, 'Una disfatta del diritto, della morale, della politica', *Critica Marxista*, 3 (1999), 18–20; Villani, 'La guerra del Kosovo', pp. 35–7.

16. In his official address to the General Assembly of the United Nations on 20 September 1999 (see B. Guetta, 'Quando l'Onu mostra i muscoli', *La Repubblica*, 2 November 1999).

17. For a comment on the International Court of Justice's decision, see P. H. F. Bekker, 'Legality of use of force: Yugoslavia versus United States et al.', *American Journal of International Law*, 93(4) (1999), 925ff.

18. Glennon, 'The new interventionism', pp. 2–7.

19. M. Albright, 'Per il Kosovo un piano Marshall europeo', *La Stampa*, 17 June 1999.

20. Simma, 'NATO, the UN and the use of force', pp. 20–2.

21. A. Cassese, 'Le cinque regole per una guerra giusta', in Beck *et al.*, *L'ultima crociata?*, p. 28.

22. Charney, 'Anticipatory humanitarian intervention in Kosovo', pp. 836–41; A. Cassese, 'Zolo sbaglia, il diritto va aggiornato', in Beck *et al.*, *L'ultima crociata?*, pp. 34–8.

23. The conditions enunciated by Cassese are, in synthesis, the following: 1. Blatant violations of fundamental human rights are taking place within the territory of the state against which force is to be used; 2. One has ascertained the incapability or refusal of the state in question to put a stop to the said violations of human rights in spite of being repeatedly enjoined to do so by the Security Council or other international institutions; 3. The Security Council is not capable of undertaking armed action because of the opposition or explicit veto of one or more of its permanent members; 4. Every possible diplomatic and peaceful solution has been attempted; 5. The use of force has been decided upon by a group of states and not by a single power, and the majority of the member states of the United Nations are not against it; 6. The use of force must have limited objectives aimed strictly at putting a stop to the violations of human rights (Cassese, '*Ex iniuria ius oritur*', p. 27). For an analytical critique of one of the first versions of Cassese's conditions, I refer the reader to my 'Il diritto internazionale e il Tribunale dell'Aia', in Cabona (ed.), '*Ditelo a Sparta*', pp. 226–9.

24. N. Bobbio, 'Perché questa guerra ricorda una crociata', interview with G. Bosetti in Beck *et al.*, *L'ultima crociata?*, pp. 18–19. The theme is brilliantly dealt with by T. Mazzarese, 'Guerra e diritti: tra etica e retorica', *Ragion pratica*, 7(13) (1999), 13–23.

25. See Pinelli, 'Sul fondamento degli interventi armati', pp. 94–5; G. Pontara, 'Guerra etica, etica della guerra e tutela globale dei diritti', *Ragion pratica*, 7(13) (1999), 51–68.

26. On this last point, see two valuable contributions: Pizzorno, 'Caro Habermas', pp. 89, 99; G. Becattini, 'È scoppiata, si fa per dire, la pace', *Il Ponte*, 55(6) (1999).

27. Spinedi, 'Uso della forza da parte della NATO in Jugoslavia', pp. 30–1.

28. See, for example, M. Walzer, 'L'idea di guerra giusta non va abbandonata', in Beck *et al.*, *L'ultima crociata?*, pp. 51–7; M. Walzer, 'Le Refus de faire la guerre se révèle souvent plus coûteux que la guerre elle-même', *Le Monde*, 10 May 1999; J. S. Nye, Jr, 'Redefining the

national interest', *Foreign Affairs*, 78(4) (1999), 22–35; R. Rorty, 'Coraggio, Europa!', *Iride*, 12(27) (1999), 241–3; E. Morin, 'Come la NATO è finita in trappola', in Beck *et al.*, *L'ultima crociata?*, pp. 110–14; J. Habermas, 'Bestialität und Humanität. Ein Krieg an der Grenze zwischen Recht und Moral', *Die Zeit*, 18 (1999); S. Veca, 'La guerra a Milosevic è giustificata', *L'Unità*, 30 April 1999; L. Bonanate, 'Guerra, politica e morale', *Ragion pratica*, 7(13) (1999), 83–93. For an opposite view, see G. Meggle, 'Questa guerra è buona? Un commento etico', *Ragion pratica*, 7(13) (1999), 69–82.

29. Walzer, 'Le refus de faire la guerre', p. 25.
30. Walzer, 'L'idea di guerra giusta', pp. 54–5, 56.
31. See M. Walzer, *Just and Unjust Wars*, New York: Basic Books, 1992. For a critique of Walzer's military ethics, especially of his moral justification of 'preventive self-defence' and the notion of 'supreme emergency', see my *Cosmopolis: Prospects for World Government*. Cambridge: Polity Press, pp. 97–104.
32. See E. N. Luttwak, 'Give war a chance', *Foreign Affairs*, 78(4) (1999), 36–44.
33. Habermas, 'Bestialität und Humanität', cit, p. 74.
34. *Ibid.*, p. 81.
35. By the term 'legal pacifism' Habermas means here a pacifism that is very different from the 'absolute pacifism' of non-violence. It is a pacifism relying, for the construction of peace, on the strengthening of international institutions and the universalization of law, according to the teaching of Kant and Kelsen, and not on individual moral virtues. Among Italian scholars, Bobbio employs the same terminology (N. Bobbio, *Il problema della guerra e le vie della pace*. Bologna: Il Mulino, 1979, p. 80).
36. Habermas, 'Bestialität und Humanität', p. 76.
37. *Ibid.*, pp. 82–3.
38. *Ibid.*, p. 83.
39. *Ibid.*, pp. 77, 85.
40. On this point, I refer the reader once again to my *Cosmopolis*, p. 82.
41. See, for example, J. Habermas, *Vergangenheit als Zukunft*. Zürich: Pendo Verlag, 1990; J. Habermas, *Staatsbürgerschaft und nationale Identität. Überlegungen zur europäischen Zukunft*. St Gallen: Erker Verlag, 1991; J. Habermas, 'Kants Idee des ewigen Friedens – aus dem historischen Abstand von 200 Jahren', *Kritische Justiz*, 28(3) (1995), 177–215; J. Habermas, *Kampf um Anerkennung im demokratischen Rechtsstaat*. Frankfurt am Main: Suhrkamp, 1996. For a critique of the Kantian–Kelsenian tradition, see my book *I signori della pace*. Rome: Carocci, 1998, and a useful recent contribution: M. Ponso, 'Zum ewigen Frieden. Letture interpretative del pacifismo kantiano', *Teoria politica*, 15(1) (1999), 143–61.

42. Pizzorno, 'Caro Habermas', p. 92; A. Scott, 'War and the public intellectual: cosmopolitanism and anti-cosmopolitanism in the Kosovo debate in Germany', *Sociological Research Online*, 4(2): <http://www.socresonline.org.uk/4/2/scott.html>.

43. For a general evaluation of Habermas's cosmopolitism, see my 'A cosmopolitan philosophy of international law? A realist approach', *Ratio Juris*, 12(4) (1999), 429–44, and Habermas's reply, *Ratio Juris*, 12(4) (1999), 450–3.

44. K. O. Hondrich, 'Was ist dies für ein Krieg?', *Die Zeit*, 22 (1999), 4.

45. P. Del Re, 'Nei Balcani e a Timor è nata la nuova Onu', *La Repubblica*, 12 October 1999.

46. Only recently has the Senate voted in favour of a partial settling of this debt; however, its actual payment is still in doubt, being subject to (illegal) conditions.

47. A. Baldassarre, 'Ma non può esserci la polizia del mondo', *Reset*, 57 (1999), 72–4.

48. Habermas deplores the fact that the Western countries' proposal to institute a High Commission of the United Nations was rejected at the Vienna Conference in 1993 owing to the opposition of a large number of Latin American and Asian countries, the latter led by China (Habermas, 'Kants Idee des ewigen Friedens', pp. 304–5).

49. As I argued in the conclusive pages of my *Cosmopolis*, pp. 194–6.

50. Actually, the application of an individualistic, democratic logic to the United Nations would subvert its hierarchical and centralized structure. It would be necessary to elect a world parliament on the basis of the principle 'one head, one vote'. But this, as Kelsen himself admitted, would be impracticable as it would assign to 'demographic powers' such as, for example, China, Indonesia and Nigeria a political representation equal to, or exceeding by far, that of the United States, Great Britain, Germany or Japan. And it is all too obvious that this would be totally incompatible with current international law and institutions (H. Kelsen, *Peace through Law*, Chapel Hill: University of North Carolina Press, 1944, p. 10).

51. H. Kelsen, *Das Problem der Souveränität und die Theorie des Völkerrechts*. Tübingen: Mohr, 1920, pp. 380, 391–3; H. Kelsen, 'Théorie générale du droit international public. Problèmes choisis', *Recueil des Cours de l'Académie de Droit International*, 42(4) (1932), 131.

52. A. Cassese, *I diritti umani nel mondo contemporaneo*. Rome and Bari: Laterza, 1988, p. 202.

53. H. Bull, 'The Grotian conception of international society', in H. Butterfield and M. Wight (eds), *Diplomatic Investigations*. London: Allen & Unwin, 1966, pp. 51–73; H. Bull, *The Anarchical Society*. London: Macmillan, 1977, pp. 26–7.

54. See L. Ferrajoli, 'Dai diritti del cittadino ai diritti della persona', in D. Zolo

(ed.), *La cittadinanza. Appartenenza, identità, diritti*. Rome and Bari: Laterza, 1994, pp. 263–92; A. Cassese, *I diritti umani nel mondo contemporaneo*. Rome and Bari: Laterza, 1999; U. Villani, 'Attuazione e sviluppi della Dichiarazione universale dei diritti dell'uomo', *Ragion pratica*, 6(11) (1998), 17–40; F. Viola, 'Dalla dichiarazione universale dei diritti dell'uomo ai Patti internazionali', *Ragion pratica*, 6(11) (1998), 41–57

55. H. Kelsen, *The Law of the United Nations*, New York: Frederick A. Praeger, 1950, p. 41. This 'legal' criticism does not apply to two later documents that certainly possess normative cogency, namely the Agreement on Civil and Political Rights and the Agreement on Economic, Social and Cultural Rights, both approved in 1966. Although influenced by the presence of Third World countries, newly freed from colonial domination, in the United Nations, these documents have also been accused of reflecting a basically Western point of view.

56. On this subject, see M. C. Davis (ed.), *Human Rights and Chinese Values: Legal, Philosophical and Political Perspectives*. New York: Columbia University Press, 1995; W. T. de Bary and T. Weiming (ed.), *Confucianism and Human Rights*. New York: Columbia University Press, 1998; E. Vitale, ' "Valori asiatici" e diritti umani', *Teoria politica*, 15(2–3) (1999), 313–24; M. Bovero, 'Idiópolis', *Ragion pratica*, 7(13) (1999), 101–6.

57. Habermas, *Vergangenheit als Zukunft*, p. 20.

58. See L. Baccelli, *Il particolarismo dei diritti*. Rome: Carocci, 1999.

59. N. Bobbio, *L'età dei diritti*. Turin: Einaudi, 1990. On this subject, see my 'Libertà, proprietà ed eguaglianza nella teoria dei "diritti fondamentali" '. A proposito di un saggio di Luigi Ferrajoli', *Teoria politica*, 15(1) (1999), 3–24; and L. Ferrajoli's answer, *Teoria politica*, 15(1) (1999), 49–92.

60. See U. Beck, *Was ist Globalisierung?* Frankfurt am Main: Suhrkamp, 1997; Italian translation Rome: Carocci, 1999; see also U. Beck and D. Zolo, 'Tutto il bene e tutto il male di Cosmopoli. Dialogo sulla globalizzazione', *Reset*, 55 (1999), 72–80.

61. H. Bull, 'Human rights and world politics', in R. Pettman (ed.), *Moral Claims in World Affairs*. London: Croom Helm, 1978, p. 81.

62. Habermas, *Bestialität und Humanität*, pp. 78, 79–80.

63. Kelsen, *Das Problem der Souveränität*, pp. 387–93. For a stern critique of Kelsen's theory of *bellum iustum*, see. H. Bull, 'Hans Kelsen and international law', in R. Tur and W. Twining (eds), *Essays on Kelsen*. Oxford: Oxford University Press, 1986, p. 329. On contemporary offshoots of the doctrine of just war, see J. B. Elshtain (ed.), *Just War Theory*. Oxford: Basil Blackwell, 1992; R. L. Holmes, *On War and Morality*. Princeton, NJ: Princeton University Press, 1989; J. T. Johnson, *Can Modern War Be Just?* New Haven, Conn.: Yale University Press, 1984.

64. H. Kelsen, *Principles of International Law*, 3rd edition. New York: Holt, Rinehart & Winston, 1967, pp. 29–33. On the subject, see my 'Hans Kelsen: international peace through international law', *European Journal of International Law*, 9(2) (1998), 306–17. It is worth remembering that Kant, unlike Kelsen, felt it to be impossible to speak of 'just war' in the absence of an international political order. According to Kant, a state that wages war upon another state is taking upon itself the role of judge in a trial in which it is one of the litigants. On Kantian internationalism, see P. P. Portinaro, 'Foedus pacificum e sovranità degli Stati: un problema kantiano oltre Kant', *Iride*, 9(17) (1996), 94–103; A. Loretoni, 'Pace perpetua e ordine internazionale in Kant', *Iride*, 9(17) (1996), 117–25; G. Marini, *Kant e il diritto cosmopolitico*, *Iride*, 9(17) (1996), 126–40.

65. By 'modern war' I mean not only war fought with nuclear or quasi-nuclear weaponry – for example, the 'fuel–air explosives' used by the United States during the Gulf War – but any military action carried out using weapons of mass destruction involving necessarily, and hence wittingly, the killing or mutilation of people, the destruction of their possessions, or the violation of their fundamental rights, totally regardless of their individual responsibilities and the reasons for their involvement in the conflict.

66. N. Bobbio, *Il problema della guerra e le vie della pace*. Bologna: Il Mulino, 1979, p. 60.

CHAPTER 4

An International 'Political Justice'

A Tribunal at War

Something unprecedented occurred in the wars in Bosnia-Herzegovina and in the Federal Republic of Yugoslavia. For the first time in history, wars were fought under the supervision of an international criminal court that was competent to judge crimes committed by either side. The International Criminal Tribunal for former Yugoslavia, instituted in May 1993 by the Security Council of the United Nations, was charged with investigating and sanctioning violations of international law committed by the parties at war. Acting somewhat like a referee during a sports match, members of the court often stepped into the fray, carrying out investigations, expressing opinions and deciding on incriminations.

The contenders in the war in Bosnia-Herzegovina were the Serbs, Croats and Bosnian Muslims, while NATO, all things considered, played a marginal military role, except towards the end of the war, when the air attacks of Operation 'Deliberate Force' against Serbian posts brought the conflict to a speedy conclusion and led to the Dayton peace talks. In contrast, during the 78 days of the war for Kosovo, NATO air forces, deployed against the Serbian army and security corps, were the main actors in the conflict. The United States accounted for about 80 per cent of the air strikes.

Unlike the Nuremberg and Tokyo tribunals, which were military tribunals set up by the victors to judge the losers, the Hague Tribunal for former Yugoslavia operated, and still operates today, as a formally impartial organ. Its courts are presided over by judges from various parts of the world, including Asia and Africa, who are not named unilaterally by any party to the conflict. When the war for Kosovo broke out, both parties – as was not the case at Nuremberg and Tokyo – had previously acknowledged the jurisdiction of the tribunal. Although the Yugoslav Federation had initially been reluctant, it was made to accept the competence of the tribunal by the Dayton agreement.[1] The military authorities of NATO had also explicitly acknowledged the jurisdiction of the Hague Tribunal, as the General Prosecutor, Louise Arbour, a Canadian, stated in May 1999. NATO had declared that it was quite willing to co-operate with any investigations by the tribunal on the activities of its members.[2]

On the basis of these elements, one might be brought to think that, for the first time in history, the so-called *ius in bello* had immediately and concretely been applied in a war theatre. An impartial authority accepted by both sides kept watch to make sure they abided by the laws of war and was ready to prosecute the offenders for any violations. Thus, the sensational incrimination of Slobodan Milošević and other high-ranking members of the Yugoslavian government while NATO bombs were falling fast and furious should be regarded as proof of a judicial response of unprecedented effectiveness and promptness. The same could be said of the $5 million reward offered by the US Department of State to whoever collaborated with the Hague Tribunal in the capture of the Yugoslavian president and his associates.

It has been argued that for once the doctrine of a 'just war' had not been a mere moral platitude or a rhetorical artifice to justify a war a posteriori. It had taken form concretely in a legal international institution entitled to apply coercive sanctions. In spite of NATO's initial violation of the United Nations Charter – which was outside the competence of the Hague Tribunal – the war in Yugoslavia, it is claimed, was fought under the aegis of international law. In May 1999, Antonio Cassese, the first president of the Hague Tribunal, declared:

> The war in Yugoslavia remains subject to the law of war in every way. All norms of the law of war must be strictly observed. Crimes committed during the war, no matter by whom, are either war crimes or crimes against humanity. Violations of the norms of the Hague and Geneva conventions

committed by states will have to be redressed. ... Thus, the law of war provides a general framework into which the behaviour of the belligerents is channelled and by which it is, to some degree, curbed.[3]

Even the armed forces of the United States, added Cassese, which had always refused to let its military personnel be judged by criminal courts other than its own, will be subject to the competence of the Hague Tribunal. Hence, it can be concluded that 'the logic of law has finally prevailed over the traditional political strategy of great powers such as the United States'.[4]

If all this were true, we would be witnessing a victory for international law and justice. And if, as has often been declared in recent years (and as the creation of the Hague Tribunal by the Security Council implies), 'international justice is the condition for peace', we ought to feel reassured and encouraged by these authoritative optimistic declarations. Having progressed beyond the controversial Nuremberg and Tokyo military tribunals, we would be entitled to believe that international criminal justice has made a valuable contribution to the cause of peace in former Yugoslavia. This objective will be achieved all the more effectively once the International Criminal Court (ICC) has been instituted, whose statute was approved in Rome in the summer of 1998. It will be impossible to start conflicts or wage genocidal nationalist campaigns without being apprehended by an international police force and hauled before a court of justice for punishment. Criminal jurisdiction will play an important role in the prevention of war and the human rights violations.

If all this were true, we would have to concede that Kelsen's maxim of 'peace through law' has given, and is still giving, a good account of itself in the Balkans. It would be a major success for 'legal pacifism', which, from Kelsen to Habermas, has hailed the international legal repression of individuals responsible for war crimes or crimes against humanity as the keystone for the construction of a stable, universal peace. We would have to applaud what has been called the 'global expansion' of judicial power, which Alessandro Pizzorno has so lucidly analysed in a recent essay.[5] We would have to conclude that today criminal justice is finally able to guarantee the defence of values and interests which was once entrusted in vain to other social subjects or institutions.

Unfortunately, it is doubtful that this is how things stand. The judicial consistency of what has actually been done so far by international criminal courts, from Nuremberg and Tokyo to The Hague, is dubious, as is the effectiveness of the 'power of judges' in bringing peace. It is doubtful that the destiny of the world can be confidently entrusted to a neutral, non-politicized judicial 'expertocracy'.[6]

My first question is: are the Nuremberg and Tokyo trials really an experience we have put behind us, as Kelsen himself hoped? Or are they not actually a precedent for today's international criminal tribunals, including the soon-to-be-instituted permanent criminal court? Is international criminal jurisdiction, from Nuremberg to The Hague, really immune from the suspicion of being, overtly or covertly, a kind of 'political justice'? What guarantees the autonomy of the judicial function in the context of modern international institutions? How can this autonomy exist outside of an international system of division of powers and rule of law? Are we quite sure that killing a limited number of individuals, or at least inflicting considerable suffering upon them – albeit in the highly symbolic context of international, judicial rites – has had or will have a truly dissuasive effect on war and civil conflicts? Does not the dark shadow of a victimizing justice lurk behind all this, demanding the cathartic relief of expiatory sacrifices?

'Vae Victis' ('Woe to the Vanquished'), from Versailles to Tokyo

From Napoleonic times to the end of World War II, international institutions never attempted to sanction individual behaviour. Indeed, individuals were not even regarded as subjects of the international legal system. International courts of justice never had binding jurisdiction over states, let alone individuals. They were always limited to marginal functions. To preserve the peace and guarantee the world order, great powers always used their political and military might, along with their diplomacy, but not courts of law. This is true of the Holy Alliance, the League of Nations, and also the United Nations.

The same goes for the philosophical tradition of European pacifism, from Erasmus to Hugo Grotius, Emeric Crucé, the Duke of Sully, William Penn, the Abbot of Saint-Pierre, Rousseau, and Kant's renowned *Zum ewigen Frieden*. Their utopian vision of a permanently and universally peaceful world was focused on the political issue of relations between states and peoples, never taking into consideration the possibility of an international judicial apparatus competent to judge individuals.

Only in the first decades of the twentieth century did Anglo-Saxon culture begin to entertain the notion that it might be useful to broaden the role of the judiciary in the international arena. This new trend started with the incrimination of Kaiser Wilhelm II of Hohenzollern as a war criminal at the end of World War I. The Treaty of Versailles accused Wilhelm II of being responsible for a 'supreme outrage to international morality and the sanctity of treaties' and demanded that he be put on trial, together with some leading German political and military figures, before an international court composed of five judges, each belonging to one of the five Allied powers (Great Britain, the United States, France, Italy and Japan). Other articles of the treaty required Germany to turn over about 900 individuals to be tried for violations of the law of war.

The trial against Kaiser Wilhelm II and his collaborators was never held because the Netherlands, where the Kaiser had sought refuge, would not grant his extradition. The German government refused to turn over the 900 persons, but said it was willing to put them on trial in their own homeland before the Supreme Court of the Reich in Leipzig. The trial was actually held, with the consent of the victorious powers, but only six were accused, and the trial ended with four light sentences. In spite of this insubstantial result, the trial was important at the normative level. It served as a precedent for making Article 3 of the Hague Convention of 1907 obsolete, which ruled that only states (and hence not individuals) could be summoned to answer for violations of the laws of war.[7]

Of course, the Nuremberg and Tokyo tribunals, created in 1945 and 1946 respectively, marked the true beginning of 'judicial internationalism'. A theoretical justification for such tribunals was ready at hand in Hans Kelsen's famous manifesto *Peace through Law*, published in 1944. Kelsen had elaborated an institutional strategy to attain peace, borrowing from Kant the ideal of perpetual peace, the federal model and the notion of 'cosmopolitan law'. Kelsen felt that the post-war situation was such that his project of a 'Permanent League' for the keeping of peace stood a good chance of being accepted by the great powers. His project was based on the old model of the League of Nations, but with an important new feature:

judicial functions had a more important role than executive and legislative functions.[8]

Kelsen believed that the main reason for the failure of the League of Nations was that it was ruled by a council – that is, a sort of international government – instead of a court of justice. In his opinion, this was a fatal 'error of construction', since the main shortcoming of an international system was precisely the lack of a judicial authority. Peace could be guaranteed only by an impartial court of justice competent to settle international controversies.[9]

Kelsen also felt very strongly about another matter: it was necessary to establish the individual penal responsibility of the members of governments that waged war in violation of international law. International courts were to try individual citizens responsible for war crimes, and all states would be bound to turn them over to the courts.[10] In spite of these premises, in *Peace through Law* Kelsen harshly criticized the Allies for repeatedly expressing their intent, between 1942 and 1943, to establish an international criminal court, composed of judges from the nations that had won the war, to judge Nazi criminals.[11] Which is precisely what happened when the Nuremberg court was instituted following the London agreement of 8 August 1945, signed two days after the atomic bombing of Hiroshima and one day before that of Nagasaki. The following year, the International Military Tribunal for the Far East, located in Tokyo, was set up along the same general guidelines (with minor changes of little consequence).[12] The Nuremberg court was made up of American, English, French and Soviet judges, and tried 22 German leaders. The trial began in November 1945 and ended about a year later with three acquittals, several jail sentences, and ten death sentences which were carried out at once.[13]

After the trial, Kelsen carried his critical argumentation further in an important essay, 'Will the Judgement in the Nuremberg Trial Constitute a Precedent in International Law?', an analysis of the procedures and decisions of the Nuremberg trial. In it, Kelsen argued against the prospect that the Nuremberg trial and its sentences might set a legal precedent. He argued that if they did, at the end of the next war the governments of the victorious states would be entitled to judge the members of the defeated states for having committed what the winners retroactively and unilaterally would define as crimes. This was something Kelsen hoped would never occur.[14]

The punishing of criminals of war should be an act of justice and not a continuation of the hostilities in forms which, while apparently judicial, are actually moved by a spirit of revenge. Kelsen felt it was incompatible with the judicial function for only the defeated states to be forced to subject their citizens to the jurisdiction of a criminal court. Furthermore, it violated the principle of *nullum crimen sine lege* (no crime without a law), which forbids retroactive laws.[15] The victor nations should have allowed any of their own citizens who were responsible for war crimes to be tried by an international court. This should have been a true international court; that is, an independent and impartial court with ample jurisdiction, not a military tribunal with strongly selective competence. According to Kelsen, it was beyond doubt that the Allies, too, had violated international law. Only if the winning nations had submitted to the authority of that same law they intended to apply to defeated nations, Kelsen warned, would it have been possible to preserve the juridical nature – that is, the generality and abstractness – of punitive norms, and thus meet the requirements for true international criminal justice.[16]

In spite of this criticism – later echoed by Hannah Arendt, Bert Röling and Hedley Bull[17] – in December 1946 the General Assembly of the United Nations unexpectedly decided that the Nuremberg sentence was binding for general international law, and charged the Committee for International Law to draw normative principles from the sentences – *rationes decidendi* (the reasons for the decision), one could say – to serve as precedents for the future. Among these were the principle of personal responsibility for war crimes and the principle that obedience to orders from a superior did not confer immunity. For decades, however, until the new international criminal courts were instituted in the 1990s, these principles were not applied. The only attempt to use the Nuremberg trial as a judicial precedent was made by Ethiopia in August 1949, when it asked Italy, in vain, to extradite Marshals Pietro Badoglio and Rodolfo Graziani as war criminals. Ethiopia meant to submit them to the judgment of an international court composed of a majority of non-Ethiopian judges. The court was to follow the principles and procedures prescribed by the statute of the Nuremberg Tribunal.[18]

The Tokyo trial was criticized even more harshly than the Nuremberg trial, especially on account of its deliberative procedures, its disregard of the rights of the defence, the professional incompetence of the judges and the dissension that exploded between members of the court, which, however, did not prevent death sentences from being handed down even by a simple majority of the judges present.[19] Japanese public opinion saw the trial as a sort of kangaroo court, the purpose of which, like the atomic bombing of Hiroshima and Nagasaki, was to sate the United States' thirst for revenge for the naval attack at Pearl Harbor in 1941. From this point of view, one might say that the seven Japanese executed by the Tokyo Tribunal could be tallied with the hundreds of thousands of victims of the atomic bombings. From 1978 onwards, the honours reserved for Japan's martyrs have also been bestowed on these seven in the temple of Yasukum.

The 'international' courts of Nuremberg and Tokyo, like the Leipzig trial in 1921, proved practically useless in terms of any dissuasive effect on the commission of war crimes. The same can be said of many other trials held by the United States at Nuremberg between 1946 and 1949, and elsewhere by other Allied powers, especially Great Britain and Australia, which held nearly a thousand between them. In the second half of the twentieth century, deportations, war crimes, crimes against humanity and campaigns of genocide did not diminish. Indeed, if one is to credit Amnesty International, violations of the fundamental rights of men and women are constantly on the increase. Moreover, many aggressive wars, some waged with impunity by the same countries that set up the Nuremberg and Tokyo trials, have caused hundreds of thousands of victims.

An Anomalous Judicial Alliance

The Security Council of the United Nations set up the International Criminal Tribunal for former Yugoslavia in 1993, half a century after the Nuremberg and Tokyo tribunals, under Chapter VII of its Charter. This tribunal is charged with prosecuting individuals responsible for serious violations of international humanitarian law committed in the territory of former Yugoslavia since January 1991.[20]

Like its twin, the International Criminal Tribunal for Rwanda, instituted in 1994 and seated at Arusha in Tanzania,[21] the Hague Tribunal for former Yugoslavia is different from the international criminal tribunals of the post-war period. First of all, it is not a military tribunal, nor has it been established by the countries that won the war so they could prosecute their defeated enemies. At first sight, the Hague Tribunal seems to respect the imperative *nemo iudex in causa sua* (no one shall be a judge in their own cause), which the Nuremberg and Tokyo Tribunals were accused of having transgressed. The Hague Tribunal does not appear prejudiced against its defendants, be they Serbs, Croats, Bosnian Muslims, or members of other Balkan ethnic groups. Article 16 of its statute, which specifies the rights and duties of the Prosecutor, formally requires the tribunal to act independently from any government or institution, in the service only of human rights and peace.[22]

By setting up this court, the official objective of the Security Council of the United Nations was allegedly to serve the general interest by defending the fundamental rights of the citizens of former Yugoslavia and promoting peace throughout the Balkans, devastated by bloody ethnic conflicts. That is why, some have argued, the Security Council created the tribunal on the authority of Chapter VII of the Charter, which grants the Council powers of intervention in the face of threats against peace or violations of peace.

But this is precisely the point that has given rise to political and theoretical doubts and objections. First of all, there is the question of whether the tribunal has been legally instituted – a question Gaetano Arangio-Ruiz has raised with particular emphasis, criticizing the doctrine of the 'implicit powers' of the Security Council.[23] One wonders whether the Council had any authority to impose upon the sovereign states of the Balkan area a drastic limitation of their jurisdiction. Challenged by the defence attorneys (as in the famous case of Dusko Tadić), the Hague Tribunal took upon itself the competence to judge whether its own authority rested on a legal foundation. Its conclusion, not surprisingly, was affirmative.[24]

But it can be argued, more in general, that the United Nations Charter does not – indeed, cannot – endow the Security Council with the power to set up an *ad hoc* judiciary body for the defence of human rights. The *ad hoc* nature of a criminal court and the retroactive character of its sanctions contradict the doctrine of the rights of man and the rule of law. These doctrines call first and foremost for respect of the principle *nullum crimen sine lege*. They prescribe that all individuals shall be subjected to the jurisdiction of ordinary courts, according to the rule of the legal predetermination of jurisdictional competence.

Second, there is the question of the autonomy of the tribunal.[25] It is odd that fifty years after the unfortunate experience of the

Nuremberg and Tokyo tribunals, the Security Council should arrogate the power to create an international law court without even attempting to take steps to favour the stipulation of an agreement or a multilateral treaty. With such a negotiational approach it would perhaps have been possible to involve the countries whose internal courts were to be subjected to the jurisdiction of the international tribunal. Furthermore, the fact that the Security Council of the United Nations set up a criminal court by vesting it, under Chapter VII of the UN Charter, with the function of promoting peace in the territories of former Yugoslavia – thus adding an explicit political purpose to its jurisdictional activity – can only be regarded as a serious normative and functional aberration.

The risk is that the international tribunal may end up by becoming a sort of subsidiary organ of the Security Council, which certainly cannot be regarded as an impartial institution, or one with a universal calling. In fact, it is subject to the control of its five permanent members, each of which has veto power. In the last analysis, the crucial question is whether the autonomy of the tribunal is in serious danger, especially as regards the activity of its General Prosecutors, who are chosen directly by the Security Council. This institutional dependency on the Council threatens to subordinate the initiatives of the tribunal to the political expectations of the great Western powers, especially the United States, which formally and practically controls the Security Council. One could add that it is no coincidence that the United States was strongly determined to have the tribunal instituted, and that President Bill Clinton and Secretary of State Madeleine Albright actively sought funds for it – quite a contrast with the American superpower's well-known reluctance to honour its financial obligations to the United Nations. Aldo Bernardini is clearly right when he says:

> Among all the measures taken by the United Nations, the institution of the Tribunal is censurable as *ad hoc*, retroactive and unprecedented. It is clearly directed against certain parties in the Yugoslav conflicts and aimed at defending situations that are artificially imposed and are among the main causes of the present, ongoing tragedy.[26]

The question of the autonomy of the Hague Tribunal appears even more serious when one looks at its connections with the political and military authorities of NATO. The statute of the tribunal has no provisions dealing with what judiciary police force its courts, and especially its General Prosecutor, should employ. There is just the hint of a prescription in Article 29, which obliges all member states of the United Nations to collaborate with the tribunal and carry out its orders. This peculiar omission was promptly taken care of. It had to be, if the tribunal were to carry out its tasks of investigation and compulsory action. Thus, starting with the last years of the war in Bosnia, a custom was established, outside of any normative provision, for the General Prosecutor of the tribunal to co-operate closely with the NATO forces deployed in former Yugoslavia. NATO's IFOR and SFOR forces have taken upon themselves the criminal police functions that the statute of the tribunal so strangely ignored. They have undertaken investigations, hunted down individuals accused of crimes, and proceeded *manu militari* (by military force) to arrest them at the tribunal's behest.

There is no point in dwelling on the obvious legal and institutional anomaly of this collaboration. NATO, as I have argued above, is a political and military alliance representing specific parties; for this reason, it can be regarded neither as one of those 'regional organizations' mentioned in Article 51 of the United Nations Charter, nor as a state police, nor as an international police organization. It is a heterogeneous body, extraneous to the tasks and objectives of the United Nations, not to mention those of a judicial organ whose main requirement should be political autonomy and impartiality.

This anomalous collaboration became an institutional synergy when Gabrielle Kirk McDonald, a US citizen, became president of the Hague Tribunal and Louise Arbour, a Canadian, became General Prosecutor. In her frequent interviews with the press, Arbour never concealed her full loyalty to the political objectives of the Western powers and her hostility towards the Yugoslav government.[27] What is even more unsettling, this synergy continued even after NATO attacked the Yugoslav Federation, openly violating the United Nations Charter. Thus, through the intercession of Madeleine Albright, the scales of justice and the swords of NATO were joined in a 'humanitarian association'.

A Presumption of Humanitarian Innocence

During the 78 days of the war for Kosovo, the Hague Tribunal clearly showed that it was in complete political agreement with the points of view and expectations of the Western powers at war with the Yugoslav Federation. It prejudicially granted NATO's political and military authorities a presumption of 'humanitarian innocence'. Ignoring behaviour by NATO that appeared prima facie against international law, paying no heed to authoritative accusations from many quarters, the General Prosecutor never investigated the NATO leadership, let alone proceeded against individual members of the Alliance.

In April 1999, when NATO air raids against the Yugoslav Federation had been going on for over a month, the 55th session of the United Nations Human Rights Committee was held in Geneva. During the meeting, Mary Robinson, delegate from Ireland and High Commissioner for Human Rights of the United Nations, denounced both the 'ethnic cleansing' enacted by the Serbs in Kosovo and NATO's bombings in former Yugoslavia. It was her opinion that the Security Council should evaluate whether the NATO military campaign was in line with the legal principles laid down in the United Nations Charter, and should deliberate on the issue, since it appeared that the human rights of the civilian victims of NATO's bombings had been severely violated. It was the Hague Tribunal's task, Robinson argued, to look closely at the behaviour of the members of UÇK and NATO, and not only that of the members of Serbian militias. In her opinion, NATO could not be regarded as the only judge competent to decide which non-military objectives could legitimately be hit during the air raids against Yugoslavia, and which were to be spared.[28] A few weeks later, while NATO was still bombing, the Brazilian diplomat Sergio Viera de Mello led a United Nations delegation to Serbia and Kosovo. In a crowded press conference in Belgrade, de Mello denounced the 'humanitarian disaster' caused by NATO's bombings and declared that UÇK militiamen, and not only the Serbs, had committed serious violations and outrages.[29]

The war went on, and in spite of these accusations, the General Prosecutor of the Hague Tribunal did not investigate the behaviour of NATO and the UÇK in the war. The General Prosecutor, Louise Arbour, declared only that NATO authorities would not object if the tribunal 'should investigate ill-aimed attacks, a disproportionate number of victims, or behaviour not in line with the Geneva Convention'.[30] The implication of this statement was clearly that she did not believe any of this to have already occurred and admitted that no investigations had been undertaken or were about to be undertaken. The war ended on 10 June. While it was being fought, no intervention of the General Prosecutor of the tribunal against subjects other than the Yugoslav Federation was recorded, in spite of the fact that many accusations were filed with the tribunal to demand condemnation of the heads of the governments of the nineteen NATO member states.

Only at the end of December 1999, some six months after the war, when Louise Arbour had been replaced by the Swiss Carla del Ponte as General Prosecutor, and Gabrielle Kirk McDonald was about to turn the presidency of the tribunal over to Claude Jorda (France), a news item apparently heralding a crucial turning point filtered through. Actually, it turned out to be nothing much. The General Prosecutor's spokesman, Paul Riley, informed the press that an accusation against NATO's political and military leaders had been filed at the beginning of June (i.e. about six months earlier) by some authoritative Western jurists, including Michael Mandel, David Jacobs and Alejandro Teitelbaum. It was supplemented by a more recent report on alleged NATO war crimes presented by a delegation of members of the Russian parliament. Well, the new General Prosecutor informed the press that she had still not decided whether to archive these accusations as manifestly unfounded, or undertake a formal investigation.[31] In the latter case, it would be the first judicial investigation against high political and military exponents of NATO, including the highest authorities of the US administration (which, as Cassese observed, have never allowed their military personnel to be judged by foreign courts). However, it is extremely unlikely that such an investigation will actually take place, because, as Charles Trueheart, an authoritative correspondent of the *Washington Post*, writes, 'The Tribunal's reliance on the military assets of Western powers makes it unlikely any prosecutor would turn against his main sources of intelligence and arrests.'[32]

Christopher Black, who belongs to a group of Canadian jurists who signed the accusation against NATO filed with the Hague Tribunal, has scrupulously documented the relations between the General Prosecutor of the tribunal and the political and military authorities of NATO:

> In 1996 the then Prosecutor met with the Secretary General of NATO and the Supreme Allied Command in Europe to 'establish contact and begin discussing modalities of co-

operation and assistance'. On May 9th a memorandum of understanding between the Prosecutor and Supreme Headquarters Allied Powers Europe was signed by both parties. That memorandum spelled out the practical arrangements of support to the Tribunal and transfer of indicted persons to the Tribunal. Further meetings have taken place including those with General Wesley Clark.[33]

Actually, any international law court that was in the least independent and neutral would have immediately recognized that the accusations of the North American jurists and the members of the Russian parliament were far from 'manifestly unfounded'. Indeed, any such law court would have undertaken investigations on its own and incriminated those responsible for the crimes, without waiting for accusations from external sources. Since the early days of the war, NATO air raids had caused easily foreseeable 'collateral damage': hundreds of civilian victims. Human Rights Watch found proof of at least 500 deaths among Yugoslav civilians in about 90 fatal accidents.[34]

NATO authority officially admitted, or did not deny, the killing, maiming or serious wounding 'by mistake' of Serbs, Kosovar-Albanians, and Roma on ten occasions. On 5 April, at Aleksinac, there were 17 dead and 30 wounded; the following day, near Priština, 9 people died in a bombing and 8 were wounded; on 9 April, 128 workers were wounded in the bombing of the Zastava car factory; on 12 April, the Salonika–Belgrade train was hit as it was crossing a bridge near Grdelica (55 people burned to death and many were wounded); on 14 April, a convoy of refugees was hit at Djakovica, near the Albanian border (82 dead and about 50 wounded); on 27 April, at Surdulica, fragmentation bombs killed more than 20 civilians – Serbs, Albanians and Roma and wounded at least 100; on 7 May, other cluster bombs were dropped on a marketplace and the civilian hospital of Nis (20 dead, 28 wounded); on 13 May, a camp of Kosovar refugees at Korisa was hit (87 dead); 23 died and 12 were wounded in the prison of Istok Kosovo, which was hit on 19 and 21 May.

On the night of 23 April a missile attack destroyed the Serbian television building in Belgrade, where 150 people – journalists and employees – were at work. This was no mistake but a pre-planned action for which the NATO command claimed responsibility. Sixteen people were killed and as many again were wounded. This action, being intentionally directed against civilians, violated the 1949 Geneva Convention, which bans deliberate attacks against civilians. Italian Foreign Minister Lamberto Dini immediately expressed his dissension, and was later to declare that it had been a deplorable initiative taken by NATO's military command, not one agreed upon previously at the political level.[35] According to the North American jurists who denounced NATO, there is probably a connection between this bombing and secret contacts between the CNN television channel and the US Department of State. In any case, the Prosecutor of the Hague Tribunal ignored the incident.

On 1 May, NATO admitted another serious mistake. A bus was hit at Luzane, near Priština, while carrying refugees across the border. About 50 people were killed. Actually, the circumstances of the attack suggest that it may have been an intentional massacre. Once again, the Hague Tribunal did not intervene.

Finally, on the night of 7 and 8 May, NATO missiles struck the Chinese embassy in Belgrade, killing 3 people and wounding 20. Chinese authorities rejected the United States' apologies and said they were convinced that the bombing was intentional. Again, the Hague Tribunal did not deem the incident worthy of an investigation.

Nor did the General Prosecutor of the Hague Tribunal investigate whether the use of cluster bombs by the United States and Great Britain was in violation of the recent international treaty banning anti-personnel mines, signed by all the countries participating in NATO's military attacks, with the sole exception of the United States. It is well known that the bomblets released by cluster bombs are just like anti-personnel mines, and that these mines strike children especially, as has happened and is still happening today in Kosovo and Serbia.

The Gulf War revealed the contaminating effects of depleted uranium (DU) projectiles. The United States used about a million of them on account of their high penetration potential. Ten thousand were used in Bosnia, although this was learned belatedly. Many were dropped in Yugoslavia, especially Kosovo, by A10 tank-buster bombers, with which only the United States was equipped. The new Secretary-General of NATO, George Robertson, from Great Britain, officially admitted that US bombers used 31,000 DU projectiles during a hundred missions.[36] After the explosion of the warhead, after contact with a solid object, the uranium, as a very fine radioactive dust, spreads out over a radius of about 100 metres. It contaminates the soil, water and air, and works its way into the food chain, increasing environmental radioactivity, which can cause malignant tumours, leukaemia, malformed foetuses, and childhood disease.[37] Thus NATO also manifestly violated the Geneva Conventions, which ban chemical and toxic weapons, and all weapons causing unnecessary suffering. In particular, NATO violated the convention, in effect since December 1983, on 'inhumane weapons', endorsed by over 30 countries.[38] After the Gulf War, several international organizations, including the United Nations Subcommittee for Human Rights, condemned the use of DU weapons. The United Nations Environment Programme (UNEP) requested data on the military operations in which DU bombs had been used, and maps of affected areas, but in vain.[39] But the General Prosecutor of the Hague Tribunal saw no reason to make a similar request or to undertake any other type of investigation. Thus, once again the tribunal ignored the serious breaches of international law committed by NATO's high command.

The Office of the General Prosecutor of the Hague Tribunal did send its representatives to the frontiers of Kosovo to gather information and testimony on the war crimes committed by Serbian militias. However, it did not investigate the intentional destruction of non-military and health infrastructures bombed by NATO, or on the environmental ravages caused by the air strikes against the chemical plants of Pančevo and Novi Sad.[40] Nor did it pay any attention to the destruction of the cultural heritage of several towns, including Priština, Peć, Djakovica, Novi Sad and Belgrade. The medieval church of Gračanica, near Priština, classified by UNESCO as a World Heritage Site, was also destroyed.[41] It is highly likely that NATO violated the Hague Convention of 1954 on the protection of cultural possessions, but in this case, too, the presumption of 'humanitarian innocence' prevailed over any deontological scruples the General Prosecutor might have had.

Putting the Enemy on Trial

To be defeated in war is normal. But to be brought to trial by one's enemy compounds that defeat, making it total and irreparable. Therein lies, as Pier Paolo Portinaro wrote, the deep symbolic meaning of the Nuremberg and Tokyo tribunals.[42] Victory would not have been complete without the celebration of a judicial rite to sanction the moral defeat of the losing side. Without that rite, a 'new order' could not have been established.

Thus, the incrimination of Slobodan Milošević and some of his closest collaborators, decided by General Prosecutor Louise Arbour on 27 May 1999, when Belgrade and all of Serbia had been bombed by NATO for over two months, seems to follow the logic of stigmatizing and morally degrading the enemy to make his defeat total. The same logic may well underlie the $5 million reward promised by Madeleine Albright to whoever might assist the Hague Tribunal in capturing Slobodan Milošević and other members of the Yugoslav government. This interpretation is borne out by the United States government's March 2000 decision to plaster Bosnia with ten thousand posters specifying the amount of the bounty in block letters and showing, in the middle, an image of President Milošević with the caption 'WANTED for crimes against humanity'.

In conclusion, according to some authoritative political observers, the war for Kosovo offers persuasive evidence that the Hague Tribunal is patterned after the military tribunals of the 1940s. While not, in the strict sense, a tribunal instituted by the victors to judge the vanquished, it is nevertheless a tribunal seconding the great Western powers in their war against an enemy, Slobodan Milošević's political regime. His military defeat they took for granted, but they intended to annihilate his regime also from a moral and legal point of view. Thus it has been maintained that the essential function of the Hague Tribunal is to contribute, with its aura of austere impartiality, to the credibility of NATO's humanitarian motivation and to dismiss NATO violations of the United Nations Charter and the international law of war as irrelevant. Apparently, this tribunal would have the same apologetic functions that Bert Röling polemically attributed to the Nuremberg and Tokyo tribunals. It could be added, following this train of thought, that President Clinton's first reaction to the news of the incrimination of the president of Yugoslavia was no coincidence: 'His incrimination confirms that our war is just'.[43]

These conclusions may seem too harsh. In any case, it can hardly be denied that the events leading to the incrimination of the Yugoslav president correspond objectively to a logic of reciprocal political and judicial collaboration between the General Prosecutor of the Hague Tribunal and the US Department of State. The close financial collaboration between the tribunal and the US government bears this out.

In early May, General Prosecutor Louise Arbour declared that in all the six years of its existence the Hague Tribunal had never been able to gather sufficient evidence to incriminate Milošević.[44] Suddenly, the 'incontestable evidence' on which the incrimination of the Yugoslav president was to be founded – an incrimination announced by Louise Arbour to President Clinton two days in advance of her official statement – was put together on the basis of intelligence provided by the United States and British governments.[45]

Thus, the General Prosecutor not only credited secret documents based on international espionage, thus mostly beyond her powers of control and investigative verification, but also committed herself to secrecy at the discretion of the political authorities involved. Obviously, this is a very serious violation. Imagine if President Clinton and his collaborators were to be incriminated on the basis of secret information from espionage activities by the Yugoslav government! Milošević was not incriminated on the basis of autonomous investigations by the Hague Tribunal in the conflict zone. No representative of the tribunal ever set foot in the Yugoslav Republic, least of all in Kosovo, after the war broke out. The only activity of the Tribunal – financed *ad hoc* by the United States – was to gather the testimony of Kosovar refugees, and probably of UÇK members, along the Albania–Kosovo border. Moreover, it should not be forgotten that the first count in Milošević's indictment is the Raçak massacre, which today no Western observer believes in, at least in the version divulged by William Walker and subscribed to by the General Prosecutor of the tribunal.[46]

Then there are the statements made to the international press by some authoritative members of the tribunal who on several occasions expressed their solidarity with the political and military activities of Western powers. Once again, the most disconcerting statements came from General Prosecutor Louise Arbour. The mere fact that Milošević had been indicted, she argued, made him an unreliable partner in the negotiations that were supposed to lead to the end of the war. Hence, one should hope for a *coup d'état* of some kind against the Yugoslav regime, and that the Yugoslav Minister of Justice would then proceed to arrest Milošević and the other accused persons.[47] One could remark that while it is true that the General

Prosecutor of the Hague Tribunal is not pledged to impartiality towards the defendants – although she has the duty to regard them as defendants and not convicts – she is certainly pledged to political independence and neutrality.

Moreover, after the end of the bombings the General Prosecutor accepted help for her representatives in Kosovo from NATO's KFOR forces, whose presence in Kosovo violated the resolution of the Security Council prescribing that the peace forces be placed under the United Nations. An even more serious circumstance is that the General Prosecutor availed herself systematically and exclusively of the collaboration of Scotland Yard and the FBI to search for proof *a posteriori* of the war crimes committed by Serbian militias. (Incidentally, on 30 September 1999, the new General Prosecutor, Carla del Ponte, formally thanked the director of the FBI for his help and expressed the wish that this profitable collaboration might continue in the future.) Press reports from Priština in the days following the end of the war mentioned that investigations were monopolized by a group of American specialists with high-tech equipment, surrounded by CNN journalists and in constant touch with CNN itself. They were led by a Department of State diplomat, and, of course, the US flag waved over their heads.[48]

It should be obvious that the General Prosecutor of the Hague Tribunal cannot continue to avail herself of the judicial assistance and technical support of the personnel of a military alliance such as NATO, which was a party in cause in the conflict, and is itself suspected of having violated the law of war on several occasions. Of course, while NATO offered assistance and support, financed directly by the United States, exclusively to investigations against its enemies, it never collaborated in investigations of its own military personnel. What need could there conceivably have been for such investigations?

The last sensational arrests were when the Bosnian Serb general Stanislav Galić was taken into custody by British soldiers of NATO's SFOR forces at Banja Luka on 20 December 1999, and the violent capture of the Bosnian Serb politician Momcilo Krajisnik by French soldiers of the same forces on 3 April 2000. In both cases, the new Secretary-General of NATO, George Robertson, immediately sent his congratulations. Both General Galić's and Krajisnik's names appeared on a list of wanted persons secretly communicated by the General Prosecutor of the tribunal to NATO's military authorities.[49] Would the Hague Tribunal consider employing Serbian militias as a judicial police to arrest secretly incriminated NATO officers or UÇK members?

'The Mother of the Tribunal'

Finally, there is the nice question of the financial relations between the presidency of the tribunal and the United States. In May 1999, at the peak of the NATO attacks against the Yugoslav Federation, Congress, acting on President Clinton's proposal, was unusually generous in allocating $27 million for the tribunal, mainly to help it gather testimony against Serbian militias on the Kosovo border and send a team of legal experts there. The president of the tribunal, US citizen Gabrielle Kirk McDonald, gladly accepted the funds.[50]

It is worth pointing out that Article 32 of the statute of the tribunal, approved by the Security Council, rules that the expenses of the tribunal should weigh on the ordinary budget of the United Nations. This norm, however, was immediately violated in a surprising joint action by three organs of the United Nations, namely the Advisory Committee on Administrative and Budgetary Questions, the General Secretariat and the General Assembly. In a resolution approved in September 1993, the General Assembly, concerned with budget problems, proposed that a temporary fund be created for the tribunal, outside the ordinary budget of the United Nations, while awaiting a final decision on how the tribunal would be funded. The General Assembly also invited the member states of the United Nations and other concerned parties to make voluntary contributions to the tribunal, either monetary or in the form of services and equipment, according to the indications of the Secretary-General.

Thus, towards the end of 1994 over $6 million flowed, or was about to flow, into the coffers of the tribunal. Moreover, the Netherlands, Denmark, Norway, Sweden and the United States – all Western countries – had lent 32 employees to the tribunal, 22 of whom were from the United States, which had also promised to donate $3 million worth of electronic equipment.[51] Of course, thanks to the success of this initiative, what had been a temporary measure became a permanent arrangement by which the Hague Tribunal is financed in violation of its statute.

As Christopher Black pointed out, the tribunal has received other sizeable funds almost exclusively from the US government and US foundations and private companies. These donations have come in the form of money or computer equipment. In the last year for which the budget of the tribunal is available, 1994/95, the United States gave the tribunal $700,000 and $2,300,000 worth of equipment and materials. In the same year, the Open Society Institute, a foundation established by George Soros, the famous American billionaire financier, contributed $150,000. The tribunal also received money from the United States Institute for Peace, founded in 1984 by Ronald Reagan and financed by the US Congress and the Coalition for International Justice; the latter is supported by American institutions such as the Central and East European Law Institute.[52]

On several public occasions, the president of the tribunal, Gabrielle Kirk McDonald, openly thanked the US government for its generosity. On 5 April 1999, before the Supreme Court of the United States in Washington she declared that the tribunal had found great support in the work of lawyers who had come to the tribunal through the Coalition for International Justice and the Central and East European Law Institute:

> We benefited from the strong support of concerned governments and dedicated individuals such as Secretary Albright. As the permanent representative to the United Nations, she had worked with unceasing resolve to establish the Tribunal. Indeed, we often refer to her as the 'Mother of the Tribunal'.[53]

On 12 May of the same year, in her address to the Council on Foreign Relations in New York, McDonald declared that the US government had generously resolved to assign $500,000 to the tribunal and to help and encourage other states to contribute to its expenses. She stressed that the US private sector, as well as the US government, felt a moral imperative to put an end to violence in former Yugoslavia, and expressed her satisfaction for a great corporation's recent donation of $3 million worth of computer ware, which would greatly increase the tribunal's operative capabilities.[54]

No doubt seems to have crossed the mind of Gabrielle McDonald, the foremost judge of the tribunal, that the autonomy of the court she presided over might be incompatible with such close ties to governments with political and economic interests at stake in the conflict, in particular the United States. Her political culture and her idea of international justice would seem totally to ignore the whole tradition of 'rule of law'. Even more paradoxically, this tradition would appear to be ignored as well by those organs of the United Nations that approved a *de facto* violation of a norm of the statute of the Hague Tribunal that should have been respected as an intangible guarantee of its autonomy.

The Two Tracks of 'Political Justice'

I hope that my arguments so far, and the evidence I have used to support them, have awakened doubts as to the independence of judgment of international criminal courts, from Nuremberg and Tokyo to The Hague (the Arusha Tribunal is hardly worth mentioning). We have seen how the judicial profile of these organs is blurred either by their adherence to a military function or by the ideological identification of their judges and prosecutors with the values and expectations of Western powers.

What normally distinguishes judicial from political acts (and, still more so, from military action) is that the judiciary strives to create an institutional space marked by separation and neutrality as opposed to a direct involvement in partisan conflict. It aims at deconstructing conflict and leashing aggression to minimize the destructive effects of social competition. Of course, the ideal of a perfectly impartial judiciary belongs among the illusions of rationalism and legal normativism. A normative idealism of this kind was certainly behind Kelsen's demand at the end of World War II that the winning powers, following a criterion of absolute formal equality, try all individuals responsible for war crimes before the same international court, having their own officers and soldiers judged alongside the Nazi enemies. The same can be said of the Ethiopian government's candid request that Italy turn over its war criminals to be tried by an international tribunal.

But when such neutrality is completely absent, or seriously compromised, we are faced with the jarring oxymoron of 'political justice'. Whenever the imperative *nulla culpa sine iudicio* (no culpability without a previous trial) is made ineffective by a presumption of guilt anticipating penal judgment, justice is taken over by politics, becoming its handmaiden, arming it with irrational symbolic weapons, and increasing its immunity and discretionary powers. As Pier Paolo Portinaro brilliantly wrote,

In our everyday vocabulary, politics and justice are normally contrasted, and certainly with good reason. Originally, politics is a matter of faction, division, struggle and strategic action aimed at success, whereas justice is a quest for impartiality, neutrality, equidistance between parties, and the pursuit of agreement within a normative framework.[55]

As Otto Kirchheimer argues in *Politische Justiz*, whenever this functional difference is lost at the national or international level, criminal trials end up by serving para- or extra-judicial purposes such as the ritual dramatization of political struggle, personalizing and stigmatizing the enemy, the procedural legitimization of measures taken against the enemy (including physical elimination), and expiatory sacrifice.[56] Trials become a sort of 'continuation of war by other means'. Countless examples of such trials are to be found in the judicial history of the past century, from the Italian Fascist *ad hoc* tribunals to Stalin's purges and, of course, the Nuremberg and Tokyo trials.

In many cases, however, argues Kirchheimer, political justice may be used by political power as an occult form of selective self-limitation, an alternative to simple amnesty, or its premise.[57] Political power may use *ad hoc* courts as a legal purge instead of continuing the war or summarily eliminating opponents. This is certainly what happened at Nuremberg. However, the 'political justice' of the Hague Tribunal did not even serve this purpose, namely the self-limitation of power, by selectively channelling the traumas of conflict and favouring pacification. On the contrary, the *ad hoc* nature of the tribunal allowed it to coexist, as we have seen, with NATO's illegal use of military force in the same territory over which the tribunal exercised its *ad hoc* competence. Indeed, Milošević's political regime was simultaneously prosecuted by an international judicial body and illegally attacked by a military alliance, a circumstance without precedent in modern history. Criminal trials, with their painstaking procedural rites, were carried out contemporarily with the indiscriminate violence of the bombings and their 'collateral effects'.

While the Security Council and the Court of Justice of the United Nations were unwilling or unable to declare that NATO's attack against the Yugoslav Republic was illegal, the tribunal for former Yugoslavia, thanks to its *ad hoc* nature, not only placed victims and aggressors on the same legal plane, but actually maintained collaborative relations with the aggressors to the detriment of those aggressed against. Since its competence was limited to violations of 'the law of war' in the restricted sense of *ius in bello* – that is, it dealt exclusively with how the war was conducted – the tribunal was in a position to overlook NATO's responsibility for a 'crime against peace', that is, a true 'aggression'. This twofold track, divorcing *ius ad bellum* from *ius in bello*, was one of the most sensational paradoxes of the war for Kosovo, and one that most Western public opinion, including authoritative jurists and experts in political affairs, has ignored.

Clearly, if NATO's attack against the Yugoslav Republic was indeed a serious violation of international law, then so were all the acts performed by NATO forces – not just the intentional killing of civilians, but also the involuntary killing of any person, whether in uniform or not, and the destruction of the peacetime infrastructures and resources of the Yugoslav Federation.

The reader will remember that the Nuremberg Tribunal included 'crimes against peace' in its competence, that is, acts of aggression by one state against another. This specific crime, however, is not provided for in the statute of the Hague Tribunal, in spite of the fact that it spells out in detail the tribunal's competence *ratione materiae* (that is, the types of crimes it is competent to deal with), to which it dedicates all of four articles (Articles 2–5). It should be mentioned that the regulations of the future permanent International Criminal Court explicitly include this competence (Article 5). This is why the United States, which urged the creation of the Hague Tribunal and has always supported and financed it, has been equally firm in opposing the creation of the International Criminal Court and refuses to approve its statute.[58]

Humanitarian Judicial Internationalism?

To draw up a balance sheet for international criminal justice and try to predict its future development, something that to an extent is anticipated by the recent approval of the statute of the new International Court, at least two other subjects need to be touched upon: the 'quality' of international criminal justice and its effectiveness in punishing and preventing crime.

In *The Anarchical Society*, Hedley Bull was the first to criticize international criminal justice for being selective and 'exemplary'. In his opinion, the principle of the formal equality of individuals before the law had been violated, and the post-war international military tribunals played an archaic and sinister sacrificial role.[59] In fact, only a select few individuals were put on trial because they were seen as having major political responsibilities, or as being the ones most involved in criminal activities.

Bull's severe judgement could just as well be applied today to the tribunals for former Yugoslavia and Rwanda. Their jurisdiction is applied only to a limited number of individuals singled out on the basis of intuitive, highly discretionary evaluations. The repressive action of these tribunals is quantitatively insignificant, especially considering the huge sums it takes to finance them. In the case of the Hague Tribunal, in its six years of activity it has incriminated 90 individuals, arrested 20, and put about 20 on trial. The disproportion is even more glaring in the case of the Arusha Tribunal. In November 1999 it had 38 individuals in custody who were accused of genocide. In the five years of its existence it tried only five individuals, whereas the individuals responsible for the extermination of 500,000 people presumably numbered several thousand. Clearly the overall picture is one of blatant violation of fundamental principles of modern law, such as the equality of individuals before the law, the certainty of law and, last but not least, the non-retroactivity of criminal law.

Moreover, one cannot help wondering about the quality of international justice when it is applied outside the social contexts in which people subject to its sanctions live and act. This is especially true for the Arusha Tribunal, but it applies to the Hague Tribunal, too, whose members were nominated without regard for the degree of their understanding of the historical, political and economic problems of former Yugoslavia.

Then there is the problem of the effectiveness and, more in general, the 'extra-judicial' consequences of the activity of the international tribunals. These consequences were remarkable, for example, in the case of the incrimination of the Yugoslav president, Slobodan Milošević. There is general consensus that the post-World War II international criminal trials had practically no deterrent effect. The same could be said for former Yugoslavia. The action of the Hague Tribunal against the atrocities committed during the Bosnia-Herzegovina war had no dissuasive effect on the contenders in the war for Kosovo. All the parties to the conflict – Serbian militias, UÇK and NATO – committed violations of the law of war, some of them very serious.

Actually, nothing guarantees that a judicial action inflicting punishment, no matter how severe, on individuals responsible for international crimes – the Hague Tribunal meted out prison sentences of as much as 40 and even 45 years[60] – will affect the macro-structural dimension of war, that is, that it will be able to influence human aggression, conflict and armed violence, the sources of which are deep-seated. On the contrary, judicial action undertaken as a sort of penal counterpoint to military conflict threatens to produce a symbolic reinforcement of hostile feelings. It introduces formal rigidities that run counter to the work of mediation and pacification traditionally handled by diplomacy, whether acting according to protocol or informally. Following Bull, one might respond to eulogies of international criminal justice by eulogizing diplomacy, especially when it is preventive.[61]

During the war for Kosovo, the interventions of the Hague Tribunal, which sometimes went so far as to ban important spokesmen from the negotiating table, countered diplomatic efforts to stop the war and spare human lives. For example, the Yugoslav president, who had been an important interlocutor of Western powers during the war in Bosnia, was suddenly turned into a 'war criminal', an untouchable pariah cut off from all possible diplomatic relations simply because he had been incriminated by the Hague Tribunal.[62]

Equally serious doubts have been expressed about the international defence of human rights. It is questionable whether this defence can be turned over to courts whose impartiality is hindered, as we have seen, by a need to entrust the armed forces of the great powers with police functions. More in general, one could argue that it is inadvisable to put the defence of human rights under the exclusive – or even predominant – control of non-national judicial bodies, even when it is the political authorities of a nation-state that violate the rights of its own citizens. This is because it is not realistic to expect that the basic liberties of the citizens of a state can be guaranteed at the international level if they are not guaranteed, first and foremost, by that state's democratic institutions.

These arguments apply not only to existing international criminal courts but also to the new one that is about to be instituted, provided its statute is ratified according to the agreed-upon formal conditions.[63] Certainly, if this court is ever set up, it will be on the basis of a broad multilateral agreement and will not be instituted in an authoritarian fashion by the Security Council.

Moreover, its criminal norms will not be retroactive. Furthermore, the court – and this is an element of great significance – will be competent to judge the 'crime of aggression', as we have seen, not merely genocide, crimes against humanity and war crimes. However, aside from these specific aspects, the general objections against international criminal courts that I have raised so far remain fully applicable.

There are two further aspects that must be stressed here, because they are markedly regressive compared to previous tribunals, since they restrict or, indeed, threaten the autonomy of this new international court. The first is the 'constitutional' contamination introduced by Article 16 of the Rome Statute: the Security Council of the United Nations will have the power to forbid or suspend, at its discretion, the initiatives of the General Prosecutor of the court.[64] Thus, the tension between the political particularism of the leading organ of the United Nations and the universalistic aspiration of a criminal jurisdiction founded on the doctrine of human rights resurfaces, and in a most exacerbated form. The second aspect is the surprising provision in Article 116, which opens the coffers of the court to voluntary contributions by governments, international organizations, private individuals, societies and other entities, thus legalizing the illegitimate funding practices of the Hague Tribunal.[65]

Finally, there is a general philosophical and legal consideration to be made. What is most puzzling in the position of those Western theorists who in the past decade have fervently advocated international criminal jurisdiction is the lack of any analysis – in terms of the philosophy of punishment and the sociology of penitentiary institutions – of the functions and possible effects of such jurisdiction. The prevailing view of the relationship between the exercise of judicial power and world order is surprisingly naive; it is based on a penal fetishism that applies a model of punitive justice to international relations which has raised serious objections as applied within national boundaries.[66] No less surprisingly, this enthusiasm for 'judicial internationalism' entrusts the destinies of democracy, peace and world order to the verdicts of a supranational judicial bureaucracy. The ultimate motivation for all this probably lies in the new insecurities and expectations of a world that is not as simplified by ideologies and religious beliefs as it used to be and has become increasingly complex, turbulent and divided, in spite of globalization.

Notes

1. See Articles 7 and 8 of the Dayton Accords, and especially Annex 6 (Agreement on Human Rights), Chapter 3 (General Provisions), Article 13 (Organizations concerned with Human Rights). The text of the Dayton Accords can be found on the Internet site <www.un.org/icty>.
2. L. Arbour, "Così porterò alla sbarra tutti i boia di Milosevic", interview with N. Lombardozzi, *La Repubblica*, 7 May 1999, p. 11.
3. A. Cassese, 'Se il massacro finisce in tribunale', in U. Beck, N. Bobbio *et al., L'ultima crociata? Ragione e torti di una guerra giusta.* Rome: Libri di Reset, 1999 p. 49.
4. *Ibid.*, pp. 49–50.
5. A. Pizzorno, *Il potere dei giudici.* Rome and Bari: Laterza, 1998; N. Tate and T. Vallinder (eds), *The Global Expansion of Judicial Power.* New York: New York University Press, 1995; on this subject, see also my 'A proposito dell'"espansione globale" del potere dei giudici', *Iride*, 11(25) (1998), 445–53.
6. P. P. Portinaro, 'Oltre la sovranità, senza la pace', *Discipline filosofiche*, 5(2) (1996), 66–8.
7. See S. Lener, 'Dal mancato giudizio del Kaiser al processo di Norimberga', *Civiltà Cattolica*, 97(1) (1946); A.-M. de Zayas, 'Il processo di Norimberga davanti al Tribunale militare internazionale', in A. Demandt (ed.), *Macht und Recht: Große Prozesse in der Geschichte,* Munich: Oscar Beck, 1990.
8. H. Kelsen, *Peace through Law.* Chapel Hill: University of North Carolina Press, 1944, pp. 13–15.
9. Kelsen is well aware that the most serious problem is the creation of an international police force, apart from and independent of the armed forces of single nations, to apply the court's sentences coercively. It is therefore realistic, he says, to put off the organization of an international police force until later and begin immediately by simply setting up the court (see H. Kelsen, *Law and Peace in International Relations.* The Oliver Wendell Holmes Lectures, 1940–1. Cambridge, Mass: Harvard University Press, 1948, pp. 145–68).
10. Kelsen, *Peace through Law*, pp. 71ff., 87–8.
11. *Ibid.*, pp. 88ff. It is well known that the British prime minister Winston Churchill would personally have preferred summary executions for the Nazi military high commanders.
12. The Tokyo trial, which lasted over two years, was held before a court of eleven judges from as many different countries designated by the supreme commander of the Allied forces, General MacArthur. Twenty-eight people were incriminated. None of them was absolved; seven were executed. See B. V. A. Röling and C. F. Rüter (eds), *The Tokyo Judgment.* Amsterdam: APA-University Press Amsterdam, 1977; B. V. A. Röling,

and A. Cassese, *The Tokyo Trial and Beyond*. Cambridge: Polity Press, 1993.

13. De Zayas, 'Il processo di Norimberga', pp. 101–4. There is an extensive literature on the Nuremberg Tribunal. See, for example, besides the works already cited, T. Taylor, *The Anatomy of the Nuremberg Trial*. New York: Knopf, 1992; M. Biddis, *The Nuremberg Trial and the Third Reich*. London: Longman, 1993; C. Ginsburg and V. N. Kudriatsev (eds), *The Nuremberg Trial and International Law*. Dordrecht: Kluwer, 1990; S. Clark, *Nuremberg and Tokyo in Contemporary Perspective*, in T. L. H. McCormack and G. J. Simpson (eds), *The Law of War Crimes*. The Hague: Kluwer Law International, 1997.

14. H. Kelsen, 'Will the judgment in the Nuremberg trial constitute a precedent in international law?', *International Law Quarterly*, 1(2) (1947), p. 115. Kelsen discusses the subject further in his *Principles of International Law*, 3rd edition. New York: Holt, Rinehart & Winston, pp. 215–20.

15. Kelsen's position on the Nuremberg Tribunal's violation of the principle of non-retroactivity of criminal law, however, is rather ambiguous. He claims that although no positive international norm existed, the Nazi criminals could not possibly have been unaware of the immorality of their behaviour, and hence the retroactive character of the law that was applied can hardly be considered absolutely incompatible with justice (H. Kelsen, 'Will the judgment in the Nuremberg trial constitute a precedent', p. 110).

16. Kelsen, *Peace through Law*, pp. 110–15. Kelsen believed that the Soviet Union, by invading Poland and declaring war on Japan, had committed war crimes punishable by an international tribunal.

17. H. Arendt, *Eichmann in Jerusalem: A Report on the Banality of Evil*, New York: Viking Press, 1963, p. 263. Bert Röling argued that the international trials of the post-war periods were used by the victors for propagandistic purposes and to draw attention away from their own offences. Cf. B. V. A. Röling, 'The Nuremberg and the Tokyo trials in retrospect', in C. Bassiouni and U. P. Nanda (eds), *A Treatise on International Criminal Law*. Springfield, Ill.: Charles C. Thomas, 1973. For his part, Hedley Bull (*The Anarchical Society*. London: Macmillian, p. 89) has argued that the symbolic function of these trials was tarnished by the selective character of their sentences. See also R. Quadri, *Diritto internazionale pubblico*. Naples: Liguori, 1974.

18. C. Miglioli, *La sanzione nel diritto internazionale*, Milan: Giuffrè, 1951, p. 69.

19. There were eleven members in the court, with a quorum of six members. Decisions, including the death sentences, were made by a simple majority; that is, if five members out of the eleven were absent, death sentences could be meted out even by three judges, since the casting vote rested with the president.

20. On the juridical and functional characteristics of the Hague Tribunal, see P. Burns, 'An international criminal tribunal: the difficult union of principles and politics', in S. Clark and M. Sann (eds), *The Prosecutions of International Crimes*. New Brunswick, NJ: Transaction Publishers, 1996, pp. 125–64; C. Bassiouni and O. Manikas, *The Law of the International Criminal Tribunal for the Former Yugoslavia*. Irvington-on-Hudson, NY: Transnational Publishers, 1996; M. Pellet, 'Le Tribunal criminel international pour l'ex-Yougoslavie: poudre aux yeux ou avancée décisive?', *Revue General de Droit General Public*, 7 (1994), 7–59; M. C. Vitucci, *Il Tribunale ad hoc per la ex-Jugoslavia*. Milan: Giuffrè, 1998. For information, documents and further bibliographic citations concerning the Hague Tribunal, consult the United Nations Internet site: <http://www.un.org/icty>.

21. The Tribunal for Rwanda is a sort of 'Siamese twin' of the Hague Tribunal, since it shares the same General Prosecutor's Office and chamber of appeal. So far it has proved totally ineffective, and by the end of 1999 was in an advanced state of crisis (I. Fisher, 'Rwanda-genocide court delays release of suspect', *International Herald Tribune*, 29 November 1999, p. 4; I. Fisher, 'Order to release suspect puts court in a bind', *International Herald Tribune*, 20 December 1999, p. 2). See, in general, D. Shraga and R. Zacklin, 'The International Criminal Tribunal for Rwanda', *European Journal for International Law*, 7(4) (1996), pp. 501–18; G. Cataldi, 'Il Consiglio di Sicurezza delle Nazioni Unite e la questione del Ruanda', in P. Picone (ed.), *Interventi delle Nazioni Unite e diritto internazionale*. Padua: Cedam, 1995, pp. 445–61; I. Bottigliero, 'Il rapporto della commissione di esperti sul Ruanda e l'istituzione di un tribunale internazionale penale', *La comunità internazionale* 4(4) (1994), 760–8.

22. Article 16, paragraph 2, of the Statute of the Hague Tribunal reads: 'The Prosecutor shall act independently as a separate organ of the International Tribunal. He or she shall not seek or receive instructions from any government or from any other source'.

23. See G. Arangio-Ruiz, 'The establishment of the international criminal tribunal for the former territory of Yugoslavia and the doctrine of the implied powers of the united nations', in F. Lattanzi and E. Sciso (eds), *Dai Tribunali penali internazionali ad hoc ad una Corte permanente*. Naples: Editoriale Scientifica, 1995; A. Bernardini, 'Il Tribunale penale internazionale per la ex Jugoslavia', *I diritti dell'uomo*, 21 (1993), 15–25; P. Palchetti, 'Il potere del Consiglio di Sicurezza di istituire il Tribunale penale internazionale', *Rivista di diritto internazionale*, 79(2) (1996), 143ff.

24. Thus, the tribunal arrogated the competence to exercise a control over the legality of the decisions of the Security Council. See J. E. Alvarez, 'Nuremberg revisited: the Tadic case', *European Journal of International*

Law, 7(2) (1996), 245–64; C. Greenwood, 'International humanitarian law and the Tadic case', *European Journal of International Law*, 7(2) (1996), 265–83; B. Conforti, *Diritto internazionale*. Naples: Editoriale Scientifica, 1997, pp. 401–2.

25. On this subject, see A. Perduca, 'Il Tribunale per i crimini nella ex Jugoslavia: giustizia sul filo della cooperazione', *Guida al diritto*, 17 (1999), 9–11.

26. Bernardini, 'Il Tribunale penale internazionale per la ex Jugoslavia', p. 21.

27. Arbour, "Così porterò alla sbarra tutti i boia di Milosevic", p. 11. It should be noted that the quotation marks belong to the original title of the interview, which allows the statement in the title ('Thus will I bring to trial all of Milošević's butchers') to be taken as a direct quotation of the interviewee rather than as an interpretation by the interviewer or the newspaper's editorial staff.

28. M. Robinson, *Report on the Human Rights Situation Involving Kosovo* (30 April 1999), <http://www.unhchr.ch/html/menu2/5/kosovo/kosovo_-main.htm>.

29. P. Sansonetti, ' "In Kosovo devastazione sistematica" ', *l'Unità*, 27 May, 1999, p. 12.

30. Arbour, ' "Così porterò alla sbarra tutti i boia di Milosevic" ', p. 11.

31. C.B., 'L'Aja, Mosca contro la NATO', *Corriere della Sera*, 30 December 1999, p. 15; R. Bultrini, 'Kosovo, indagine sui piloti NATO', *La Repubblica*, 29 December 1999, p. 20; C. Trueheart, 'Tribunal reviews anti-NATO charges', *International Herald Tribune*, 20 January, 2000, p. 1. In an interview granted after his resignation from the Hague Tribunal, Antonio Cassese admits that 'an investigation' of crimes committed by NATO pilots 'would be a dutiful act' (cf. 'Noi, giudici di guerra sconfitti dall'odio etnico', ed. N. Lombardozzi, *La Repubblica*, 26 March 2000, p. 17).

32. Trueheart, 'Tribunal reviews anti-NATO charges', p. 1.

33. C. Black, 'The International Criminal Tribunal: instrument of justice?', Proceedings of the 25 October 1999 Paris Conference on Justice and War, special issue of *Dialogue*, 31–32 (2000), 109.

34. Human Rights Watch is an independent international organization investigating the most serious violations of human rights. Its Internet site is <www.hrw.org>.

35. Prime Minister D'Alema, however, disavowed his Minister of Foreign Affairs and praised the scrupulousness and transparency of NATO's behaviour during the war, which showed the world 'how the armed forces of democratic countries should behave' (G. Luzi, 'L'attacco alla televisione divide il governo italiano', *La Repubblica*, 24 April 1999, p. 2; G. Luzi, 'Dietrofront di Dini', *La Repubblica*, 25 April 1999, p. 7).

36. From the declarations of the Italian Under-Secretary of Defence, Paolo Guerrini, who, however, called the polemics about DU 'senseless' and tried to play down the consequences for human health. See M. Nese, 'Allarme insensato, le radiazioni restano nella media', *Corriere della Sera*, 11 March 2000, p. 10.

37. See C. Giannardi and D. Dominici's thorough scientific analysis, 'Danni collaterali dell'uranio impoverito: stima per la guerra del Kosovo', *Il Ponte*, 55 (11–12) (1999), pp. 118–29. See also F. Gustincich, 'I misteri del Kosovo radioattivo', *Limes*, 4 (1999), 231–3; Depleted uranium emits alpha particles with an energy of 4.2 mega-electron volts, capable of disrupting the DNA of the human cells they come in contact with, transforming them into cancerous cells (6 electronvolts is enough to produce that effect). It is worth mentioning General Wesley Clark's statement that 'depleted uranium is a very heavy metal from which radioactivity has already been removed. It is no more dangerous than lead' ('Milosevic punta ancora sul Kosovo', interview with M. Nese, *Corriere della Sera*, 26 March 2000, p. 11).

38. A. Cassese, *Il diritto internazionale nel mondo contemporaneo*. Bologna: Il Mulino, 1984, pp. 283–319. The 'Convention on Inhuman Weapons', held in December 1983, bans the use of projectiles whose fragments are not detectable by X-rays, bans or restricts anti-personnel mines and explosive devices that look harmless, and bans or restricts the use of incendiary weapons.

39. In August 1996, the Subcommittee of the United Nations on the Prevention of Discrimination and the Protection of Minorities voted a resolution against weapons of mass destruction, especially weapons containing DU; see UN Press Release, 4 September 1996, <http://southmovement.alphalink.com.au/antiwar/UNres.htm>; M. Nava, 'Kosovo, i veleni della pace', *Corriere della Sera*, 11 March 2000 p. 10.

40. The destruction and burning down of chemical plants caused large quantities of mercury, dioxins, and other highly toxic substances to be disseminated into the air, soil, and water. The *Ostdeutsch Rundfunk Brandeburg* has produced the film *Bomben auf den Chemiewerken* ('Bombs on chemical industries') by Sascha Adamek, documenting the ecological repercussions of NATO's attack against the Yugoslav Federation, especially in Pančevo and Novi Sad, the towns that were hit the hardest. The Italian edition was edited by Alberto Tarozzi with the collaboration of the Laboratory of Visual Sociology of the University of Bologna (<tarozzi@spbo.unibo.it>).

41. A. Lodovisi, 'La grande dissipazione', *Guerre e pace*, 7(60) (1999), 19.

42. P. P. Portinaro, introduction to A. Demandt (ed.), *Processare il nemico*. Turin: Einaudi, 1996, pp. xvi-xvii.

43. A. Zampaglione, 'La soddisfazione di Clinton: "la nostra guerra è giusta"', *La Repubblica*, 28 May 1999, p. 4.

44. L. Arbour, '"Così porterò alla sbarra tutti i boia di Milosevic"', p. 11.

45. M. Ricci, 'Tutti i delitti di Milosevic', *La Repubblica*, 28 May 1999, p. 2.

46. M. Nava, 'Kosovo, dubbi sulla strage di Raçak', *Corriere della Sera*, 16 April, 2000, p. 9. Roberto Morozzo della Rocca mentions that, on the morrow of the 'Raçak massacre', Louise Arbour went personally to the Yugoslav border, accompanied by Christiane Amanpour, a CNN reporter who is very well known for her professional activity, as well as for being the wife of James Rubin, an influential spokesman of the US Department of State (R. Morozzo della Rocca, 'La via verso la guerra', *Limes*, supplement to no.1 of 1999, p. 25). Paolo Soldini adds that 'many will remember the image of Ms Arbour blocked by the Serbs as she tried to enter Kosovo to investigate the Raçak massacre. Few know, however, that the whole TV scene was directed by Amanpour herself and organized by the CNN, which provided the equipment and cameras. And it was thanks to her friendship with the General Prosecutor that the CNN correspondent was able to anticipate the news of Milošević's incrimination' (P. Soldini, 'La guerra dello scoop sul fronte del Kosovo', *L'Unità*, 8 August 1999, p. 15).

47. M. Ricci, 'Tutti i delitti di Milosevic', p. 2.

48. J. Kifner, 'FBI begins sifting sites of alleged massacres', *International Herald Tribune*, 25 June 1999, p. 1.

49. C. Trueheart, 'British troops arrest key Bosnian Serb', *International Herald Tribune*, 21 December 1999, p. 6. Obviously, the fact that the incriminations were secret is in itself another serious violation by the Prosecutor of the tribunal.

50. M. Cavallini, 'Albright: nessuna immunità per Milosevic', *L'Unità*, 28 May 1999, p. 4.

51. These data are drawn from the 1994 *Yearbook of the International Criminal Tribunal for former Yugoslavia* (under the headings 'Budget and finance', pp. 24–6, and 'Voluntary contributions by states', pp. 65–6), which can be consulted at the United Nations site: <www.un.org/icty/basic/yearbook/1994/year-94.htm>.

52. Black, 'The International Criminal Tribunal: instrument of justice?', pp. 109–10.

53. *Ibid.*, p. 109.

54. *Ibid.*, p. 110.

55. Portinaro, introduction to Demandt (ed.), *Processare il nemico*, pp. xii–xiii.

56. O. Kirchheimer, *Politische Justiz*. Frankfurt am Main: Europäische Verlagsanstalt, 1981.

57. *Ibid.*, pp. 607–8.

58. 'Statuto di Roma della Corte penale internazionale', *Rivista di studi politici internazionali*, 66(1) (1999), 25–95. On the subject, see G. Vassalli, 'Statuto di Roma. Note sull'istituzione di una Corte Penale Internazionale', *Rivista di studi politici internazionali*, 66(1) (1999), 9–24.

Abundant information and documents are available on the United Nations' Internet site: <www.un.org/law/icc/>.

59. Bull, *The Anarchical Society*, p. 89.

60. In March 2000 the Hague Tribunal sentenced the Croatian-Bosnian general Tihomir Blaskić to 45 years of prison. Thousands of Croats rallied in protest in front of the US Embassy in Zagreb, thereby clearly showing that they regarded the United States as politically responsible for the tribunal's repressive actions (cf. 'Protest in Zagreb', *International Herald Tribune*, 7 March 2000, p. 7).

61. Bull, *The Anarchical Society*, pp. 162–83, stresses the importance of diplomacy for the preservation of the world order.

62. A. Baldassarre, 'Ma non può esserci la polizia del mondo', *Reset*, 57 (1999), 73.

63. So far (as of March 2000), only six states have ratified the statute approved in Rome in July 1998, namely Brazil, Fiji, Italy, Trinidad and Tobago, San Marino, and Senegal. Unless at least 60 countries ratify it, the tribunal will not begin to function.

64. 'Statuto di Roma della Corte penale internazionale', p. 34.

65. *Ibid.*, p. 87.

66. See E. Santoro's recent book, *Carcere e società liberale*. Turin: Giappichelli, 1998.

CHAPTER 5

The Consequences of the War

An Effective War?

No war can be judged exclusively, or even mainly, on claims for its initial legal or ethical legitimacy. It has been argued that a war might be illegal or immoral at its outset but then gain credibility by its practical results and thus earn full ethical and legal legitimacy. Norberto Bobbio was the first to argue that the war for Kosovo should be judged above all on its results; that is, its effectiveness in reaching its stated objectives, namely putting an end to 'ethnic cleansing' in the territories of former Yugoslavia, restoring civil and democratic life in Kosovo, and re-establishing peace and order in the Balkans.

In Bobbio's opinion, NATO's attack against the Yugoslav Federation could only be regarded as an international offence. There would be every reason to deplore the 'war from the sky' waged by the United States – one of the few countries that had never suffered an aerial bombing – as an act of cowardice.[1] Nor could one deny that the NATO offensive was very ideological, donning the trappings of a 'holy war', a 'new crusade'. Still, if in the end the illegal war proved effective, we should set aside all legal formalism and moral scruples, be realistic, and once again express our gratitude to the United States.[2]

Reasoning along the same lines, Giancarlo Bosetti argued that aside from qualms over its legal and moral aspects, the war waged by NATO against Milošević was a worthwhile initiative. Once again the United States acted on behalf of Europe, which lacked identity and political determination, and made up for its military and diplomatic fragility. NATO did what Europe should have done in the first place, possibly on its own. It thwarted the criminal plans of a nationalist dictator who was jeopardizing European peace and world order, as other dictators had done in the past. The war was effective; hence, it was just.[3]

In principle, one might agree with Bobbio's and Bosetti's approach, although not, from my point of view, with their conclusions. A realistic reflection on the 'humanitarian war' should include an examination of its political effects, going beyond mere criticism of its ethical motivations and international illegality. However, a realistic approach should not attempt to judge the effectiveness – or ineffectiveness – of the war only on its immediate outcome; it should also gauge the impact it has had and may have in the near future on the regional and international political balance of power.[4] In a realist perspective, what counts most is how collective resources are concentrated and distributed internationally, first and foremost power itself, considered as a resource.

Therefore it is important to analyse, first of all, the direct consequences for the Kosovo area of the 78 days of bombing and the subsequent military occupation. It is not enough to ascertain whether the intervention actually put a stop to the violence of 'ethnic cleansing' and gave back to the hundreds of thousands of Kosovar refugees a home and civil living conditions. We should also try to understand what sort of international control has been installed in the territories of former Yugoslavia following the war. Moreover, we should address the issue of the war's long-term effects in the Balkan region, the area that the war was allegedly supposed to pacify and stabilize, meeting its demand for political autonomy and protecting its territorial integrity from disruptive nationalist tensions.

Second, it is important to evaluate the impact of NATO's military initiative on Europe's fragile, complex political structure. It is worthwhile to analyse the response of public opinion in the major European countries to the political and military hegemony wielded by the United States during the war. The post-war period seems to have highlighted how hard it is now for some European countries to make the dynamics of regional integration coexist with the strategic unilateralism of the United States. From this standpoint, Italy, as we shall see, is in a very special position, having been the epicentre of

NATO operations and strategic decisions for geopolitical and military reasons.

Third, it is important to examine the reactions of the whole non-Western world to the display of power staged by the Atlantic Alliance and the United States in the Balkans. The management of the war and its political and military results have shown that today the Western countries can boast of an absolute economic, technological and military supremacy. In the present circumstances, nobody can stand up against them. Even great nuclear and demographic powers such as Russia, India and China, while explicitly and sometimes firmly condemning NATO's intervention, did so in very cautious terms. They were well aware of the risks involved in even the slightest allusion to a possible military reaction on their part. NATO's offensive projection, its new philosophy of humanitarian interference, and especially its appeal to a *ius ad bellum* not subject to international law, were all manifestations of the United States' and NATO's awareness of their military invincibility.

However, this unprecedented concentration of international power may turn out to be a factor of instability. As Samuel Huntington has argued, the United States' hegemonic unilateralism is not matched by a perfectly unipolar structure of the world. It is true that vast areas of the planet – notably the African continent and much of the Latin American subcontinent – have no choice but to stand by powerlessly and watch the Western powers in action, only to legitimize their deeds once they are an accomplished fact by passing over them in silence. But it is unlikely that the strong political and diplomatic tensions the United States' offensive provoked, and continues to provoke, in the Eurasian continent will be reabsorbed readily and painlessly. In this area there are regional powers which, while they were not involved in the conflict, perceive the overwhelming might of the 'last' world empire as a threat to their integrity.

As we shall see, this applies first of all to Russia, which feels threatened and besieged by NATO's military presence, partially because of the geopolitical nearness of the war theatre. It also applies to India, and even more so to China. The latter reacted firmly to NATO's military initiative, especially after the Chinese embassy in Belgrade was bombed on 7–8 May 1999. Finally, one should not forget the variable of international terrorism – now customarily referred to as 'global terrorism' – which NATO's display of force has radicalized into a bloody hostility against 'American imperialism'. It is no coincidence that the United States is increasingly haunted by the nightmare of terrorism, fearful of the revenge of countries that the United States itself has offended by labelling them as 'rogue states', banning them from civilized world society, and subjecting them to economic and military retaliatory measures in open contempt of international law. So now the United States hopes to defend itself from them by using a costly, dangerous instrument: the new anti-missile shield.

Camp Bondsteel

At least since the Congress of Berlin, near the end of the nineteenth century, interventions in the Balkans by Western powers have produced the same effects over and over again with remarkable consistency. Normally, as we have seen, these interventions have exacerbrated Balkan ethnic nationalism, reinforced its most radical fringes, and caused further fragmentation of Balkan political groups, while undermining their cultural and territorial integration and making the Balkans poorer and more dependent on foreign economies. Western intervention has also subjected the Balkan states to the logic of imperial competition, which dominated the Eastern Question from the break-up of the Ottoman Empire to the Italian and German invasion of the 1940s.

NATO's first intervention in the territories of former Yugoslavia was no exception to the rule. The *pax americana* of Dayton, like the imperial pacification imposed by tsarist Russia or Habsburg Austria, resulted in political and military control over the area by the intervening powers.

The whole Bosnian region has already been occupied for five years by NATO troops only formally dependent on the United Nations. The economy of the region depends on Western aid. The West has even built commercial facilities there, including huge supermarkets bankrolled by foreign capital and often controlled by organized crime, all of which are extraneous to the economic and cultural fabric of the country.[5] Ethnic tension still runs high, and economic conditions, in spite of the almost $5 million Western countries have lavished on the region, are still very precarious.[6]

The 'humanitarian war' for Kosovo, at least to judge from its immediate consequences and the events of the post-war period, would seem to follow the traditional pattern. The imperial mapping of Rambouillet was imposed on Yugoslavia by force of arms. The sole exception to this was the fact that NATO was not present in Serbia and Montenegro, as had been demanded at Rambouillet. Under the formal guise of a temporary administration by the United Nations, Kosovo has in fact become a military protectorate of NATO, that is, in practice, of the five powers that were most involved in the war, especially the United States, with a small contingent of Russian soldiers as a picturesque touch.

United Nations Resolution 1244 of 10 June 1999, which ratified the war and its results, by then accomplished facts, has papered over the deep ambiguity of the 'imperial mapping' of Rambouillet with a sanction by protocol. Western powers were careful not to reaffirm the general principle of the self-determination of ethnic and cultural minorities; it would have sounded too threatening to world stability and, furthermore, incompatible with the theory of the universality of human rights. Besides, formal homage had to be paid to Russian diplomacy and Chinese requests by mouthing again a ritual formula about the autonomy of Kosovo within the Yugoslav Federation and the free, democratic and multi-ethnic character of the political institutions the Western powers intended to establish. This meant that any chance for Kosovo's gaining independence was formally out of the question.[7]

However, much more lurked behind the threadbare cover of diplomatic formalism. Ever since Rambouillet, the US administration had acknowledged the UÇK's claims to independence and pledged to favour the rise to power of its leaders within the political structures of the post-war period, along with the definitive marginalization of Ibrahim Rugova and the moderate, democratic wing of Albanian nationalism. In spite of formal declarations to the contrary, this is the line that was followed in the post-war period by KFOR authorities and the civil administration, led by the Frenchman Bernard Kouchner for the United Nations, without the participation of the Serbs.[8]

This double-dealing, along with the exacerbation of feelings of hostility and revenge caused by the war, lies at the heart of the situation of anarchy, violence and fear that has prevailed in Kosovo in spite of the presence of over 40,000 KFOR soldiers and a (fragile) civil administration. NATO's humanitarian intervention did *not* put a stop to 'ethnic cleansing'; it merely switched targets. In the post-war period, the violence of the Albanian majority – as even Italian Foreign Minister Dini confirmed[9] – was unleashed on the Serbs and

Roma who had not yet chosen (or had been unable to choose) to emigrate. According to an OSCE report, violence, harassment, discrimination and intimidation carried out with impunity against ethnic minorities in Kosovo are an everyday occurrence.[10] The Albanian mafia has colonized Kosovo. Its turnover allegedly runs at about $8 billion (twice the gross national product of Albania). As journalists Paolo Rumiz and Pietro Del Re report, in 'liberated' Kosovo many Kosovar women, when they go out of their houses, fear they will be abducted by Albanian bandits from Tiranë and Durrës and forced into the international prostitution trade.[11] That is why there are families which, after having rebuilt their houses, are thinking of emigrating again. Marco-Antonio Gramegna, who investigates sexual exploitation in Kosovo for the International Organization for Migration in Geneva, writes, 'Priština itself has become a centre of prostitution where Ukrainian, Moldavian, Russian and Romanian women converge, thanks to the presence of a great number of KFOR and United Nations soldiers. It is a market in full expansion.'[12]

Before the war, 30,000 Serbs lived in Priština, the capital of Kosovo. After the war, only a few hundred were left. All told, since the end of the war 170,000 people, most of them Serbs and Roma, have abandoned Kosovo, mainly seeking refuge in Serbia, in the Kraljevo area. This means that 87 per cent of the non-Albanian population of Kosovo has fled.[13] According to the United Nations High Commissioner for Refugees, the resident Serbian population of Kosovo has fallen from the original 250,000 to about 65,000. Moreover, according to data provided by the KFOR, 360 people were killed in Kosovo between July and October 1999. Over 35 per cent were Serbs, and about 38 per cent were Kosovar Albanians. Many of the latter were eliminated either by the UÇK itself because they were regarded as spies, or by other groups in struggles for power among the Albanian guerrilla forces.[14]

In the months following the end of the war, the UÇK turned into a structure for the political and military management of the territory, the so-called 'Temporary Government of Kosovo'. Its fighters did not comply with the obligation to disarm, aside from turning in their heavy weaponry, which could no longer be used. This 'temporary government', while maintaining relations with heroin-peddling Balkan and European mafias,[15] co-operates with many civil and military agencies of the occupation forces and is treated as an important interlocutor. This not only violates the resolution of the Security Council of the United Nations, but in fact legitimizes an organization that is fighting for the complete independence of the whole territory of Kosovo from Serbia and is fanning the coals of hatred and vengeance to achieve its purpose.[16] Since January 2000 the UÇK, under the name of 'Eastern Kosovo Liberation Army', has even managed to infiltrate the territory of southern Serbia near the administrative border with Kosovo, where it has repeatedly engaged the Serbian police in gunfights.[17] Its objective is to take the three main towns near the north-eastern border of Kosovo away from Serbia: Presevo, Medvedja and Bujanovac (hence the acronym UÇPMB used by the guerrillas), all with Albanian majorities.

The outbreak of violence in Kosovska Mitrovica in February 2000 is an emblematic example of how unstable the region is. Kosovska Mitrovica is the only city in Kosovo that still has a sizeable enclave of Serbs (about 10,000 people). In February a mass of Kosovar-Albanians repeatedly laid siege to the Serbs on the other side of the Ibar River, threatening to kill them all. The KFOR troops barely managed to protect the Serbs. The Kosovar-Albanians had been instigated and mobilized by UÇK militants. It is on them, and not on the Serbs, that responsibility for these serious incidents falls, according to the Italian Mario Morcone, administrator of Mitrovica for the United Nations, thus contradicting General Wesley Clark's public statements. The spiral of murderous violence that led to the clash between the two ethnic groups was sparked by an attack, almost certainly by the UÇK, that cost the lives of two Serbian civilians.[18]

It can hardly be denied that the original responsibility for all this falls on the Western powers – actually, much more on the United States than on the European members of NATO. The United States has pursued a strategy of tacit collaboration with Kosovar-Albanian extremist groups. This strategy will inevitably bring about the separation of Kosovo from Serbia, and this in turn will entail the total expulsion of the Serbs from a land they regard, rightly or wrongly, as the 'cradle' of their civilization. The leadership of this new Balkan state will probably fall into the hands of the corrupt, anti-democratic elite of the UÇK, whose methods will be no better than those of the hated Serbian authorities.

Thus, even overlooking the emigration of hundreds of thousands of Kosovar-Albanians, indirectly caused by NATO's bombings but for which the Serbian militias' ruthless retaliation was immediately responsible, it is clear that the war did not honour its 'humanitarian' pledge. It did not keep its two main promises, namely to put a stop to ethnic violence and give rise to a democratic government in Kosovo and in the whole Yugoslav Federation. On the contrary, the results were of the sort that has always followed armed interventions by Western powers in the Balkans: ethnic tensions were exacerbrated, extremist and anti-democratic groups were bolstered, the political structures were fragmented and subordinated to Western strategies, local culture was devastated, and the area was impoverished.

The 'reconstruction' of Kosovo and the other war-torn regions threatens to make things still worse, in spite of rhetorical prattle about a 'Marshall plan for the Balkans'. As has already occurred in Bosnia-Herzegovina, reconstruction will probably create cultural uprooting, economic and financial subordination (in Kosovo, as is well known, the German mark has been introduced as official currency), and political dependence.[19] In many respects the reconstruction will most likely be just as destructive as the war.

Serbia has been excluded from the projects and funds allocated for reconstruction, unless Milošević's regime be voted out or overthrown by force. To achieve this result, the United States has shown no scruples in bringing all available means of political, economic and communicational pressure to bear. The *pax americana*, as Madeleine Albright has repeatedly said,[20] requires the total isolation of a defeated and economically annihilated Serbia: Milošević must be brought out and turned over to the Hague Tribunal. But until this happens, there is little likelihood of stability in the region. One has only to think of Montenegro, Vojvodina, Macedonia, Bosnia and Serbia itself, which has no intention of giving up its historical ties with Kosovo, and has been quick to respond to UÇK provocation along the north-eastern border of Kosovo.[21] On the other hand, the creation of an independent Kosovo under the protection of NATO, the most probable outcome of the United States' ambiguous strategy, will strengthen the movement for a 'Greater Albania', and call all the frontiers of the region into question, unleashing a new wave of violence and political instability.

The summit for a Stability Pact in the Balkans, held at Sarajevo in July 1999 with the participation of President Clinton and leading exponents of NATO and South-East European countries, was somewhat of a personal victory celebration for Clinton, confirming the United States' intention to turn Kosovo into a permanent base from which to control the whole Balkan peninsula. During a later trip to the Balkans, President Clinton reaffirmed this intention while visiting Camp Bondsteel near Urosevac in east-central Kosovo. Camp Bondsteel is the largest military base the United States has built since the Vietnam War. So far it has cost almost $40 million. It can house about 5000 troops in comfortable quarters. It is equipped with a heliport used by fighter helicopters, including a dozen Apaches. It will soon be provided with a landing ground for planes as well. The base covers a surface of 3 square kilometres. Facilities include a fitness centre, a sports field, a library, two chapels and, of course, a Burger King. Besides being very well equipped, Camp Bondsteel is exceptionally well defended and secure. It was built in record time on an artificial plateau obtained by levelling three hills once covered with wheat fields.[22]

It is inevitable that the majority of the inhabitants of Kosovo view this fortress erected in the heart of their country as the resplendent emblem of the success of the United States' war for universal human rights and democratic freedom. A few weeks after Clinton's visit, however, a young sergeant stationed at Camp Bondsteel raped and killed an 11-year-old Albanian girl, Merite Shabiu. Of course he will be put on trial, but in a US military base, and by a US military court.[23]

The Scognamiglio Doctrine

As we have seen, some European observers believe that the United States' war on the Yugoslav Federation was intended first of all to hamper Europe's political integration. According to this theory, the US government was following the guidelines of the 'Brzezinski doctrine', which holds that the European defence system should be fully integrated with that of the United States. Europe should continue to be the 'American bridgehead' on the Eurasian continent. NATO's new projective and aggressive stance is believed to have been motivated by the United States' strategic plan to prevent Europe's political integration, added to its economic and financial integration, from widening the distance between the two shores of the Atlantic. Europe must not be allowed to adopt autonomous political and military strategies.

Whether one accepts this interpretation or not, it is unquestionable that the major decisions in the war for Kosovo were made by the United States alone. The decision to wage a 'war from the sky' was American, as was the choice of the targets and the resolve to bomb with implacable continuity. Some of the targets of military operations involving the most sophisticated US planes or missiles remained a secret even to the allies, including Great Britain.[24] It is well known that the overall military contribution of European countries during the war did not reach 20 per cent of the total, and was technologically a low-profile contribution.[25] At the same time, however, US diplomacy was scrupulously careful to ensure the consensus and collaboration of European countries, however insignificant their military contribution.

With the exception of Greece, which opposed the war from the beginning and refused to take part in it, and allowing for some lukewarm reservations expressed by Germany and Italy, the Europeans bowed to the will of the United States, almost as if they had been collectively mesmerized by the 'Brzezinski doctrine'. They showed their acquiescence both within the decision-making structures of NATO, and when the European Union decided on its own, as was the case with the European economic and financial sanctions (especially the oil embargo) against the Yugoslav Federation. It is true that criticism was sometimes voiced. Both the French and the Italians guardedly remarked that some of the military operations decided by General Wesley Clark were outside the purview of NATO's own norms and procedures.[26] But never at any time did the political unity of the Atlantic forces wobble, as the Yugoslav regime possibly hoped it would. Clinton's praise of Italian prime minister Massimo D'Alema – 'Massimo is a rock of loyalty' – could be lavished on all the leaders of the nineteen NATO countries – first and foremost, of course, on Tony Blair.

However, since the end of the conflict an unease has been growing between the United States and Europe that would seem to spring directly from the 'humanitarian war'.[27] The Europeans have realized that their increased economic and financial weight and their progress in economic integration is not matched by their military potential. For decades, with the exception of the resistance of Gaullist and neo-Gaullist France, they have left it to the United States to represent the West in foreign policy and defence matters, placing themselves under the United States' nuclear umbrella. What transatlantic crises there were had to do mainly with trade and financial policies, and were always solved without serious traumas.

It is no coincidence that up till now the process of European integration has developed much more in the economic and financial sectors – as the Schengen and Maastricht treaties clearly bear out – than on the much more delicate ground of foreign politics and defence, which have remained the exclusive domain of Europe's American ally.

One of the consequences of the war for Kosovo was a widespread conviction among European governments that Europe should develop its own strategic capabilities in defence, military commands and computer espionage. Following the example of the United States, Europe should convert its traditionally static and defensive military forces into troops capable of rapid, dynamic offensive missions, like those deployed in the war for Kosovo. Even Great Britain agrees with this European sentiment, in spite of a long-standing, deeply rooted ambiguity in its relations with continental Europe.[28] Javier Solana, who after the end of the war left his post of Secretary-General of the Atlantic Alliance to become the European High Representative for Foreign Affairs and Common Security, immediately began working in this direction. The Kosovo crisis, Solana declared,

> has been a wakeup call for European leaders and European public opinion. It has revealed the shortcomings of European national and collective military capabilities. Europeans can produce only a small fraction of the capabilities needed to project and sustain forces as to manage the kind of security challenges we are presently facing and will face in the future. ... It is not an ambition to set up a new military alliance in Europe that would compete with or replace NATO. It is a positive effort to play a more committed, responsible role.[29]

The new Secretary-General of the Atlantic Alliance, George Robertson, replacing Javier Solana, admitted that in spite of the European countries' conspicuous military investments – amounting altogether to about 60 per cent of those of the United States - their military potential is less than 10 per cent of that of the United States. Hence the European Union must absolutely equip itself with a modern and efficient 'European army' of its own.[30]

On the basis of these premises, European Union Foreign and Defence Ministers gathered for a series of meetings for the creation of a European army numbering 40,000–60,000 men, which should become operative by 2003. The final decision was made in

November 1999 at Helsinki. But there is this crucial point: the new military force will be 'separable', but not at all 'separate', from NATO. The European army will be truly autonomous only when NATO entrusts Europe with the task of intervening. The head of this new military force will be Javier Solana, who will also assume the functions of Secretary-General of the WEU, the old and by now moribund defensive alliance of the major countries of Western Europe, sooner or later to be dismantled.

The Helsinki agreement is supposed to become something very similar for European defence to what Maastricht was for the European currency. An elaborate structure has been created that was made up of several different military bodies. Following the model adopted at Maastricht, 'convergence criteria' have been defined; that is, standards by which to determine the military services and expenses each country must bear and to evaluate each country's progress. The idea of using Maastricht as a model was suggested by the Italian Minister of Defence, Carlo Scognamiglio, at the Anglo-Italian summit of July 1999. It was later accepted by the French and finally adopted by all the Ministers of Defence of the European Union.[31]

Europeans, with Solana in the front rank, have hastened to declare that the purpose of the projected European defence system is to strengthen the 'European pillar' of the Atlantic Alliance, that this was already in NATO's plans, and that it will conform to the 'new strategic concept' approved in Washington.[32] For his part, Tony Blair has peremptorily declared that 'NATO remains the landmark of European defence'.[33] In spite of this, the reaction of Europe's American ally was not long in coming, notwithstanding the fact that during the war the United States had criticized the European countries for their lack of military competence. The US Assistant Secretary of State, Strobe Talbott, warned the allies against the risk that this new military project might undermine NATO's cohesion and harm NATO countries not belonging to the European Union, such as Turkey, Hungary, the Czech Republic, Poland, Norway, Iceland, as well as the United States itself and Canada.[34]

It is evident that these worries on the part of the United States make sense only within a rigidly unilateral vision, à la Brzezinski, of hegemonic strategy. The statements of personages such as Solana, Blair and Robertson, whose Atlantic loyalty is beyond doubt, can hardly be anything but sincere and reliable. It is beyond doubt that their purpose is to improve Europe's military efficiency without detriment to Atlantic solidarity. At the most, their intention might be to make Europe's relationship of military co-operation with the United States less unbalanced, and hence more dignified in European eyes and those of the world. Nor can there be any doubt about the intentions and objectives of what could be called the 'Scognamiglio doctrine'. It is hardly plausible that Europe, by creating its army, can be planning to enhance its political identity to the point of attaining to a significant autonomy with respect to the United States. It is highly improbable that the war for Kosovo can restore to Europe a strong international role, let alone allow it to compete with the United States.

For years the issue of European political identity has fuelled an important theoretical discussion involving some of the best minds of the continent, especially Germans, such as Ralf Dahrendorf, Jürgen Habermas and Fritz Scharpf. These and other scholars have debated under what conditions European politics can achieve legitimacy, at both the national and the European Union level. They have highlighted a threefold 'democratic deficit' marking the current phase of the process of European integration: the lack of a European sense of collective identity, the lack of communication and political debate on a regional scale, and the lack of a European institutional structure capable of guaranteeing that politicians answer to a European electorate.[35]

Ralf Dahrendorf has identified three variables that a democratic Europe should seek to keep in a synergic balance: the production of economic resources, the defence of human rights, and the political loyalty of citizens. He also denounced the imbalance resulting from excessive emphasis on technological development, production and consumption, to the detriment of the defence of rights and the promotion of shared political values and a sense of membership in a 'European civil society'.[36] Dieter Grimm and Richard Bellamy, among others, devoted special attention to the theme of the defence of the fundamental rights of European citizens and the alternative between a protection entrusted to norms established by the existing treaties and judicial practice, on the one hand, and one founded on a written constitution, on the other.[37]

The impact of the 'humanitarian war' on the process of European integration seems to have had, *pace* Habermas's optimistic expectations,[38] one main consequence: it has sacrificed the whole issue of Europe's political identity and democratic development to what I may call the 'Scognamiglio doctrine'. Today, alongside the

Europe of Maastricht – the Europe of money and banks – there is the Europe of Helsinki. This Europe has resolved to give priority to its military dimension and to carrying out the aggressive strategy of promoting the 'new world order' and 'global security' within the 'new NATO' and under the hegemonic direction of the United States.

The 'Noble Circle of the Great'

Among European countries, Italy was the most directly involved in the war for Kosovo, because of both its intense participation in the military action – in which Italy was second only to France and far surpassed Great Britain and Germany[39] – and its geopolitical contiguity with the territories of former Yugoslavia. In fact, this closeness explains the special attention Italy, as a 'great power', has given to the other bank of the Adriatic throughout the twentieth century, from the 'Fiume question' to the invasion of Greece, the claim to Istria, the Pellicano mission, and Operation Alba in 1997.

Italy took part in the war with 50 of its own planes, which carried out more than 1300 defensive and offensive incursions. And it put no fewer than twelve military bases (especially the Aviano base in Friuli) and the ports required for the 20 ships involved in the military operations at the disposal of NATO, the United States in particular. The most significant military decisions of the war were made in Italy by the four regional and sub-regional NATO commands, stationed at Vicenza and Naples. Moreover, Italy sent over 5000 troops and police into Kosovo, in addition to the 4000 already deployed in Bosnia, Albania and Macedonia. When the partial withdrawal of the multinational troops from Bosnia is completed, Italian forces in the Balkans will be second in size only to the British.[40]

We see, then, that in spite of the low profile affected by the Italian government for the benefit of its domestic public opinion, Italy served, so to speak, as an immense aircraft carrier, and hosted the main headquarters of the war. Without Italy's co-operation, as US Defense Secretary William Cohen acknowledged, it would not have been possible to fight the war, or it would have had to be fought in forms very different from the 'war from the sky'.

Thus, one of the immediate results of the war for Kosovo and NATO's expansive and aggressive metamorphosis was an increase of

Italy's strategic – and, hence, political and military – importance within NATO, due to its contiguity with the Balkan area, its projection in the Mediterranean, and especially its full reliability as a political ally. The duty of taking part in the war of the 'new NATO' was seen by the D'Alema government as a strategic imperative for Italy, which wanted to 'count as a great country'. 'If we had not done it', wrote the Italian prime minister,

> we would have undermined the prestige newly acquired by Italy with the Alba operation. We would have failed to fulfil one of the functions that the new European equilibrium has assigned to our country as a frontier facing extremely turbulent areas in the Mediterranean and the Balkans: the role of a country that is called upon to project stability.[41]

Italy's participation in the war for Kosovo was rewarded with its immediate advancement. For the first time, as Massimo D'Alema wrote with satisfaction, Italy had become part of the so-called 'Quint':

> The Kosovo crisis has *de facto* created a new network of relationships; for example, the daily teleconferences among the Foreign Ministers of five countries: United States, Germany, Great Britain, France and Italy. As a consequence of Kosovo, we have become part of that group. It is not written in any official document, but in fact a sort of club sprang up around Kosovo. ... It is hard to define rules for membership of the noble circle of the great, which has no statute. You just realize you are on a certain agenda of phone calls of the president of the United States.[42]

The prime minister's patriotic pride, while it seems to have little to do with the humanitarian universalism for which the war was allegedly fought, is probably justified. However, it can hardly be claimed that Italy's political leaders sought their people's political participation and democratic consensus. As Ralf Dahrendorf stressed, the main effect of the war for Kosovo on Western political systems was to aggravate and highlight the erosion of their democratic institutions. To quote D'Alema, the war brought out the overwhelming power of 'networks of relationships' and transnational 'clubs'. These networks and clubs not only claim, as NATO did, a *ius ad bellum* of their own, not obliged to bow to the provisions of international law, but also can act without being empowered by the

national representative assemblies of their countries. In fact, the war
for Kosovo was decided, in Italy as in other European countries, by
certain political and military elites without a democratic *ad hoc*
mandate – indeed, sometimes operating, as in Italy, in open
violation of the Constitution.[43] Dahrendorf wrote:

> [F]ew today raise questions of sovereignty when NATO is in
> cause. But who made the decision to conduct the war in
> Kosovo the way it was conducted? What if the people had not
> wanted the war; to what political authority would they have
> been able to appeal to express their will? To the NATO
> council? Or maybe to the government of the United States, in
> confirmation of the funny joke that, since the United States
> exercises its power over the rest of the world, the rest of the
> world should have the right to vote in the American
> presidential elections?[44]

But D'Alema did not only bow loyally to the decisions made,
overruling international law, by the 'club' of the powerful that
'sprang up around Kosovo'. He also proposed a presidential reform
of Italian institutions in order to disengage the decisions of the
executive branch from 'the fragility of parliamentary majorities' in
wartime. In foreign policy, argued D'Alema, the need for stability is
crucial. One cannot risk a governmental crisis during a war, even if
it may be necessary 'to make decisions it is hard for the majority to
accept'.[45] This does not mean 'suspending the rules of democracy',
D'Alema explained, because

> the worse risk is to live in a country that does not count for
> anything, banned from the places where decisions are made.
> This is a case in which an excess of democracy prevents true
> democracy, because it bans you from the places where
> decisions are made for you, too. ... Delegating power to a
> few is a prerequisite for an efficient modern democracy. We
> live in a time when the decision-making circuit is no longer
> national.[46]

Besides being objectionable from both the theoretical and the
political point of view, D'Alema's worries are also rather surprising,
since his government did not need to overcome much resistance to
bring Italy to war. The centre-left government's warlike orientation
went hand in hand with the natural Atlantic bent of many Italians.
This inclination, which even the Cermis incident did not under-

mine, found its emblematic expression in the thousands of Italian citizens who, during the war, chose the green fields of Aviano for their family picnics. Here they could watch, with innocent, technological glee, the great flying machines taking off from the US military base to bring death and destruction to a nearby country.

This 'post-modern' *qualunquismo*, as if to say 'philistinism', was encouraged by public and private television channels, which engaged in an obsessive, almost subliminal, insistence on the humanitarian motivation, illustrating it with images of the (authentic) sufferings of Kosovar refugees and the atrocities of the civil war. This subliminal manipulation reached its climax when national television channels broadcast images of the most famous Italian comic actor, Roberto Benigni, warmly embracing President Clinton, who had surprisingly been invited to Florence to take part in a meeting of European social democrats on the 'third way' advocated by Anthony Giddens and Tony Blair.

Thus, arguably, the 'humanitarian war', besides earning the Italian government membership in the exclusive 'noble circle of the great', has caused Atlanticism to become even more deeply rooted in the feelings of a large majority of Italians. Fabio Mini argued, I believe with reason, that the Italians' current Atlanticism is not so much based on rational reasons for supporting a political and military alliance as it is a sort of mental attitude as well as an existential condition even more deeply ingrained than the favour with which they look on the perspective of European integration.[47] It is an emotional conviction, one might say, refractory to rational discussion of the pros and cons of Italy's membership in the 'new NATO' and the presence of US military bases on Italy's 'European' soil.[48] Indeed, it is well known that Italy is the only European country which, after the end of the Cold War, did not arrange with the United States for the withdrawal of at least a small part of its military forces.

The war for Kosovo has confirmed that a majority of Italians are increasingly attracted by the perspective of their country's acquiring a 'global' role alongside the other great powers of the planet, thanks to its entry into Europe and its admission to the great international economic, political and military institutions. This Italy, being aligned with the strategy of 'new world order' and 'global security', feels perfectly at its ease within the 'new NATO', and is ready to turn its back on its Mediterranean history and roots.

What really seems to count for most Italians, including Massimo

D'Alema, is that the Italian flag waves over the Balkans and that Italian companies are taking part in the post-war reconstruction of Kosovo and thus may somehow manage to stop the big trans-Adriatic flows of migrants that are seen as threatening the Italian peninsula. What counts is that even in East Timor, in the remote Indonesian archipelago, Italy is proclaiming its role as a Western power, freed from its old inferiority complex towards its mighty partners, and, at the same time, in complete harmony with them. That is why US and NATO military bases in Italy must not be reduced or renegotiated. Indeed, they must be strengthened. While the Italian bases of Camp Darby, Camp Ederle, La Maddalena and Sigonella, as well as the Naples complex, remain in function, it has been decided to turn the USAF base at Aviano into a sort of functional twin of the Camp Bondsteel base just built in Kosovo. Project 'Aviano 2000' for the restructuring and doubling of the Aviano base will cost at least half a billion dollars, to be paid by NATO, the United States, and to a large degree by the Italian government as well. The capacity of the base was scheduled to be increased from 1700 to 3000 troops by the year 2001. As Domenico Pecile wrote with commendable sincerity in the *Corriere della Sera*, this imposing renovation was meant to 'convert the USAF base, entrusting it with the role of armed guard not just of the Balkans but of the Middle East as well, within the framework of the strategy of the United States and NATO'.[49]

Several serious terrorist attacks have already taken place against Italian companies involved in renovating the base.[50]

The Mirror of Russia

Giulietto Chiesa wrote that Russia saw a reflection of its own agony in the collapse of Yugoslavia and the humiliation of Serbia.[51] He argues that Russia's solidarity with the Serbs is not due merely to their common ethnic and religious roots. The rapid collapse of post-Titoist Yugoslavia shattered Russia's dream of making a powerful comeback from its present economic and political breakdown. The traumatic realization has dawned on the Russians that the destiny of the Russian Federation may no longer be in their own hands but is dictated by the evolution of the global balance of power. It has suddenly become clear that the Serbs' defeat, like that of the

Russians, depended on a single 'external' factor, that is, the absolute supremacy of a world power – the United States of America – which the Soviet Union once confronted on equal terms, and against whose plans for world hegemony it is presently powerless.

NATO's transformation and its expansion eastwards threaten to isolate the Russian Federation by gathering in the loose pieces of the former Soviet empire. The resulting political geography of the Euroasian continent will be very different from what was outlined at Yalta. Western Europe itself has been briskly steered away from its process of regional integration and back into its role as a bridgehead of US supremacy in Eurasia. Even the network of international institutions has been dismantled or marginalized, beginning with the United Nations. The result was a further humiliation of what was left of Russia's international prestige, which today hangs on its veto power in the Security Council of the United Nations.[52]

This stimulating interpretative approach accounts, at least in part, for the behaviour of Russian diplomacy during the war for Kosovo. It is unquestionable that in Russia the first consequence of the war was a strong wave of anti-American feeling that was manifested at once in the shoot-out in front of the American embassy in Moscow. The Russian Centre for Studies on Public Opinion ascertained that the NATO war had spread disillusionment, fear and resentment among a broad majority of Russians. Aleksandr Solzhenitsyn gave voice to these feelings in his usual apocalyptic style.[53] The Russian people were dismayed by their country's impotence to heed the explicit request for help of their Serbian 'brothers'. At the same time, tragically deluded, they feared that a power they had regarded as friendly was about to open a new era of 'cold war'.[54] After the fall of communism, the rich, free countries of the West had told the Russians they were ready to help them build a democracy and a market economy that would save them from the disruption and poverty into which the country had sunk. But, as Roy Medvedev writes, what the Russians believe now is that the West has robbed them, driven them into debt, and placed them under an armed siege.[55]

All the political forces represented in the Duma – not just the right- and left-wing nationalists, but also the centralist 'Westernists' – have taken very firm stands against NATO's 'humanitarian war'. This unanimous reaction of Russian political forces and public opinion alike provides a key for understanding the frantic, often clumsy diplomatic duplicity of Boris Yeltsin's government. It explains its attempts to meet the demands of national political opinion by protecting the Serbs and, at the same time, its willingness to give in, through the conniving mediation of Viktor Chernomyrdin, to the political pressure and economic retaliatory measures of the all-powerful United States, which holds the purse strings of the international credit that debt-ridden Russia so desperately needs. Thus, Boris Yeltsin made a decisive contribution to the victory of the West, as in the end he accepted the results of the war and legitimated NATO's protectorate over Kosovo with Russia's awkward and marginal participation in the military occupation of the territory.

All this, while it can hardly be denied, is still not the whole story. The Russian people are not motivated only by depression, fear and an elementary need for security. Nor were the Kremlin and Muscovite intelligentsia merely forced to acknowledge their defeat. There is a third element which became more evident after the war and has been quite clear ever since Boris Yeltsin's retirement and the rise to power of former KGB lieutenant colonel Vladimir Putin at the beginning of 2000. The war for Kosovo has forced Russia onto a hard, dangerous course: it is seeking to regain its role as a great power on a planetary chessboard where the game of politics is being played for high stakes.

As Vitaliy Tetryakov, director of the influential *Nezavisimaya Gazeta*, wrote, the results of the 'humanitarian war' are forcing Russia to change its domestic and foreign policies radically. In order to survive within the *pax americana*, it must regain a military deterrent, first and foremost a nuclear one, by pursuing immediate, extensive rearmament. But to boost military and, hence, economic power would take a strong, even authoritarian regime, able to fight corruption and crime and put all democratic illusions to rest.[56]

In a nutshell, Russia's aim is to be able once again to stand up to the United States and NATO, as the Soviet Union and the Warsaw Pact would have done. The difference is that to win this new 'cold war', Russia would have to broaden its strategic alliances to take in all international political subjects not subordinated to the hegemony of the United States, including the Islamic countries. After the 'humanitarian war' Russia has no choice but to become anti-American, anti-democratic and generally hostile to the global dimension of market economy, which is increasingly ruled by the great Western corporations. This new Russia will also be mistrustful of Europe, and especially of the Eastern European countries that have sided with NATO or already joined it, such as Poland, the Czech Republic and Hungary.[57]

Are these inordinate, irrational ambitions induced by a boundless imperial frustration, with no chance of success? Possibly. However, there are signs that under the leadership of Vladimir Putin, a man little inclined to idealism, Russia is shifting away from several aspects of the political strategies of the Yeltsin era, and these shifts all go in the direction Tetryakov indicated. Russia is trying to respond to the overwhelming military and technological supremacy displayed by NATO in the Balkans. To this end it has launched itself on a policy of rearmament, extensive militarization of society, ruthless repression of the Chechnyan struggle for independence, and a new strategy of alliances focusing mainly on the Asiatic theatre. It is especially important for Russia not to yield an inch in the Caucasus, not just to keep its military prestige, but because that is where the Great Game of energy sources is being played, and where the political and diplomatic initiative of Western powers is especially aggressive.

At the beginning of the war for Kosovo, the Yeltsin government closed off the diplomatic channel between Russia and the Western powers that had been opened within the framework of the 'Partnership for Peace', NATO's programme involving many countries not yet in the Atlantic alliance but wishing to join it, or at least to orbit around the American superpower. But Vladimir Putin has gone much further. He has revived the Russian 'doctrine of security', with a strong emphasis on nuclear weapons. In spite of the serious crisis it is going through, Russia wants to remind the world that it is still the second nuclear power of the planet, and that it counts on its nuclear armaments to redeem itself. Russia has warned that it will use them to reply to attacks with conventional weapons by states equipped with nuclear weapons. But Russian has also warned that it will not limit itself to giving up, as Yeltsin had already proposed, the principle of 'no first strike'. Putin's Russia has declared that it will use its nuclear weapons indiscriminately against any external aggressor, even if the latter does not use or possess nuclear weapons and is not allied with states equipped with such weapons. In line with this new conception of security, Putin has launched a process of militarization of Russian society. He has reinstated compulsory military training for reservists, extended this obligation to students of public and private secondary schools, and done away with the possibility to opt for civil instead of military service upon finishing school. Military spending, as the new Minister of Finances announced, will be drastically increased, perhaps by as much as 150 per cent of what was allotted by the previous budget.[58]

The purpose of this increase in military expenditures is first of all to pay for the war in Chechnya, which Western powers, while mouthing criticism over its destructive ferocity, made no move to stop. After pitching in to bring the 'humanitarian war' to a happy end, now the Kremlin cashes its cheques, with the opportunistic complicity of the West. However, as Vladimir Putin has made very clear, the main objective of the war against Chechnyan independence is strategic. Russia intends to maintain control of the whole trans-Caucasian area in order to keep the routes open to South-Central Asia.[59] It is clear that in northern Caucasus the Kremlin is not merely seeking to turn back an attack on the territorial integrity of the Russian Federation and repress what the Russians regard as an intolerable terrorist threat. The Chechnyan war is first and foremost an answer to the strategy launched by NATO expansion in the Balkans and continued at the Istanbul summit of November 1999, where the project for the Baku–Ceyhan oil pipeline was approved, having been personally promoted by President Clinton. The Kremlin is trying to oppose the Western powers' plan to exclude Russia from the 'corridors' through which petrol and combustible gas will be conveyed to the European continent. At stake in this 'Great Game' is control over the immense energy resources of the Caucasian and Caspian region. Russia is still not out of the running; it has played the card of the Blue Stream project, managed by the Russian industrial colossus Gazprom, the aim of which is to lay an underwater pipeline through the Black Sea from north to south to reach Turkey.[60]

The big new military investments planned by the Kremlin are also earmarked for the resumption of projects for space control, anti-missile defence and the production of intercontinental vectors, which had been started during the Reagan era and then abandoned. Today, faced with the new US anti-missile defence project announced by President Clinton, over which controversy is raging both in the East and in the West, Russia is responding by resuming experimental long-distance missile launching and speeding up its strategic weapons production.[61]

The rearmament and militarization programme of the new Russian leadership goes hand in hand with a plan to restrict democracy and further centralize the state. It has been argued that this project aims at making President Putin's party the 'Kremlin party'.[62] In March 2000 a group of intellectuals, including Andrei Sakharov's wife, Yelena Bonner, signed an open letter stating that the rise to power of the former KGB official is a serious danger for the new Russian democracy. According to the signatories, there is even the risk of a return to Stalinist methods: a hierarchical involution of society, limitation of the freedom of the press, abuse of power and contempt for human rights.[63]

But the most ambitious strategic objective of the new Russian leadership focuses on East Asia. Having abandoned its pan-Slav and pan-Orthodox rhetoric, the Kremlin now seems to be seeking an alliance with the two great eastern powers – nuclear and demographic powers – that opposed the NATO war, namely India and China. In December 1999 the then Prime Minister, Yevgeni Primakov, had already explicitly announced this new strategic perspective in a visit to New Delhi: Russia, India and China were to unite almost 3 billion people in a 'strategic triangle' to defend their common interest against the United States' global hegemony.[64] The 'Primakov doctrine', it has been observed, presents a scenario bristling with obstacles. For one thing the relations of each of the three Asiatic powers with the United States are more important than the relations each one has with the other two. Relations between India and China have often been tense. Since the collapse of the Soviet Union, political and especially commercial relations between India and Russia have been rather insignificant. Nevertheless, many believe that the war for Kosovo has alarmed India and China as much as it has alarmed Russia. They are worried by the many-faceted US supremacy – at once military, economic and technological – as much as by the ease with which NATO used force without any previous authorization by the United Nations.

This global framework helps us to understand why relations between Russia and China – and between the latter and India – have improved so quickly after the war for Kosovo. Significantly, recent Russian and Chinese joint documents criticize NATO harshly. In a joint declaration concluding Boris Yeltsin's visit to Beijing in December 1999, China and Russia bluntly accused the United States of violating the sovereignty of states in the name of a pretended right of humanitarian intervention to impose on the whole world 'a single cultural model, an exclusive conception of values, and a dominating ideology'.[65] It is equally significant that in

June 1999 Beijing and New Delhi resumed negotiations for the regulation of their frontiers, and the two countries for the first time started a diplomatic dialogue on international security.[66]

The Empire at the Centre of the World

During the night of 7 and 8 May 1999, three NATO missiles hit the Chinese embassy in Belgrade, destroying a wing of the building, killing three Chinese officials and wounding 20 people, six of them seriously, including the military attaché Ven Bo Koy. It is a puzzling incident for many reasons and may well be at the core of this 'humanitarian war'. This bombing will probably have more significant and longer-lasting consequences on the global equilibrium of the planet than any other event of the war. Perceived by China and many Asiatic countries as a blatant expression of the aggressiveness and dangerousness of the Western world, the war for Kosovo is going to affect not only relations between the United States and China, but also, more in general, relations between the West, including Europe, and the Far East. Bates Gill wrote authoritatively:

> The NATO bombing of the Chinese embassy in Belgrade exacerbates all the more China's long-simmering resentment over what it sees as abusive American unilateralism. Indeed, all that China opposes in the U.S.-led NATO action in Serbia – American aggression, the trampling of state sovereignty, excessive use of force – has been intensely magnified by the single action of destroying the Chinese embassy. This tragic event cuts to the very core of Chinese grievances with the current world order, illustrating U.S. dominance, highlighting China's relative weakness, and violating China's long and passionately held principle of noninterference in the internal affairs of other states.[67]

The bombing of the Chinese embassy in Belgrade happened during a complex, delicate phase in the political and economic evolution of post-Maoist China. On the one hand there is the Confucian tradition, with its sense of authority, family and organic membership in the social body. This tradition is largely synergetic with the centralized, authoritarian structure of the Communist Party, the custodian of what little remains of the Maoist heritage. On the other hand, there is China's burgeoning market economy, with its implicit pragmatic and technological conception of the world, the 'modernizing' of lifestyles, and the adoption of the formal aspects of the European legal tradition.[68] The Chinese political and military class is trying to harmonize these different functional components. At the same time, it must deal with thrusts for independence that threaten the elephantine structure of the state in several places, as well as with corruption and the increasing economic inequalities caused by the country's impetuous capitalist development.[69] This difficult balance has very high costs. Today, a policy of decentralization of power, pluralistic democratization of political structures, and respect of the fundamental rights of citizens and the basic elements of the rule of law seems impracticable in post-Marxist China, although some weak attempts in this direction have been made.[70]

China knows that in many respects it lags behind the West, but it is aware, at the same time, of its great potential and of a growing strength and prestige coming from its age-old civilization, its past history as a great economic and political power, its demographic potential (a quarter of the world population is Chinese), its nuclear armaments and its booming economy. Finally, its market, far from saturated, holds out promises of economic growth for the whole planet. China proudly senses its 'difference' from the rest of the world and is fostering a new nationalism that will allow it to say 'no' to whoever tries to assimilate and subordinate it. Evidence of this attitude is the huge success of recent works such as *China Can Say No* by Zhang Xiaobo and *Containing China* by Sun Yiqin and Cui Hongjian, which have truly become a bible of Chinese patriotism.[71]

For all these reasons, the Chinese authorities reacted very harshly to the bombing of their embassy. Anti-American protest, fuelled by the new nationalism, exploded in Beijing and in many other Chinese cities. It was the most imposing popular protest since the demonstrations in Tiananmen Square in 1989, with the difference that in this case it was a protest encouraged, at least in part, by the regime, which in substance tolerated acts of violence against the embassies of the United States and Great Britain. China requested and obtained an emergency meeting of the Security Council, which, however, declined to express any formal censure of NATO. The US president, Bill Clinton, wrote a personal letter to the Chinese president, Jiang Zemin, to apologize for the mistake, alluding to an exchange of maps for which the CIA was claimed to be responsible.

But the Chinese authorities did not accept the apologies and expressed their conviction that the bombing was intentional. The high technology and detailed intelligence the American superpower had access to – which most Chinese look up to with admiration – were incompatible with such a clumsy mistake. In about 38,000 attack missions, only once had NATO's air force mistaken one fixed target for another.[72] The only reasonable doubt regarded the political level at which the decision to hit the Chinese embassy had been made. But whoever was responsible for the decision, China insisted, had to be identified and punished.[73]

Hundreds of articles appeared in the Chinese press to denounce the iniquities of the 'hegemonic politics' of the United States and voice the feeling of impotence and frustration on the part of China, a great regional power and permanent member of the Security Council, which, however, could not afford to reply to the insult because of its relative military and economic inferiority. If the Chinese embassy was attacked on purpose, it is a sign of a major shift in the political strategies of the great powers of the planet that has caught China unawares. As in Boris Yeltsin and Vladimir Putin's Russia, so in Jiang Zemin and Zhu Rongji's China the war for Kosovo was perceived as a warning sign. China has only about 20 ballistic missiles against the thousands that the United States has deployed all over the world, many surrounding China. The Chinese gross domestic product is barely a tenth of that of the United States and the economy, while developing rapidly, lacks industrial and financial projections on an international scale. The United States, by constrast, exports its technological products all over the world and controls the energy resources, economy and finances of much of the world through transnational corporations based in the United States.[74] The major powers of the planet, with the United States and the European Union in the lead, have imposed economic and political conditions for China's admission to the World Trade Organization. These conditions risk putting China up for grabs once again, turning it into an immense satellite of Western capitalism. The Chinese people are said to have a keen memory. The Opium War has certainly never been forgotten, nor the endless rapine and humiliations inflicted upon them by European colonial powers, especially Great Britain and France.

Hence, China needs to refocus its diplomatic strategy and military politics, laying aside the idyllic, pro-American trend of the Deng Xiaoping era. First, there are the problems in the north-east theatre. There is the threat from South Korea, a military outpost of the United States. There is the danger that Japan will pursue a rapid rearmament. These perils are compounded by a project for a missile shield, called 'Theater Missile Defense', which the United States has developed for its Asian allies and plans to extend to Taiwan (the United States is already present in the area, with at least 100,000 soldiers deployed in South Korea and Japan). To the west, China faces the push for independence by Tibetan Buddhists, instability in Xinjiang, where the population is largely Muslim,[75] and the traditional reciprocal mistrust with India and Pakistan, both of which are nuclear powers. In the south-east there is the controversy over the southern islands of the China Sea – the Spratly and Paracel islands – claimed by Vietnam, the Philippines, Malaysia and Brunei. There is, above all, the crucial question of the independence of Taiwan, a long-standing cause of tension between China and the United States, and a very dangerous potential source of conflict.[76]

Given this context, when the United States struck the embassy, the already existing suspicions, resentment and tensions were amplified. The Chinese regard the war for Kosovo, with NATO's side-lining of the United Nations Security Council and its flouting of international law, as an extremely dangerous precedent, the true purpose of which is to legitimate future 'humanitarian interventions' by Western powers in East Asia and the Pacific. That is why China feels the need to become a centre of planetary resistance to the hegemony of the United States and the other Western powers, in the Asiatic quadrant as well as elsewhere. (One of the first signals of this attitude was China's surprise decision in March 2000 to send thousands of its citizens to northern Serbia. Their mere presence there would automatically involve China in any new crisis in the area.) Western observers believe that Chinese resistance to US hegemony will be very cautious as long as the United States' economic and military supremacy lasts, but will become increasingly competitive and aggressive as the present gap is reduced.

After the attack on the embassy, China changed its course at once. It shut down all the diplomatic channels through which it had kept up a dialogue with the United States on the control of strategic weapons and the defence of human rights. In August 1999 China tested a new nuclear missile, the 'Dong Fend 31', capable of carrying a nuclear warhead without being intercepted by anti-ballistic defence systems for 8000 kilometres; that is, until it is far into the territory of the United States. China has even threatened to withdraw from the pool of countries that subscribed to the Nuclear Non-Proliferation Treaty. The director of the Department for the Control of Disarmament, Sha Zukang, has declared that if the United States persists in its new anti-missile defence scheme, 'the current equilibrium will be subverted and the process of nuclear disarmament halted or even reversed'.[77]

China has been equally resolute in launching a large-scale diplomatic offensive for the purpose, first of all, of improving its relations with other North-East Asian countries. In November 1999, China, South Korea and Japan held the first trilateral summit in the history of modern Asia. The meeting was concluded with a declaration of intent in favour of the creation of a 'co-operative structure in North-East Asia' resembling the one already established in the South East.[78] At the same time, Chinese diplomacy seeks to revive the process of regional integration in Pacific Asia. This process was begun in the 1970s by the Association of South East Asian Nations (ASEAN), but progress since then has been rather slow. With a market of half a billion people, a gross domestic product of about $750 billion and a volume of trade of roughly the same value, ASEAN today has already become the fourth economic concentration in the world, after the United States, the European Union and Japan. Beijing's new strategic project, patterned after the process of integration of the European Union, aims at an economic, financial, scientific and technological amalgamation of North-East and South-East Asia, drawing these areas away from the influence of the United States.

China, Japan, South Korea and the ten ASEAN countries – Vietnam, the Philippines, Brunei, Indonesia, Singapore, Malaysia, Burma, Thailand, Cambodia and Laos – met in Manila in November 1999. On this occasion, for the first time the creation of a free exchange area (East Asia Free Trade Area, EAFTA) was discussed, as well as the creation of a single currency for these thirteen countries. Japan went so far as to propose the institution of an Asian Monetary Fund, a project opposed by the United States. Chinese prime minister Zhu Rongji, confirming previous declarations of President Jang Zemin during a visit to Thailand, stated China's readiness to discuss not just financial matters, but political issues and collective security as well, with all East Asiatic countries.[79]

Today, Asia's aspiration to emancipate itself appears at least as strong as it was forty years ago, when the three most populous countries of the continent – China, India and Indonesia – organized a conference at Bandung which was to lay the foundation for the ideology of 'Third World' and 'non-aligned' countries. At the core of this movement is China's determination to begin the long journey that will lead it to become what it was for thousands of years and what it has never ceased to think of itself as being: 'the empire at the centre of the world'. An ancient Chinese proverb says that even a thousand-mile journey begins with a first step. China took the first step immediately after the bombing of its embassy in Belgrade.[80]

Notes

1. N. Bobbio, 'L'America ricorda la lezione del Vietnam?', *La Stampa*, 28 March 1999, p. 3.
2. See N. Bobbio, 'Perché questa guerra ricorda una crociata', interview with G. Bosetti, in U. Beck, N. Bobbio *et al.*, *L'ultima crociata? Ragioni e torti di una guerra guista*. Rome: Libri di Reset, 1999, pp. 16-24; L. Ferrajoli and D. Zolo, 'Una crociata illegale, ma necessaria solo perché americana?', *ibid.*, pp. 39-43; N. Bobbio, 'Non siate prigionieri dell'antiamericanismo', *ibid.*, pp. 44-6.
3. G. Bosetti, 'I lati oscuri della guerra umanitaria', *ibid.*, p. 9.
4. On the local, regional and international consequences of the war, see G. Scotto and E. Arielli, *La guerra del Kosovo*. Rome: Editori Riuniti, pp. 158-73.
5. R. J. Smith, 'In Bosnia, free enterprise has gotten way out of hand', *International Herald Tribune*, 27 December 1999, p. 5.
6. M. Thompson, 'This peace accord failed to create a multiethnic Bosnia', *International Herald Tribune*, 20-21 November 1999, p. 6.
7. Italian Minister of Foreign Affairs Lamberto Dini insisted on the formula of autonomy within the Yugoslav Federation. See his interview with U. De Giovannangeli, 'Giusto l'appello per allentare l'embargo', *L'Unità*, 15 November 1999, p. 5.
8. See E. Caretto, 'Gli Usa: "Kosovo indipendente" ', *Corriere della Sera*, 25 September 1999, p. 12.
9. 'Ever since the United Nations has been in Kosovo, all reprisals are directed against the Serbian population. This is intolerable' (from an interview edited by M. Ansaldo and V. Nigro in *La Repubblica*, 4 March 2000, p. 17).
10. See G. Rampoldi, 'Kosovo, regno dell'impunità', *La Repubblica*, 4 November 1999, p. 13; M. Ansaldo, 'Kosovo, l'Onu accusa La Kfor', *La Repubblica*, 19 November 1999, p. 21; S. Erlanger, 'Chaos and revenge erode Kosovo peace', *International Herald Tribune*, 23 November 1999,

p. 1. In the four months following the war, the OSCE reported 348 murders, 116 kidnappings, 1070 lootings and 1106 acts of arson against Serbs, Roma, Slav Muslims or moderate Albanians.

11. P. Rumiz, 'Primavera da brividi nelle tre polveriere pronte a saltare', *La Repubblica*, 24 March 2000, p. iii of the insert 'Album', dedicated to Kosovo; P. Del Re, 'Kosovo, lager albanesi per "addestrare" prostitute', *La Repubblica*, 3 April 2000, p. 17.

12. Del Re, 'Kosovo, lager albanesi per "addestrare" prostitute', p. 17.

13. M. Mastroluca, 'In colonna da Pristina un altro carico di profughi', *L'Unità*, 12 June 1999, p. 1.

14. S. Erlanger, 'For Serbs of Kosovo, reprisals spread fear', *International Herald Tribune*, 20 December 1999, p. 7. By 20 December at least 146 Serbs had been killed in Kosovo since its occupation by NATO.

15. See J. Peleman, 'Gli Stati-mafia: dietro le quinte dei regimi balcanici', *Limes*, supplement to no. 1 of 1999, pp. 59-72; A. Negri, 'Alle radici della violenza', in E. Berselli, A. Calabrò, C. Jean, P. Matvejevic, A. Negri, M. C. Platero, S. Silvestri and D. Siniscalco, *La pace e la guerra. I Balcani in cerca di un futuro*. Milan: Il sole 24 Ore, 1999, pp. 48-53. In an address to the House of Commons in March 2000, British Foreign Secretary Robin Cook claimed that 40 per cent of the heroin entering Europe comes from Kosovo.

16. G. Rampoldi, 'Gli errori della dottrina Clinton', *La Repubblica*, 13 August 1999, p. 1.

17. See S. Erlanger, 'Explosive section of Mitrovica is called off-limits to U.S. troops', *International Herald Tribune*, 29 February 2000, p. 5; 'Mitrovica, battaglia sul ponte', unsigned reportage, *La Repubblica*, 4 March 2000, p. 16.

18. See S. Di Lellis, 'La lunga notte di Mitrovica', *La Repubblica*, 5 February 2000, p. 16; S. Erlanger, 'Divided Mitrovica damages hopes for peace in Kosovo', *International Herald Tribune*, 21 February 2000, p. 8; F. Battistini, 'Noi serbi, assediati in Kosovo', *Corriere della Sera*, 23 February 2000, p. 14; J. Fitchett, 'Nato warns Serbs against new clash', *International Herald Tribune*, 24 February 2000, p. 1.

19. On the theme of the 'Marshall plan' for the Balkans, see Adriaticus, 'Italia–Europa–Usa: la grande partita della ricostruzione', *Limes*, 2 (1999), 55-66; Miles, 'I Balcani in Europa: tra utopia e magia nera', *Limes*, 2 (1999), 67-77; D. Siniscalco, 'Per un nuovo Piano Marshall', in E. Berselli et al., *La pace e la guerra*, pp. 165-80.

20. M. Albright, 'Croatia has joined the democracies, showing Serbia the way', *International Herald Tribune*, 18 February 2000, p. 8.

21. On the future of Kosovo, see M. Roux, 'Spartire il Kosovo? Elementi per un dossier', *Limes*, 2 (1999), 199-213; on Macedonia and Vojvodina, see F. Strazzari, 'Macedonia: requiem per uno Stato-caserma', *Limes*, supplement to no. 1, 1999, pp. 79-86; F. Strazzari, 'Una, due, molte

Macedonie', *Limes*, 2 (1999), 225-36; P. Quercia, 'Voivodina o Vajdaság?', *Limes*, 2 (1999), pp. 243-53.

22. M. J. Jordan, 'Settling in for a long Kosovo run', *Christian Science Monitor*, 22 November 1999.

23. E. Rosaspina, 'Ha violentato e ucciso una bimba: in cella soldato Usa', *Corriere della Sera*, 1 / January 2000, p. 13. The sergeant will be tried at Mannheim military base, in Germany.

24. F. Fubini, 'Il paradosso italiano: siamo importanti ma contiamo poco', *Limes*, 4 (1999), 21.

25. See W. Pfaff, 'Europe is moving forward with its new defence "identity"', *International Herald Tribune*, 25 November 1999, p. 5; A. Nativi, 'Spendere di più o rassegnarsi a contare di meno', *Limes*, 4 (1999), 99-106.

26. 'Parigi: Gli Usa hanno ignorato le regole della Nato', *Il Manifesto*, 11 November 1999, p. 9; G. Luzi, 'L'attacco alla televisione divide il governo italiano', *Il Manifesto*, 11 November 1999, p. 2.

27. P. W. Rodman, 'The fallout from Kosovo', *Foreign Affairs*, 78(4) (1999), 50–1.

28. At Saint-Malo, in December 1998, the British and French had signed a joint declaration in which the London government, for the first time after its rejection of the Euro, expressed the intention to play a leading role in Europe's military defence and security. For a lucid critique of Great Britain's ambiguity, see M. Riva, 'Il doppio volto inglese, paradosso dell'Europa', *La Repubblica*, 9 December 1999, p. 13. For an authoritative confirmation of this ambiguity, see T. Blair and G. Brown, 'Il futuro dell'Inghilterra è nella nuova Europa', *La Repubblica*, 26 October 1999, p. 15.

29. J. Solana, 'Decisions to ensure a more responsible Europe', *International Herald Tribune*, 14 January 2000, p. 8.

30. See A. Polito, 'La Nato non diventerà il poliziotto del mondo', *La Repubblica*, 30 September 1999, p. 21; Rodman, 'The fallout from Kosovo', pp. 50-1; L. Rosenzweig and D. Vernet, 'Le richieste della Nato all'Europa', *La Stampa*, 4 November 1999, p. 8.

31. V. Nigro, 'Eurodifesa, i piani della Ue per un esercito comune', *La Repubblica*, 29 November 1999, p. 15; Polito, 'La Nato non diventerà il poliziotto del mondo', p. 21.

32. A. Cagiati, 'La nuova Alleanza Atlantica', *Rivista di studi politici internazionali*, 66(3) (1999), pp. 343-4; A. Cagiati, 'La sicurezza europea nel XXI secolo', *Rivista di studi politici internazionali*, 67(1) (2000), 35-44.

33. T. Buerkle, 'EU force no threat to NATO, allies say', *International Herald Tribune*, 26 November 1999, p. 1; A. Polito, 'Più forza all'Eurodifesa', *La Repubblica*, 26 November 1999, p. 13.

34. See C. R. Whitney, 'Europe's mobile force: an uncertain factor for

United States strategists', *International Herald Tribune*, 13 December 1999, p. 5; W. Drozdiak, 'Europe force plan draws a United States caution on NATO', *International Herald Tribune*, 16 December 1999, p. 1.

35. See F. W. Scharpf, *The Problem Solving Capacity of Multi-Level Governance*. Florence: Istituto Universitario Europeo, 1997, pp. 185-200; J. Tarantino, 'Non c'è nessuna Europa possibile oltre l'Europa di Maastricht', *Diorama letterario*, 21(2-3) (2000), 16-19. For an interesting discussion of the theme of continental – and hence not Atlantic – identity of Europe, see C. M. Santoro, *Occidente. Identità dell'Europa*. Milan: Franco Angeli, 1998.

36. See R. Dahrendorf, *Quadrare il cerchio*. Rome and Bari: Laterza, 1995, pp. 45-56; R. Dahrendorf, *Warum Europa? Nachdenkliche Anmerkungen eines skeptischen Europäers*. Wiesbaden: Hessische Landeszentrale für Politische Bildung, 1996.

37. See D. Grimm, 'Una Costituzione per l'Europa?', in G. Zagrebelsky, P. P. Portinaro and J. Luther (eds), *Il futuro della Costituzione*. Turin: Einaudi, 1996, pp. 339-67; J. Habermas, 'Una Costituzione per l'Europa? Osservazioni su Dieter Grimm', *ibid.*, pp. 369-75; R. Bellamy, V. Bufacchi and D. Castiglione (eds), *Democracy and Constitutional Culture*. London: Lothian Foundation Press, 1995; R. Bellamy (ed.), *Constitutionalism, Democracy and Sovereignty: American and European Perspectives*. Aldershot: Avebury, 1996; M. Telò, 'L'Europa attore internazionale: potenza civile e nuovo multilateralismo', *Europa Europe*, 8(5) (1999), 37-56.

38. See J. Habermas, *Die Normalität einer Berliner Republik*. Frankfurt am Main.: Suhrkamp, 1995; J. Habermas, *Staatsbürgerschaft und nationale Identität. Überlegungen zur europäischen Zukunft*. St. Gallen: Erker Verlag, 1991.

39. M. D'Alema, *Kosovo. Gli italiani e la guerra*. Milan: Mondadori, 1999, p. 33.

40. Fubini, *Il paradosso italiano*, p. 23.

41. D'Alema, Kosovo, pp. 21-2.

42. *Ibid.*, pp. 52-3.

43. See L. Ferrajoli, 'Guerra "etica" e diritto', *Ragion pratica*, 7(13) (1999), 117-28; U. Villani, 'La guerra del Kosovo: una guerra umanitaria o un crimine internazionale?', in G. Cotturri (ed.), *Guerra–individuo*. Milan: Angeli, 1999, p. 36.

44. R. Dahrendorf, 'Nel mondo senza nazioni la vecchia democrazia perderà', *La Repubblica*, 26 January 2000, p. 15.

45. D'Alema, *Kosovo*, pp. 36-7.

46. *Ibid.*, pp. 37-8.

47. See F. Mini, 'L'alternativa è l'asse Roma–Washington', *Limes*, 4 (1999), 65-80. The Italians' Atlanticism is almost a religion. The attempts of

dissident groups to undermine it have been largely unsuccessful, in spite of the effectiveness of some of their protests, especially those enacted through the Internet. The Catholics' pacifism has been insignificant, with the important exception of the Sant'Egidio Community. It was possibly neutralized by the 'useless sermons' of the Roman Pontiff, who once again chose to address his generic appeals to heads of state, instead of speaking to the conscience of the faithful. (For criticism of the generic character of the Pope's appeals, see A. Cassese, 'L'ingerenza di Woityla', *La Repubblica*, 15 December 1999, p. 1.) A declaration of Cardinal Ruini, secretary of the Italian Episcopal Conference, is also worth mentioning. The cardinal stated that, according to Catholic ethics, 'ethnic cleansing' is a much more serious sin than the involuntary killing of civilians by NATO bombings.

48. Fascicle 4, 1999, of *Limes* offers an example of a rational discussion of the reasons why Italy must stick with NATO.

49. D. Pecile, 'Attentati terroristici ad Aviano', *Corriere della Sera*, 11 December 1999, p. 15; A. Desiderio, 'Paghiamo con le basi la nostra sicurezza', *Limes*, 4 (1999), 38.

50. Pecile, 'Attentati terroristici ad Aviano', p. 15.

51. See G. Chiesa, 'La Russia allo specchio', *Limes*, supplement no. 1, 1999, pp. 109-12. Chiesa offers insightful analyses of Russia in the Yeltsin era in *Da Mosca*. Rome and Bari: Laterza, 1993; *Russia, addio*. Rome: Editori Riuniti, 1997.

52. Chiesa, 'La Russia allo specchio', pp. 111-12.

53. See G. Chiesa, 'La Russia si sveglia fuori dal mondo', *Limes*, 2 (1999), pp. 174-5.

54. F. Tuscano, 'La guerra vista dai Russi', *Guerre e paci*, 7(60) (1999), 33-5; V. Zavlassky, 'Mosca resterà a guardare', *Reset*, 54 (1999), 13-14.

55. R. Medvedev, 'La rabbia dei russi', *La Repubblica*, 20 April 1999, p. 1.

56. V. Tetrjakov, 'Il triangolo strategico della Russia', *Limes*, 2 (1999), 167-71.

57. *Ibid.*, p. 171.

58. M. Gessen, 'Russian society regresses to a military mind-set', *International Herald Tribune*, 1 March 2000, p. 11.

59. V. Putin, 'Nel Caucaso una minaccia strategica all'esistenza della Russia', *Corriere della Sera*, 11 February 2000, p. 15.

60. The project is supported by the Turkish government, which at the same time has declared itself in favour of both the American project and a similar Iranian project. See D. Ignatius, 'Watch the Caspian "great game" getting rough', *International Herald Tribune*, 27 January 2000, p. 6.

61. P.C. Bleek and F. N. von Hippel, 'A missile defence system isn't what America needs', *International Herald Tribune*, 13 December 1999, p. 8.

62. M. McFaul, 'Don't allow Putin to undermine Russia's freedoms',

International Herald Tribune, 4–5 March, p. 8.

63. S. Viola, 'Un uomo forte per la Russia', *La Repubblica*, 7 March 2000, p. 25.

64. R. Thakur and Y. Zhang, 'China, India, Russia: eyeing new alignments', *International Herald Tribune*, 30 November 1999, p. 8.

65. E. Eckholm, 'Laws on Taiwan irritate U.S.–China relations', *International Herald Tribune*, 14 December 1999, p. 4.

66. Thakur and Zhang, 'China, India, Russia', p. 8.

67. See B. Gill 'Limited engagement', *Foreign Affairs*, 78(4) (1999), pp. 70-1; B. Gill and J. N. Mak (eds), *Arms, Transparency, and Security in South-East Asia*. Oxford: Oxford University Press, 1997.

68. See M. Bell, H. E. Khor and K. Kochhar, *China at the Threshold of a Market Economy*. Washington, DC: International Monetary Fund, 1993; K. Fukasaku, D. Wall and M. Wu, *China's Long March to an Open Economy*. Paris: OECD, 1994; R. F. Ash and Y. Y. Kueh (eds), *The Chinese Economy under Deng Xiaoping*. Oxford: Clarendon Press, 1996; J. Tao and W.-N. Ho, 'Chinese entrepeneurship', in A. Scott (ed.), *The Limits of Globalization*. London: Routledge, 1997, pp. 143-77.

69. See S. Cook and G. White, *The Changing Pattern of Poverty in China: Issues for Research and Policy*. Brighton: Institute of Development Studies, 1998.

70. See M. C. Davis (ed.), *Human Rights and Chinese Values: Legal, Philosophical and Political Perspectives*. Hong Kong: Oxford University Press, 1995; C. Wang and X. Zhang (eds), *Introduction to Chinese Law*. Hong Kong: Sweet & Maxwell, 1997; S. Lubman, *Bird in a Cage: Legal Reform in China after Mao*. Stanford, Calif.: Stanford University Press, 1999; E. Olson, 'China aims to thwart censure by UN rights group', *International Herald Tribune*, 21 March 2000, p. 4.

71. See X. Zhany, *Zhongguo keyi shuo bu* (China Can Say No), Beijing, 1996; Y. Sun and H. Cui, *Ezhi Zhongguo* (Containing China), Beijing, 1997. On the theme of China's otherness, see F. Jullien, 'Pensare un altrove: la Cina', *Iride*, 11(24) (1998), 239-49. As I have said, there is a rich debate on 'Asian values'. I refer the reader to my 'The "Singapore Model": democracy, communication and globalization', in K. Nash and A. Scott (eds), *Blackwell Companion to Political Sociology*. Oxford: Blackwell, 2000.

72. Thakur and Zhang, 'China, India, Russia', p. 8; F. Sisci, 'Washington e Pechino in rotta di collisione', *Limes*, 2 (1999), 177-9; P. Noubel, 'Kosovo: A Cold War shadow over Sino-United States relations', *China Today*, 16 July 1999.

73. V. Loeb and S. Mufson, 'Warning on air raid that hit Chinese Embassy was ignored', *International Herald Tribune*, 25 June 1999, p. 4. According to the accurate reconstruction by the British weekly *The Observer*, the attack on the Chinese embassy in Belgrade was deliberately planned by NATO because the Embassy's computers were being used to transmit

information to the Yugoslav armed forces.

74. F. Sisci, 'Anche noi cinesi potremmo chiedere di entrare nella Nato', *Limes*, 4 (1999), 170-1.

75. J. Pomfret, 'Ethnic unrest continuing in China, despite crackdown', *International Herald Tribune*, 28 January 2000, p. 4.

76. See M. J. Valencia, *China and the South China Sea Disputes: Conflicting Claims and Potential Solutions in the South China Sea*. London: International Institute for Strategic Studies, 1995; Gill, 'Limited engagement', pp. 73-4.

77. F. Dragosei, 'Lo scudo spaziale USA', *Corriere della Sera*, 25 November, 1999, p. 13.

78. M. Richardson, 'China, Japan and South Korea agree with ASEAN on Trade Co-operation', *International Herald Tribune*, 29 November 1999, p. 5. See also R. Taylor, *China, Japan and the European Community*. London: Athlone Press, 1990; C. Howe (ed.), *China and Japan: History, Trends and Prospects*. Oxford: Clarendon Press, 1996.

79. See R. Severino Jr, 'Listen to Southeast Asia in Seattle', *International Herald Tribune*, 25 November 1999, p. 4; T. Koh, 'Progress toward an East Asia free trade area', *International Herald Tribune*, 14 December 1999, p. 8. See also G. Segal, *China Changes Shape: Regionalism and Foreign Policy*. London: International Institute for Strategic Studies, 1994.

80. B. Gill, 'Limited engagement', p. 76; but see G. Segal, 'Does China matter?', *Foreign Affairs*, 78(5) (1999), 24-36.

Conclusion

I

As I write these final pages, exactly a year has gone by since NATO began bombing the Federal Republic of Yugoslavia, on 24 March 1999. The war is behind us, and by now everyone realizes that its humanitarian claims were baseless. The objectives announced at the beginning of the war have not been attained, even though this does not mean that the war was not a victory for the United States and the West.

As was easily foreseeable, military force not only has failed to protect human rights, but has violated them as well. NATO's ambition to act as the champion of universal values, with little concern for legal norms and political legitimacy, has proved equally incongruous. True international protection of human rights would have to be entrusted to an international institution of a quite different sort, not to a military alliance. Furthermore, such an institution would intervene using economical and civil rather than military means. It would favour intercultural dialogue instead of coercively imposing a particular world-view. Finally, it would act preventively instead of after the fact.

The 'war from the sky' has not brought peace, democracy and stability to the Balkans. Instead, like other Balkan wars, it has left a legacy of hatred, violence, corruption, poverty, prostitution and environmental disaster. The territories and towns laid waste during the 78 days of uninterrupted bombing – from Priština to Niš,

Belgrade, Novi Sad and the Danubian area – have been reduced to a pre-industrial condition.

In Kosovo, 'ethnic cleansing' has not ended; it has just changed direction. The same can be said for the tragedy of the refugees. The Kosovar-Albanians who had left their homeland, most of them after the beginning of NATO's bombings, soon returned. But the hundreds of thousands of Serbs and Roma who were expelled by force from Krajina and eastern Slavonia are still encamped in Serbia, homeless and without assistance. Over 200,000 Serbs and Roma who lived in Kosovo have met with the same fate, a direct consequence of the 'liberation' of their region by NATO. Milošević's execrated regime has not fallen, and the Serbian people, bombed and subjected to economic sanctions, have paid and are continuing to pay for crimes they did not commit. Thousands of Serbs and Albanians have lost their lives or been maimed by NATO bombs. More innocent people will continue to fall victim to the mines strewn by cluster bombs and the contamination caused by the tens of thousands of depleted uranium projectiles shot from US planes.

The fate of Kosovo (autonomy? independence? incorporation into 'Greater Albania'?) is written in the inscrutable plans of Western governments and will be determined, at least in part, by the interests of criminal organizations which the war has made richer and stronger. NATO's protectorate seems destined to last *sine die* in the shadow of the military strongholds of Camp Bondsteel and Aviano 2000. War threatens to break out in Bosnia, Montenegro, Macedonia and especially southern Serbia, on the border with Kosovo, where new UÇK militias are preparing for a second onslaught against the Serbs.

II

Is it to be expected that NATO will undertake more 'humanitarian' wars to pacify and democratize the Balkans? Will humanitarian interference become a regular *modus operandi* not just in the Balkans, but in any other area of the planet where the United States, with or without its European allies, sees fit to employ military force in the name of human rights? The answer to both questions should probably be affirmative, because these are precisely the objectives of the strategy of a 'new world order' that the United States has been developing since the early 1990s.

This is a crucial issue. The 'humanitarian war' has definitively ushered us into the new global order; that is, into a deeply changed scenario with respect to the bipolar system of the period following World War II. The main lesson of the Kosovo war is that the globalization of the world and the increasing spread of information and communication technology call for new forms of international use of force. As Alvin and Heidi Toffler argue, at the time of the Gulf War the United States was already prepared to deal with the new world situation, relying on a sophisticated technological and military strategy, as well as its absolute nuclear supremacy. It was secretively co-operating with other English-speaking countries to establish a system of satellite monitoring and electronic espionage controlling the whole planet. Having left the rigid geopolitical strategies of the past behind, it was developing new, intelligent weapons, increasingly selective and automated. As the 'war from the sky' has shown, in little more than ten years the military structures of the United States have undergone radical changes – technological, organizational, strategic and logistical – to adapt to the new relationship between war, economy and society imposed by globalization and information technology.

After the end of the Cold War and the gradual erosion of the Westphalian system of sovereign states, international power has been centred in the hands of a restricted *directoire* of industrial countries under the hegemony of the 'global sovereignty' of the American superpower. This new situation has had a violent impact on post-war international institutions. The whole system of international law, including international criminal jurisdiction, has been subordinated to the needs of 'global security' and the new modes of war (which NATO inaugurated in the Balkans).

The best starting point for a realistic reflection on these events is to analyse the imbalances that globalization is causing in the international distribution of power and wealth among countries, among the regions of the planet, and within individual countries. The gap in wealth, information, scientific and technological power, and job opportunities is growing. Rich elites are getting richer; the poor, who are the majority, are getting poorer. This is what Eric Hobsbawm has called the 'new wall of poverty'. The income of the wealthiest 20 per cent of the world population is 150 times that of the poorest 20 per cent. At least a billion people live in absolute poverty and without enjoying even the most elementary rights, while another billion enjoy increasing prosperity on a planet that is becoming smaller, more integrated, and under their control. This gap keeps widening, thanks to the liberalization of the world economy and foreign debt, which is draining the blood of the poorest countries. As was seen at the Euro-African summit held in Cairo in April 2000, these developments have brought about an increasing divergence between the cognitive perceptions and symbolic universes of different human communities.

Zygmunt Bauman has recently referred to a new division of the world population between globalized rich and localized poor, and has denounced the inability of neo-liberal policies to prevent a planet-wide disintegration of cultures and societies. Ulrich Beck has observed that this trend also affects civilized and prosperous Europe, which today boasts 50 million poor, 20 million unemployed and 5 million homeless people. The considerable increase of world production is going hand in hand with a true 'Brazilianization' of the planet. The widening international gap in economic power is accompanied by an irresistible drift towards the creation of more rigid hierarchies in international relations, a fall in the standards for the legitimization of political power, a levelling of cultural differences, turbulent migratory flows, and transnational infiltration by criminal organizations.

These trends are the background against which the hegemonic strategy of the United States is being played out. Indeed, globalization is not, as a common neo-liberal cliché has it, a spontaneous process by which the world is becoming unified thanks to the laws of the marketplace. It requires constant military surveillance, as lucid analyses written by US 'cartographers' clearly bear out. The most serious threats to collective security come from the poorest areas of the planet, where powerful terrorist organizations have their bases and even a small country can become a formidable antagonist. One has only to think of the organization led by the Saudi Osama bin Laden. Moreover, the increasing complexity and interdependence of the world has made the interests of industrial countries more vulnerable, especially regarding access to energy sources, the safety of sea and air transportation, the stability of markets, and control over the production of biological, chemical and nuclear weapons.

Hence, the use of force in the peripheries of the world is on the agenda of the Western powers for the simple reason that it is inevitable. Globalization relies necessarily on a strong military arm. Hence the obsession with terrorism that has induced the Clinton administration to refurbish Reagan's old plan for an anti-missile shield to protect the United States and, perhaps, its allies as well, a project that has already alarmed Russia and China and seems destined to generate strong tensions in Europe, too.

The Western doctrine of humanitarian intervention, NATO's aggressive new vocation, and the international criminal court for former Yugoslavia were all conceived in the framework of the doctrine of 'global hegemonic stability'. One specific result of the 'humanitarian war' in the context of this global strategy is that the United Nations has been sent to the bench and international law has been subverted in the name of an absolute *ius ad bellum* that NATO claims for itself. All this, as we have seen, has sparked a new, generalized arms race, involving nuclear as well as conventional weapons, against which, in vain, the US Secretary of State has launched less than credible appeals. Moreover, the 'humanitarian war' has cast discredit on international criminal justice. During the war the Hague Tribunal repeatedly and consistently demonstrated its dependence on the political expectations of the United States, from which it gets its funds and military assistance. Today some wonder, in the East as well as the West, what ideal international court one could possibly turn to for a fair judgment on the violations committed not just by NATO, but also by the Hague Tribunal itself.

III

Do viable political strategies exist to counter the effects of 'hegemonic globalization', which is to say economic anarchy on the one hand, political and military authoritarianism on the other? Ulrich Beck has suggested a way of recovering political democracy at the global level, considering that the politics of and within national states is less and less effective and increasingly far removed from the model of representative democracy. After all, there was the sensational rebellion against the World Trade Organization in December 1999 on the occasion of the Millennium Round in Seattle, which was then replayed at the Davos Summit and during other, later meetings. Thanks to a grassroots international mobilization, thousands of young people besieged the seat of the summit and staged imposing protest demonstrations. The environmentalist movements were joined by a vast, diversified group of representatives of American and European workers and young people opposing the overwhelming power of the great corporations over global production and trade.

Was this a mere extemporaneous explosion of antagonistic energies, with no future perspective? Or are we seeing, instead, a renewal on a global scale of democratic political struggle, with the birth of a new movement that can take the new dimensions and forms of international power in its stride? This is not an easy question to answer. One can certainly say that the project for a 'cosmopolitan democracy', conceived by Beck on the example of better-known Western globalists such as Richard Falk and Jürgen Habermas to counter the destructive, authoritarian effects of globalization, is an illusion. These authors are strongly influenced by the philosophical idealism of Kant and Kelsen, with its characteristic over-reliance on international law and institutions and scarce attention to economic, scientific-technological and military phenomena. A realist consideration of globalization processes would suggest, instead, a much more cautious attitude concerning the potential and probable results of such a cosmopolitan project. As Kenichi Ohmae has shown, albeit indirectly, powerful economic forces oppose such projects in the name of the primacy of the self-regulating mechanisms which, it is claimed, steer, or should steer, global markets. Besides, as I have argued elsewhere, in the present climate of increasing differentiation and turbulence of the international scene, there is every reason to doubt that a project for the political unification of the world could possibly have positive results.

In my opinion, instead, the objective to pursue in the name of such values as pluralism and cultural diversity is the defeat of the hegemonic unilateralism of the United States. This view, as we have seen, is shared by respected US analysts such as Samuel Huntington, Joseph Nye and Bates Gill. Instead of advocating a political and legal unification of the world, which would inevitably be dominated by Western powers, it might be wiser to strive for a redistribution of global wealth and power to promote new forms of multipolar balance. Paradoxically, in the long run some unforeseen and unwanted effects of the 'humanitarian war' may perhaps converge in this direction.

Possibly, as Carlo Maria Santoro hopes, Europe may eventually regain an identity and a Western destiny in a continental and Mediterranean prospective, instead of an Atlantic one. This may lead the countries involved in the process of European integration to emancipate themselves from their present subjugation to the political and cultural hegemony of the Anglo-Saxon powers. Thus, Europeans might seek different relations both with the African continent, especially the countries along the Mediterranean coast, and emergent – or re-emergent – countries of the Eurasian continent, especially China. China, a nation that firmly opposed the 'humanitarian war', is the great variable in the global balance of powers of the decades to come.

Map of the former Yugoslavia (1945–1991), showing the six
republics and two autonomous regions

From Kosovo Polje to Seattle: Historico-political Chronology, 1389–1999

1389

From the second half of the fourteenth century onwards, the history of the Balkans was marked by the continuous effort of the autochthonous populations of the region to resist the expansion of the Ottoman Empire. In 1389, Albanians, Bosnians, Bulgarians, Herzegovinians, Serbs and Wallachians fought side by side against the Ottoman Turks on the plain of Vardar, which became famous as the 'Field of Blackbirds' (in Serbian, *'Kosovo Polje'*). The Serbs and the Bosnians were defeated, and the Serbian Empire, established in 1150, came to an end.

1453–1521

On 29 May 1453 the Turks conquered Constantinople and, shortly thereafter, the entire Balkan region, including Serbia. Only the city of Belgrade managed to retain its independence. In 1464, Bosnia and Herzegovina were forced to surrender to the Turks. Finally, in 1521, Belgrade too capitulated.

1529–1699

Suleiman the Magnificent laid siege to Vienna, but in October 1529 the Turks were defeated for the first time. In 1690 the Serbs attempted to rebel against the Turks but were defeated and forced to abandon Kosovo, which during the Ottoman Empire had been included, with Sanzak and Macedonia, in the *vilajet* of Kosóva and Manastir. In 1699 the Turks were ousted from Slavonia, Transylvania and many other Balkan territories. Turkish control over the region weakened and Austria began to replace the Ottomans, occupying the territories inhabited by the Romanians, Serbs and Croats.

1780–1815

During the eighteenth century a new protagonist appeared on the Balkan scene, Russia, which was seeking an outlet on the Sea of Azov and, hence, to the Black Sea and the Mediterranean. In 1780, Austria and Russia signed the Petersburg agreement, with which they split up the former Balkan territories of the Ottoman Empire between themselves. In 1815, Great Britain obtained a protectorate over Corfu and the Ionian islands.

1815–40

The Serbs tried to regain their independence. The Greeks, Albanians and Wallachians also revolted, as did the Bulgarians a few years later (1836–41).

1840–76

Russia started negotiations with Great Britain to divide Turkey into zones of influence. In 1853 the Crimean War broke out, fomented by Great Britain to contain Russian expansionism. In 1876, Tsar Alexander II yielded Bosnia-Herzegovina to Franz Josef I of Austria.

1878

At the Berlin Congress, European powers addressed the 'Oriental question'. They solved it by following a colonial logic, giving priority to strategic and geographic factors, to which ethnographic considerations were only secondary. They recognized the independence of Bulgaria, Romania, Serbia and Montenegro. Austria-Hungary obtained a protectorate over Bosnia-Herzegovina and became the main actor on the Balkan scene. Cyprus was turned over to Great Britain. The Prizren League, which was to become the hub of the Albanian national movement, was founded at Prizren, in southern Kosovo.

1908

By an act of force, Austria-Hungary annexed Bosnia-Herzegovina.

1909–12

The Albanian national movement managed to gain control of Kosovo and occupy Shkup (Skopje). But the Serbian army took over Kosovo again at the start of the 'Balkan Wars' (1912-13). In November 1912 the independent state of Albania was proclaimed at Vlorë.

1912–13

The 'Balkan wars' were fought by a coalition formed by Bulgaria, Greece, Montenegro and Serbia against the Ottoman Empire, which had been weakened by the conflict with Italy over the control of Libya. The Ottomans were forced to cede most of the European territories they had occupied in the previous centuries.

1913

With the Peace of London, the great European powers, in redistributing the lands taken from the Turks among the Balkan states, decided to create a new state, Albania. The region of present-day Kosovo was divided up between Serbia and Montenegro, and the first tensions between Serbs and Albanians arose.

1914

On 28 June the hereditary Archduke of Austria-Hungary, Franz Ferdinand, was assassinated at Sarajevo. The tensions between the Habsburgs and the Serbs for the control of Bosnia were the detonator that sparked World War I.

1914–18

During World War I, Kosovo was temporarily occupied and divided up between the Austrian-Hungarian and the Bulgarian armies, which competed for its control. Then it was conquered again by the Serbs.

1917–18

The independence of Albania (under an Italian protectorate) was proclaimed. The Corfu Pact (of 30 July 1917) paved the way for the unification of the Serbs, Croats and Slovenians under the crown of the Karagjorgjević family, a process favoured by the collapse of the Habsburg Empire. In 1918 the Kingdom of Yugoslavia was proclaimed.

1919–21

The treaties of San Germano, Neuilly, Trianon and Sèvres (1920) limited the Turkish state to Constantinople and Anatolia. The Treaty of Versailles assigned Kosovo (Kosovo-Metohija, or Kosmet) and Macedonia to the Kingdom of Yugoslavia. On 28 June 1921, with the Constitution of San Vito, the 'Kingdom of the Serbs, Croats and Slovenians' became a hereditary parliamentary monarchy with a centralized government. It was under the hegemony of the Serbs, and the Albanian population of the kingdom was not recognized as an ethnic and cultural minority.

1939–40

In April 1939, Italy attacked Albania and occupied Durrës and Vlorë. Even the capital, Tiranë, was taken, and Victor Emanuel III was crowned King of Albania. In October 1940 the Italians invaded Greece as well.

1941

On 6 April, Germany and Italy attacked Yugoslavia. Italy occupied Kosovo and part of Macedonia, and annexed them to Albania. In the meanwhile, partisan forces were organizing, led by a charismatic Croatian communist leader, Marshal Josip Broz Tito.

On 10 April, Croatia – supported, armed and financed by Hitler and Mussolini – became an independent state and annexed Bosnia-Herzegovina. A ruthless 'ethnic cleansing' directed against Jews, Roma and Serbs began under the leadership of the *Duce* (*poglavnik*), Ante Pavelić, head of the *ustaše* Nazi–Fascist movement. Hundreds of thousands of Serbs were killed or forced to flee. In Serbia, too, nationalist movements cherishing the ideal of a 'Greater Serbia' arose.

1941–4

Italy set up the protectorate of Albania and established schools in which the teaching was done in Albanian. A conference of the Albanian communists of Kosovo and Albania held at Bujane, near Prizren, declared in favour of the right of Kosovo to self-determination and the reunification of Albania after the end of the war. After the surrender of the Italian army, the Albanian territories were occupied by German troops. During their occupation, the Nazi–Fascists maintained the administrative unity of the Albanian territories and promoted the creation of a 'Greater Albania'.

1944–6

On 20 October 1945, after the end of World War II, the Yugoslav federal state was proclaimed under the leadership of Marshal Tito.

Map of 'Greater Albania' (1941–4)

The federation included the six republics of Slovenia, Croatia, Serbia, Bosnia-Herzegovina, Montenegro and Macedonia, and the two autonomous regions of Vojvodina and Kosovo. Strong tensions arose between the Albanian National Front and the Yugoslavian police forces.

1948

On 28 June, Tito's Yugoslavia was expelled from the Kominform and abandoned the Soviet bloc.

1961

A sharp ideological conflict broke out between the USSR and Albania.

1966–72

Yugoslav Minister of the Interior Alexander Ranković, an intransigent Serbian nationalist, was deposed, and tensions with Albanian nationalists were eased. The use of Albanian in Kosovo schools was extended and the language was introduced into university teaching. A debate was begun on the Federal Constitution, in the course of which the representatives of the Albanian people demanded that Kosovo be granted the status of a republic. The police repressed student demonstrations at Priština. The University of Priština, the academic centre of the Albanians in Yugoslavia, was founded. Forty thousand students enrolled. The Orthographic Congress in Tiranë, also attended by delegates from Kosovo, decided to maintain a unified writing system for the Albanian language in all the territories peopled by Albanians.

1974

On 21 February, under the new federal constitution Kosovo and Vojvodina gained considerable autonomy. Kosovo was granted the status of 'autonomous province' and, as such, recognized as one of the partners in the federation, with its own constitution and institutions, independent of those of Serbia.

1980

Upon the death of Marshal Tito on 4 May, nationalist aspirations surged again and ethnic tensions were rekindled. The Yugoslav economy declined quickly, public debt reached $20 billion, and inflation rocketed to sky-high levels (2500 per cent a month).

1981

The Albanian population of Kosovo called publicly for the proclamation of a 'Republic of Kosóva'. Student demonstrations in Priština and other towns of Kosovo were harshly repressed.

1986

On 28 May Slobodan Milošević was elected president of the Serbian Communist Party.

1988

An all-out strike by more than 1000 Albanian miners was called at Trepca, a large mining complex in Kosovo. Popular demonstrations of solidarity with the miners took place all over the region.

1989

On 28 June, on the six hundredth anniversary of the battle of Kosovo Polje, Milošević organized a demonstration in support of the Serbs' claim to Kosovo. A state of national emergency was proclaimed and the Kosovo parliament was forced to accept the cancellation of its autonomy. Mass protest broke out and was repressed by the police. The 'League of the Communists of Kosovo' was dissolved and the first free parties were formed, including the

Democratic League for Kosovo (DLK), which gathered the most support.

On 9 November, with the fall of the Berlin Wall, the Cold War came to an end and the Soviet empire collapsed.

On 15 November Milošević was elected president of Serbia.

1990

In January, Yugoslavia sent troops and tanks into Kosovo to quash an uprising. Between June and July the representatives of the Albanians of Kosovo proclaimed the independence of the region from Serbia. Milošević harshly repressed the independence movement.

1991

On 25 June, Slovenia declared its independence from Yugoslavia. Croatia followed suit immediately thereafter, with the support of Germany and the Vatican. The Serbs of Krajina, in their turn, proclaimed their independence from Croatia. The leader of Croatia was the nationalist Franjo Tudjman, who, like the Nazi–Fascist Pavelič before him, had himself called *poglavnik* (*Duce*).

On 1 July, the Warsaw Pact was dissolved. Croatia declared war on Yugoslavia.

On 1 September, the University of Priština was shut down. From 26 to 30 September a referendum was held, and 87.5 per cent of the population of Kosovo voted in favour of an independent and sovereign state.

On 8 September, Macedonia declared its independence from the Yugoslav Federation, provoking a reaction on the part of Greece.

In October, the Bosnian parliament voted for independence. Albania recognized the independence of Kosovo.

In November, after a long siege, the town of Vukovar, the emblem of the autonomy of Croats in Slavonia, was taken by the Yugoslav army. Thousands died or were deported.

1992

In April the European Community recognized the independence of Bosnia. A war broke out at once between Serbs, Croats and Bosnian Muslims. The Serbs put Sarajevo under siege. Serbia and Montenegro joined to form a new Federal Republic of Yugoslavia.

On 24 May, the first multi-party election in Kosovo was held. The majority of the votes went to the DLK. Slav Muslims and Kosovar Turks also took part in the elections. Ibrahim Rugova of the DLK was elected president of the Republic with 99 per cent of the votes.

On 30 May, the Security Council of the United Nations voted Resolution 757, which called for an embargo against Serbia, accused of supporting the rebellion of the Serbs in Croatia and Bosnia.

On 4 June, at the Atlantic Council in Oslo, NATO declared that it was at the disposal of the United Nations and the Conference on Security and Co-operation in Europe (CSCE) for a peacekeeping intervention in the territories of former Yugoslavia. It was the first occasion on which NATO announced its intention to operate 'out of area' and for non-defensive purposes.

On 7 July, following the Brioni Agreement, hostilities between Croatia and the Yugoslav Republic were suspended, but this did not put an end to strife. The forced emigration of the Serbs began from the territories conquered by Croatia (especially Krajina). Eventually the number of Serbian refugees reached 200,000.

On 15 December, Yugoslavia was expelled from the International Monetary Fund.

1993

In April, NATO sent air patrols into Bosnia. The Serbian authorities denied Amnesty International and the CSCE access to the whole territory of Serbia in retaliation for the economic sanctions against Serbia.

On 31 March, with Resolution 816, the Security Council of the United Nations assigned NATO the task of guaranteeing a 'no fly zone' in the Bosnian airspace.

On 25 May, following a preliminary resolution of 22 February (no. 808) and in conformity with Chapter VII of its charter, the Security Council of the United Nations passed Resolution 827 instituting the International Criminal Tribunal for Former Yugoslavia, seated at The Hague. Its stated purpose is to prosecute individuals responsible for 'serious violations of international humanitarian law' in the territories of former Yugoslavia dating from 1 January 1991.

On 4 June, with Resolution 836, the Security Council of the United Nations authorized the sending of new military forces in support of those already operative in Bosnia-Herzegovina. The United Nations Protection Forces (UNProFor) thus came to number 23,000 troops.

1994

On 6 February, about 70 people were killed in Sarajevo market.

On 28 February, NATO carried out its first war action in the Balkan skies with the tacit assent of the United Nations.

1995

On 26 May, the Serbs bombarded Sarajevo heavily and shortly thereafter (11 July) massacred Muslims at Srebrenica. The United Nations Protection Forces proved incapable of protecting the civilian population.

On 29 August NATO decided on a massive air attack against Serbian military posts. Operation 'Deliberate Force' lasted until mid-September. A total of 3515 air missions were flown, and over 1000 bombs were dropped.

On 1 November, peace talks began at Dayton, Ohio, chaired by the United States. The participants were the Bosnian Alija Izetbegović, the Croat Franjo Tudjman and the Serb Slobodan Milošević.

On 16 November, the International Tribunal in The Hague incriminated the Bosnian Serb leader Radovan Karadžić and the Serb general Ratko Mladić for genocide and other war crimes.

On 21–22 November, the Dayton peace agreement was signed. The United Nations lifted the sanctions against Serbia and Montenegro.

On 5 December, the Ministers of Foreign Affairs and Defence of the NATO countries decide to send 60,000 soldiers to Bosnia

(SFOR) to enforce application of the peace agreement for the United Nations.

On 14 December, representatives of the three conflicting ethnic groups of the Balkans (Izetbegović, Tudjman and Milošević) signed a peace treaty in Paris in the presence of the president of the United States, Bill Clinton. The representative of the United Nations was invited to attend, but as a mere observer. At the end of the month, a NATO peacekeeping mission was sent to Bosnia.

1996

On 1 September, Milošević and Rugova came to an agreement on the opening of public buildings for Albanian schools, but its application was repeatedly put off.

On 7 November, strong popular protest exploded in Belgrade against Milošević, who refused to recognize the victory of the opposition in the local elections.

1997

On 19 May, the first posters of the Kosovo Liberation Army (in Albanian: Ushtria Çlirimtare ë Kosovës or UÇK) appeared. In autumn, tens of thousands of Albanian students and teachers marched in the streets to protest against their exclusion from state schools.

1998

On 28 February, Serbian units carried out a violent repression in the area of Drenica. The fighting went on until June and caused more than 300 casualties.

On 2–5 March, at Priština, Serbian police forces attacked thousands of Albanian demonstrators. A battle at the village of Prekaz kindled tensions even further.

On 22 March, Kosovo again voted to elect its president and parliament. Ibrahim Rugova was re-elected and the Democratic League for Kosovo once again gained a majority of the votes.

On 31 March, with Resolution 1160 (approved with the abstention of China), the Security Council of the United Nations addressed an appeal to the Serbian forces and the UÇK guerrillas to cease fighting and open peace negotiations. An embargo on weapon supplies to Belgrade was also decided.

Between 8 and 11 June, the United States, immediately followed by Europe, resolved to put further economic and financial pressure on Serbia. NATO prepared to intervene militarily.

On 23 September, Resolution 1199 of the Security Council of the United Nations – also approved with the abstention of China – called for a ceasefire, the opening of negotiations, and the admission of international observers and members of humanitarian associations into the territories of former Yugoslavia. The Belgrade government was warned to abstain from repressive actions ('indiscriminate and excessive use of force') against civilians.

By the end of September, more than 1000 Albanians and Serbs had died in the conflict in Kosovo. Over 200 villages were uninhabitable and tens of thousands of Albanians had taken to the mountains.

On 13 October, an 'Activation Order' of the Atlantic Council authorized NATO to begin air raids against targets in the Federal Republic of Yugoslavia. Milošević was given four days to withdraw his troops from Kosovo.

On 16 October, the American envoy Richard Holbrooke and Slobodan Milošević reached an agreement providing for a ceasefire guaranteed by the presence of an international force (Kosovo Verification Mission) organized by the Organization for Security and Co-operation in Europe (OSCE), as well as a reduction of Serbian forces in Kosovo. The agreement also provided for aerial surveillance by NATO and, later on, for the deploying of NATO forces in Macedonia to protect the mission of the OSCE verifiers.

On 24 October, Resolution 1203 of the Security Council of the United Nations – approved with the abstention of Russia and China – authorized the presence of OSCE verifiers and aerial monitoring by NATO in the skies of Kosovo.

On 27 October, Serbian security forces were withdrawn *en masse* from Kosovo.

1999

On 16 January, evidence of a massacre was discovered at Raçak, in southern Kosovo, where 45 horribly mutilated bodies of Albanians were discovered. A controversy broke out over the responsibility for the massacre and its authenticity. The General Prosecutor of the Hague Tribunal, the Canadian Louise Arbour, showed up at the border between Albania and Kosovo in the company of Christiane Amanpour, a CNN reporter, with the intention of carrying out an investigation. The two women were not allowed to cross the border.

On 18 January, William Walker, a US citizen and leader of the OSCE mission, called the Raçak massacre a crime against humanity and blamed it on the Yugoslav political authorities, army and police forces. Two days later the Belgrade government declared William Walker *persona non grata* and ordered him to leave the country. Thanks to Russian and French mediation, the order was rescinded.

On 29 January, the Contact Group (Italy, France, Germany, Great Britain, the United States and Russia), meeting in London, invited the Belgrade government to comply immediately with the resolutions of the United Nations. The UÇK's military actions were condemned and the parties in the conflict were convoked to the castle of Rambouillet, France, on 6 February.

On 6 February, the Rambouillet talks began under joint French and British chairmanship. The Serbian delegation was led by Yugoslav vice-president, Ratko Marković, while the Albanians of Kosovo were represented by Ibrahim Rugova, Hashim Thaci and Veton Surroi. Negotiations went on without achieving any results.

On 23 February, the Contact Group decided on a suspension of negotiations and convened a new session, to be held in Paris on 15 March.

On 12 March, the Czech Republic, Hungary and Poland joined NATO.

On 15 March, the Paris peace talks were resumed but only to be broken off definitively after five days. The text of the agreement was signed only by the Kosovar-Albanian delegation. The signature was accompanied by a controversial declaration of interpretation that reaffirmed the Albanian Kosovars' intention to hold a referendum on the independence of Kosovo after a transitional phase. Belgrade's representatives were especially opposed to the clauses allowing the presence of NATO forces in both Kosovo and other territories of the Federal Republic of Yugoslavia.

On 20 March, the OSCE verifiers began to withdraw from Kosovo.

On 22 March, Milošević denounced the 'activation order' of the Atlantic Council to the Security Council of the United Nations as an illegal threat to use force against a sovereign state.

On 23 March, the Serbian parliament rejected NATO's conditions. The Secretary-General of NATO, Javier Solana, put into effect the 'activation order' without waiting for the authorization of the Security Council of the United Nations, or even soliciting it.

On 24 March, NATO launched an air attack against the territory of the Yugoslav Federation. Thus began Operation 'Determinate Force', commanded by the US general Wesley Clark. It lasted 78 days. At the request of Russia, an urgent session of the Security Council of the United Nations was convened on 26 March. India, Russia and Belarus proposed a resolution condemning the NATO intervention against the Federal Republic of Yugoslavia. The document, approved by China, Russia and Namibia, was rejected by the other twelve members of the Council, including the three Western permanent members: the United States, Great Britain and France.

On 24–25 March, the heads of state of the European Union, meeting in Berlin, reaffirmed their support of NATO's military action.

On 26–27 March, air raids continued all over the territory of the Federal Republic of Yugoslavia, causing the first civilian casualties among both the Serbian and the Kosovar-Albanian populations. A mass exodus of Albanians from Kosovo to Albania and Macedonia began.

On 30 March, Slobodan Milošević offered to withdraw Yugoslav forces from Kosovo in exchange for a suspension of the bombings. His offer was rejected.

On 2 April, Russia requested a reunion of G8 ministers and announced its intention to send naval units into the Adriatic Sea to monitor the situation.

On 3–4 April, NATO decided to launch its first missile attack against the centre of Belgrade and bombed the first bridge over the Danube.

On 5 April, NATO admitted that a missile had missed its target. About 20 Serbian civilians were killed in the town of Aleksinac.

On 6 April, NATO attacks destroyed a refinery at Novi Sad and a second bridge over the Danube. The Yugoslav Foreign Minister called in vain for an intervention by the Secretary-General of the United Nations to stop the bombing of Belgrade. Milošević announced a unilateral truce during the Orthodox Easter (11 April), but NATO authorities decided to continue bombing.

On 7 April, the Contact Group discussed and, in substance,

confirmed NATO's five conditions for the suspension of the bombings: cessation of hostilities and repression by the armed forces of Belgrade; withdrawal of Yugoslav military units and police forces from Kosovo; admission of an international security force into Kosovo; return of the Kosovar-Albanian refugees; a political solution based on the Rambouillet draft agreement.

On 9 April, NATO bombers missed their target again, hitting civilian structures near Priština, with at least twelve casualties. One hundred and twenty-eight workers were wounded in the bombing of the Zastava car factory. In an official declaration, Kofi Annan imposed upon Belgrade a series of conditions basically coinciding with those of NATO. The G8 group, meeting at Dresden, also sided with NATO's position.

On 12 April, a NATO missile struck a passenger train crossing a bridge at Grdelicka, not far from Belgrade, killing over 50 people, most of whose bodies were carbonized.

On 14 April, another mistake by NATO bombers caused the death of over 70 people in a convoy of Kosovar refugees in flight near Djakovica. About 100 others were wounded.

On 21 April, NATO missiles destroyed the seat of the Serbian Socialist Party in Belgrade and Milošević's private residence. Another bridge over the Danube was destroyed in Novi Sad, in Vojvodina.

On 23 April, the Russian envoy at Belgrade, Viktor Chernomyrdin, said that Milošević would be willing to allow foreign troops to be deployed in Kosovo.

On 22–24 April, NATO forces bombed the building of the Serbian television company in Belgrade, killing and wounding many reporters and TV operators. Italian Minister of Foreign Affairs Lamberto Dini protested strongly, but Italian prime minister D'Alema disavowed him and praised the scruples and transparency of NATO's conduct of the war. The electric plant at Obrevonaz was also hit. Belgrade was blacked out, its hospitals were left without electricity, and its water supply system and public transportation were put out of order.

On 23–25 April, NATO celebrated its fiftieth year in Washington. On this occasion, it confirmed its intention to continue the war until victory.

On 27 April, Strobe Talbott for the United States met with the Russian envoys, Igor Ivanov and Viktor Chernomyrdin. Belgrade declared that NATO's bombings had caused at least 1000 casualties among the civilian population.

On 28 April, yet another mistake by NATO resulted in the death of more than 20 civilians, hit by cluster bombs at Surdulica.

On 30 April, a petrol embargo, declared by the European Union on 23 April, was put into effect against the Yugoslav Federation. NATO also threatened to begin a naval blockade. Civilian targets continued to be bombed in Belgrade. The population was prostrate. The fifty-fifth session of the United Nations Committee for Human Rights was held in Geneva. During the meeting, Mary Robinson, United Nations High Commissioner for Human Rights, denounced the devastation caused by NATO's bombing of Yugoslavia.

On 2 May, Slodoban Milošević turned over three US soldiers captured by the Serbs to the Reverend Jesse Jackson of the United States. NATO made yet another mistake: a bus carrying refugees over the border was hit at Luzane, near Priština. At least 20 people Serbs, Albanians and Roma – were killed, and as many others were wounded. Graphite bombs were used to cause short circuits in Serbia's power plants: 70 per cent of the country was blacked out.

On 6 May, in Bonn, the G8 countries reached an agreement for a possible political solution, but the NATO bombings went on.

On 7 May, the Yugoslav authorities accused NATO of having dropped cluster bombs on the hospital and marketplace of Nis, killing more than 20 people and seriously wounding at least 70 more. NATO belatedly admitted the error.

On the night of 7 May, NATO missiles hit the Chinese embassy in Belgrade, killing 3 people and wounding 20. China demanded an emergency meeting of the Security Council, which however refused to censure NATO in any way.

On 10 May, Yugoslavia announced the beginning of its withdrawal from Kosovo, but NATO authorities did not confirm it.

During the period 11 to 20 May, NATO continued to bomb Serbia, while the search for a political solution went on. On 14 May, another convoy of refugees was destroyed at Korisa (79 dead). Schröder went to Peking, while Chernomyrdin returned to Belgrade. The President of Finland, Martti Ahtisaari, also took part in negotiations as the representative of the European Union. About a hundred cluster bombs dropped by NATO planes returning from raids in Yugoslavia were caught in the nets of fishermen in the Adriatic Sea, only a few miles from the lagoon of Venice.

On 27 May, the International Tribunal in The Hague incriminated Slobodan Milošević and four other civil and military members of his government, accusing them of a series of very serious crimes. On a visit to Yugoslavia, the Brazilian diplomat Sergio Viera de Mello, leader of the United Nations humanitarian mission, denounced the 'humanitarian disaster' caused by the NATO bombings.

On 28 May, following a new mission by Chernomyrdin to Belgrade, the Yugoslav president accepted the plan proposed by the G8 countries and requested an immediate stop to the bombings.

On 1 June, in continued NATO bombings, civilians were again killed at Novi Pazar. The political authorities of Belgrade sent a letter to the President of the European Union, confirming their acceptance of the conditions put forward by the G8.

On 3–4 June, the Serbian Parliament and the federal government accepted the peace plan presented by Chernomyrdin and Ahtisaari.

On 8 June, the Foreign Ministers of the G8 countries, meeting in Cologne, drew up a draft of a resolution to be submitted for approval to the Security Council of the United Nations.

On 10 June, the withdrawal of the Serbian troops began and the Secretary-General of NATO, Javier Solana, declared that he had ordered air raids to be suspended. The Security Council of the United Nations adopted Resolution 1244, proclaiming an end to the conflict in Kosovo. China abstained from the vote.

On 12–13 June, stealing a march on the United States and Great Britain, two hundred Russian soldiers left Bosnia, camped on the administrative border between Serbia and Kosovo, and then entered Kosovo and occupied Priština Airport.

On 18 June, NATO forces entered Kosovo, where they discovered dozens of corpses, as well as 'torture rooms' attributed to the Serbian militias. Great Britain and the United States sent teams of experts with high-tech equipment to investigate acts of violence committed by Serbs against the Albanian population of Kosovo and report them to the Hague Tribunal. The Kosovar-Albanians began their revenge against the Serbs. UÇK militiamen occupied the towns of Kosovo, refusing to turn over their light weapons and becoming, *de facto*, the political and military arbiters of the situation.

On 20 June, the G8 summit in Cologne decided to extend humanitarian aid to the Serbian population, but only selectively, to avoid benefiting Milošević's regime.

On 25 June, the United States offered a reward of $5 million to anyone offering information leading to the arrest of Slobodan Milošević.

On 4 July, the Frenchman Bernard Kouchner was named United Nations civil administrator for Kosovo.

On 30 July, a summit for a stability pact in the Balkans was held in Sarajevo with the participation of President Clinton and leaders from the NATO countries and those of South-Eastern Europe. Serbia was excluded from the summit and denied the funds allocated for its reconstruction while Milošević's regime remained in power.

On 11 September, the crisis in East Timor became worse. The United States, while criticizing the Indonesian government, declared that it did not consider itself the policeman of the world and did not intend to carry out a humanitarian military intervention against Jakarta. The new Secretary-General of NATO, the Briton George Robertson, issued similar statements.

On 18 October, Javier Solana, former Secretary-General of NATO, became High Representative for Foreign Affairs and Common Security of the European Union. He declared his intention to strive for the creation of a common European military defence apparatus destined to absorb the Western European Union (WEU).

On 28 October, on a visit to Priština, the new General Prosecutor of the Hague Tribunal, Carla del Ponte, declared that the tribunal was evaluating the possibility of adding genocide to the counts for which Slobodan Milošević was being incriminated.

On 2 November, an international polemic broke out concerning the number of victims of the massacres attributed to the Serbian army and militias in Kosovo. A US intelligence agency, STRATFOR, reported that the corpses discovered by the FBI numbered only in the lower hundreds, a far cry from the 11,000 dead mentioned by Kouchner or the 100,000 claimed in May by US Defense Secretary William Cohen to justify a posteriori the humanitarian intervention.

On 15 November, at a meeting held in Brussels, the Ministers of Foreign Affairs and Defence of the European Union drafted a project to create a European army of 40,000 men. This new military force would be separable (but not separate) from NATO. The head of this new structure would be Javier Solana, who was also designated as the next Secretary-General of the WEU. Fifteen days before the beginning of the Millennium Round at Seattle, the governments of United States and China underwrote an agreement to prepare for China's entry into the World Trade Organization (WTO).

On 18–19 November, at the OSCE summit in Istanbul, Western leaders harshly criticized the Russian government for its repression of the Chechnyan rebels, but did not threaten to use military force. The United States resolutely pushed for, and reached, an agreement (from which Russia was excluded) for the construction of the new Baku–Ceyhan pipeline, which is to convey crude oil from South-West Asia (Azerbaijan) to the Mediterranean (Turkey) without crossing the territories of Russia and Iran. Georgia and Turkmenistan took part in the agreement, as well as Azerbaijan and Turkey.

From 30 November to 3 December a WTO summit met in Seattle for the 'Millennium Round'. The meeting highlighted a conflict between rich and poor countries, and between the commercial interests of the United States and those of Europe. A large-scale international mobilization brought thousands of demonstrators to Seattle, who laid siege to the summit. The demonstrators protested against economic inequalities induced by globalization processes.

On 3 December, the violence of Kosovar-Albanians against the Serbian minority continued. An elderly university professor was killed, and his wife and mother-in-law, who were with him in his car, were brutalized and seriously wounded by a crowd of Kosovar-Albanians celebrating a national holiday out in the streets. Other localities in Kosovo also witnessed homicidal violence against Serbs and Roma who would not or could not emigrate.

On 10 and 11 December, at the Helsinki summit of European heads of state, the European Union decided to develop, by 2003, an autonomous military force to be able to take initiatives promptly in international crisis situations (but only when NATO was not already involved).

Selected Bibliography

Asmus, R. D., Kluger, R. L. and Larrabee, F. S. 'Building a new Nato', *Foreign Affairs*, 72(5) (1993), 28–40.

Baccelli, L., *Il particolarismo dei diritti*. Rome: Carocci, 1999.

Badie, B., *La Fin des territoires: Essai sur le désordre international et l'utilité sociale du respect*. Paris: Fayard, 1995.

Bassiouni, C. and Manikas, O., *The Law of the International Criminal Tribunal for the Former Yugoslavia*. Irvington-on-Hudson, NY: Transnational Publishers, 1996.

Bauman, Z., *Globalization: The Human Consequences*. New York: Columbia University Press, 1998.

Bauman, Z., *In Search of Politics*. Cambridge: Polity Press, 1999.

Beck, U., *Was ist Globalisierung?* Frankfurt am Main: Suhrkamp, 1997.

Beck, U., 'Der militärische Pazifismus. Über den postnationalen Krieg', *Suddeutsche Zeitung*, 19 April 1999.

Beck, U., Bobbio, N. *et al.*, *L'ultima crociata? Ragioni e torti di una guerra giusta*. Rome: Libri di Reset, 1999.

Benedikter, T., *Il dramma del Kosov:. dall'origine del conflitto tra Serbi e Albanesi agli scontri di oggi*. Rome: Datanews, 1998.

Berselli, E., Calabrò, A., Jean, C., Matvejevic, P., Negri, A., Platero, M. C., Silvestri, S. and Siniscalco, D., *La pace e la guerra: i Balcani in cerca di un futuro*. Milan: Il Sole 24 Ore, 1999.

Bianchini, S., *La questione jugoslava*. Florence: Giunti, 1999.

Bobbio, N., *Il problema della guerra e le vie della pace*. Bologna: Il Mulino, 1979.

Borejsza, J.W., *Il fascismo e l'Europa orientale: dalla propaganda all'aggressione*. Rome and Bari: Laterza, 1981.

Brzezinski, Z., *The Grand Chessboard*. New York: Basic Books, 1997.

Bull, H., *The Anarchical Society*. London: Macmillan, 1977.

Cabona, M. (ed.), *'Ditelo a Sparta': Serbia ed Europa contro l'aggressione della Nato*. Genoa: Graphos, 1999.

Caccamo, D., 'Kosovo: vincitori e vinti', *Rivista di studi politici internazionali*, 66(3) (1999), 339–60.

Cagiati, A., 'La nuova Alleanza Atlantica', *Rivista di studi politici internazionali*, 66(3) (1999).

Cassese, A., '*Ex iniuria ius oritur*: are we moving towards international legitimation of forcible humanitarian counter-measures in the world community?', *European Journal of International Law*, 10(1) (1999).

Castellan, G., *Histoire des Balkans, XIV–XX siècle*. Paris: Fayard, 1991.

Chinkin, C. M., 'Kosovo: a "good" or "bad" war?', *American Journal of International Law*, 93(4) (1999), 841–7.

Clark, R. and Sann, M., *The Prosecution of International Crimes: A Critical Study of the International Tribunal for the Former Yugoslavia*. New Brunswick, NJ: Transaction Publishers, 1996.

Corm, A., *L'Europe et l'Orient: de la balkanisation à la libanisation*. Paris: La Découverte, 1989.

Cotturri, G. (ed.), *Guerra–individuo*. Milan: Angeli, 1999.

Cvijic, C., *Remaking the Balkans*. London: Pinter, 1991.

D'Alema, M., *Kosovo: gli italiani e la guerra*. Milan: Mondadori, 1999.

Daniel, J., 'Les deux surprises du Kosovo', *Nouvel Observateur*, 22 July 1999.

de Benoist, A., 'Ripensare la guerra', *Trasgressioni*, 14(1) (1999).

Debray, R., *Croire, voir, faire*. Paris: Éditions Odile Jacob, 1999.

Demandt, A. (ed.), *Macht und Recht: große Prozesse in der Geschichte*, Munich: Oscar Beck, 1990.

Di Francesco, T. (ed.), *La Nato nei Balcani*. Rome: Editori Riuniti, 1999.

Dogo, M., *Kosovo: Albanesi e serbi: le radici del conflitto*. Cosenza: Marco Editore, 1992.

Emerson, M., *Ridisegnare la mappa dell'Europa*. Bologna: Il Mulino, 1998.

Falk, R. A., 'Reflections on the war: postmodern warfare leads to severe abuses of the community that is supposed to be rescued',

The Nation, 28 June, 1999.

Falk, R. A., 'Kosovo, world order, and the future of international law', *American Journal of International Law*, 93(4) (1999), 847–56.

Ferrajoli, L., 'La guerra della Nato: una disfatta del diritto, della morale e della politica', *Critica marxista*, 3 (1999), 17–24

Franck, T. M., Luck, E. C., Rockler, W. J. and Glennon, M. J, 'Sidelined in Kosovo?', *Foreign Affairs*, 78(4) (1999), 116–22.

Galtung, J., 'Faschismus ist überall', *Suddeutsche Zeitung*, 7 June 1999.

Gardam, J. (ed.), *Humanitarian Law*. Aldershot: Ashgate, 1999.

Garde, P., *Vie et mort de la Yugoslavie*. Paris: Fayard, 1992.

Gill, B., 'Limited engagement', *Foreign Affairs*, 78(4) (1999), 65–76.

Glennon, M. J., 'The new interventionism', *Foreign Affairs*, 78(3) (1999), 2–7.

Glenny, M., *The Balkans, 1804–1999: Nationalism, War and the Great Powers*. London: Granta Books, 1999.

Graziosi, A., *Dai Balcani agli Urali: l'Europa orientale nella storia contemporanea*. Rome: Donzelli, 1999.

Grmek, M., Gjidara, M. and Simac, N., *Le 'Nettoyage ethnique'*. Paris: Fayard, 1993.

Grove, E. (ed.), *Global Security: North American, European and Japanese Interdependence in the 1990s*. London: Brassey's, 1991.

Haass, R. N., *The Reluctant Sheriff: The United States after the Cold War*. New York: Council of Foreign Relations, 1997.

Haass, R. N., 'What to do with American primacy', *Foreign Affairs*, 78(5) (1999), 37–49.

Habermas, J., 'Kants Idee des ewigen Friedens – aus dem historischen Abstand von 200 Jahren', *Kritische Justiz*, 28(3) (1995).

Habermas, J., 'Bestialität und Humanität. Ein Krieg an der Grenze zwischen Recht und Moral', *Die Zeit*, 18, (1999).

Hagen, W., 'The Balkans' lethal nationalism', *Foreign Affairs*, 78(4) (1999), 52–64.

Handke, P., 'Der Krieg ist das Gebiet des Zufalls', *Süddeutsche Zeitung*, 5–6 June 1999.

Harding, J., 'Europe's war', *London Review of Books*, 21(9) (1999), 9.

Hedges, C., 'Kosovo's next masters?', *Foreign Affairs*, 78(3) (1999).

Hirst, P. Q. and Thompson, G., *Globalization in Question: The International Economy and the Possibilities of Governance*. Cambridge: Polity Press, 1996.

Hondrich, K. O., 'Was ist dies für ein Krieg?', *Die Zeit*, 22 (1999), 4.

Huntington, S. P., *The Clash of Civilizations and the Remaking of World Order*. New York: Simon & Schuster, 1996.

Huntington, S. P., 'The lonely superpower', *Foreign Affairs*, 78(2) (1999), 35–49.

Iuso, P., *Il fascismo e gli ustascia, 1929–1941: il separatismo croato in Italia*. Rome: Gangemi, 1998.

Janigro, N., *L'esplosione delle nazioni: le guerre balcaniche di fine secolo*. Milan: Feltrinelli, 1999.

Jelavich, B., *History of the Balkans*. Cambridge: Cambridge University Press, 1983.

Kaldor, M., *New and Old Wars: Organized Violence in a Global Era*. Cambridge: Polity Press, 1999.

Kelsen, H., *Das Problem der Souveränität und die Theorie des Völkerrechts: Beitrag zu einer Reinen Rechstlehre*. Tübingen: Mohr, 1920.

Kelsen, H., *Peace through Law*. Chapel Hill: University of North Carolina Press, 1944 (2nd edition: New York: Garland Publishing, 1973).

Kelsen, H., 'Will the judgement in the Nuremberg trial constitute a precedent in international law?', *International Law Quarterly*, 1(2) (1947), 153.

Kelsen, H., *Law and Peace in International Relations*. The Oliver Wendell Holmes Lectures, 1940–1, Cambridge, Mass.: Harvard University Press, 1948.

Kirchheimer, O., *Politische Justiz*. Frankfurt am Main: Europäische Verlagsanstalt, 1981.

Kissinger, H., 'US intervention in Kosovo is a mistake', *Boston Globe*, 1 March 1999.

Kissinger, H., 'New world disorder', *Newsweek*, 31 May 1999.

Kissinger, H., 'The end of NATO as we know it?' *Washington Post*, 15 August 1999.

Kitsikis, D., *L'Empire ottoman*. Paris: Presses Universitaires de France, 1985.

L'Abate, A., *Kossovo: una guerra dimenticata*. Bari: La Meridiana, 1999.

Lattanzi, F. and Sciso, E. (eds), *Dai tribunali penali internazionali* ad hoc *ad una corte permanente*. Naples: Editoriale Scientifica, 1995.

Lejbowicz, A., *Philosophie du droit internationale*. Paris: Presses Universitaires de France, 1999.

Lind, M., 'Civil war by other means', *Foreign Affairs*, 78/5 (1999), 123–42.

Luthard, C., *Géopolitique de la Serbie-Monténégro*. Paris: Éditions Complexe, 1998.

Luttwak, E. N., 'A post-heroic military policy', *Foreign Affairs*, 75(4) (1996), 33–44.

Luttwak, E. N., 'Give war a chance', *Foreign Affairs*, 78(4) (1999), 36–44.

McCormack, T. L. H. and Simpson, G.J., *The Law of War Crimes*. The Hague: Kluwer Law International, 1997.

Malcolm, N., *Kosovo: A Short History*. New York: New York University Press, 1998.

Malcolm, N., Djilas, A. *et al.*, 'Is Kosovo real?', *Foreign Affairs*, 78(1) (1999), 130–9.

Mandelbaum, M., 'A perfect failure', *Foreign Affairs*, 78(5) (1999).

Matvejevic, P. (ed.), *I signori della guerra: la tragedia dell'ex Jugoslavia*. Milan: Garzanti, 1999.

Morozzo della Rocca, R., *Nazione e religione in Albania*. Bologna: il Mulino, 1990.

Morozzo della Rocca, R., *La guerra in Europa: origini e realtà di un conflitto etnico*. Milan: Guerini e Associati, 1999.

Mortellaro, I., *I signori della guerra; la Nato verso il XXI secolo*. Rome: Manifestolibri, 1999.

Nye, J. S., Jr, 'Redefining national interest', *Foreign Affairs*, 78(4) (1999).

Ohmae, K., *The End of the Nation State: The Rise of Regional Economies*. New York: Free Press, 1995.

Peric, A., *Origine e fine della Jugoslavia nel contesto della politica internazionale*. Milan: Lupetti, 1998.

Picone, P. (ed.), *Interventi delle Nazioni Unite e diritto internazionale*. Padua: Cedam, 1995.

Pipa, A. and Repishti, S., *Studies on Kosova*. New York: Columbia University Press, 1984.

Pizzorno, A., *Il potere dei giudici*. Rome and Bari: Laterza, 1998.

Portinaro, P. P., *Il realismo politico*. Rome and Bari: Laterza, 1999.

Prévélakis, G., *Les Balkans: cultures et géopolitique*. Paris: Nathan, 1994.

Rodman, P. W., 'The fallout from Kosovo', *Foreign Affairs*, 78(4) (1999), 45–51.

Röling, B. V. A. and Cassese, A., *The Tokyo Trial and Beyond*. Cambridge: Polity Press, 1993.

Röling, B. V. A. and Rüter, C. F. (eds), *The Tokyo Judgment*. Amsterdam: APA-University Press Amsterdam, 1977.

Roux, M., 'Di chi è il Kosovo? Cento anni di conflitti', *Limes*, 3 (1998).

Roux, M., *Le Kosovo: dix clefs pour comprendre*. Paris: La Découverte, 1999.

Rugova, I., *La Question du Kossovo*, eds M.-F. Allain and X. Galmiche. Paris: Fayard, 1994.

Santini, G., *Dall'Illirico romano alla Jugoslavia moderna: le strutture territoriali della penisola balcanica attraverso i secoli*. Milan: Giuffrè, 1997.

Santoro, C. M., *Occidente. Identità dell'Europa*. Milan: Franco Angeli, 1998.

Schmitt, C., *Der Nomos der Erde im Völkerrecht des Jus Publicum Europaeum*. Berlin: Duncker & Humblot, 1974.

Scotti, G., *Croazia, Operazione Tempesta. La liberazione della Krajina e il genocidio del popolo serbo*. Rome: Gamberetti, 1996.

Scotto, G. and Arielli E., *La guerra del Kosovo*. Rome: Editori Riuniti, 1999.

Shraga, D. and Zacklin, R., 'The International Criminal Tribunal for Rwanda', *European Journal for International Law*, 7 (1996), 501–18.

Simma, B., 'NATO, the UN and the use of force: legal aspects', *European Journal of International Law*, 10(1) (1999), 1–22.

Singer, M. and Wildavsky, A., *The Real World Order: Zones of Peace, Zones of Turmoil*. Chatham: Chatham House Publishers, 1993.

Sisci, F., 'Washington e Pechino in rotta di collisione', *Limes*, 2 (1999).

Sorel, L., 'Il nuovo atlantismo contro l'Europa', *Diorama letterario*, 20(5) (1999).

Spinedi, M., 'Uso della forza da parte della NATO in Jugoslavia e diritto internazionale', *Quaderni Forum*, 12(3) (1999).

Stark, H., *Les Balkans: le retour de la guerre en Europe*. Paris: Ifri/ Dunod, 1993.

Suganami, H., *The Domestic Analogy and World Order Proposals*. Cambridge: Cambridge University Press, 1989.

Sweeney, J. and Holsoe, J., 'Nato bombed Chinese deliberately', *Observer*, 17 October 1999.

Toffler, A. and Toffler, H., *War and Anti-War: Survival at the Dawn of the Twenty-first Century*. New York: Little, Brown, 1993.

Vickers, M., *Between Serb and Albanian: A History of Kosovo*. New York: Columbia University Press, 1998.

Vickers, M. and Pettifer, J., *Albania: From Anarchy to a Balkan*

Identity. London: Hurst, 1997.

Vitucci, M. C., *Il Tribunale ad hoc per la ex-Jugoslavia*. Milan: Giuffrè, 1998.

Waltz, K. N., *Theory of International Politics*. New York: Newbery Award Records, 1979.

Walzer, M., *Just and Unjust Wars*. New York: Basic Books, 1992.

Weller, M. (ed.), *The Crisis in Kosovo, 1989–1999*. Cambridge: Documents and Analysis Publishers, 1999.

Wight, M., 'Why is there no international theory?', in H. Butterfield and M. Wight (eds), *Diplomatic Investigations*. London: George Allen & Unwin, 1969.

Zolo, D., *Cosmopolis: Prospects for World Government*. Cambridge: Polity Press, 1997.

Zolo, D., 'Hans Kelsen: international peace through international law', *European Journal of International Law*, 9(2) (1998), 306–24.

Zolo, D., 'Jürgen Habermas' cosmopolitan philosophy', *Ratio Juris*, 12(4) (1999), 429–44.

Zolo, D., 'The lords of peace: from the Holy Alliance to the new international criminal tribunals', in B. Holden (ed.), *Global Democracy*. London: Routledge, 2000.

Name Index

NAME INDEX

Subject Index